= Evolutionary psychol
= Religion.
= key points
C000212804

Witches, Feminism, *and* The Fall of the West

Edward Dutton

Radix & Washington Summit Publishers
P.O. Box 1676
Whitefish, MT 59937

email : hello@WashSummit.com
web: www.WashSummit.com

Cataloging-in-Publication Data is on file with the Library of Congress

hardback: 978-1-59368-078-7
paperback: 978-1-59368-079-4
eBook: 978-1-59368-080-0
audio: 978-1-59368-081-7

Printed in the United States of America
10 9 8 7 6 5 4 3 2 1

Contents

Acknowledgments

I would like to thank Dr. Bruce Charlton for his valuable advice on developing this book and for his many important ideas on its subject matter. I would also like to thank Professor Guy Madison for reading through and commenting on earlier versions of this manuscript. Mr. Richard Spencer, Mr. Nils Wegner, and Ms. CK edited the work and prepared it for press, and Mrs. J. LeDarc designed the cover. I'm grateful to all of them.

I was inspired with the idea that modern feminists are the descendants of Early Modern witches by a comment by the Internet content creator Mrs. Robyn Riley. I would like to thank her for her thought-provoking interviews. I would like to thank all of my followers on my Internet channel, *The Jolly Heretic*, for their stimulating suggestions and, in particular, John Oliver Allen Rayner-Hilles, Esq. I would also like to thank Professor Ray Blanchard who gave me a very helpful interview.

This book mainly developed out of an earlier project entitled "The Taming of the Gene" which was funded by the Ulster Institute for Social Research, I wish to thank them for their financial support. The development of the ideas herein has benefited from discussions with Dr Michael Woodley of Menie, so I would like to acknowledge my intellectual debt to him. Parts of this book have previously appeared in: *At Our Wits' End* by myself and Michael Woodley of Menie and in my books *How to Judge People By What They Look Like, The Silent Rape Epidemic;* "The Victorian Spinster and the Rise of Feminism" in *Family Tree* (July 2013), and Edward Dutton and J.O.A. Rayner-Hilles (In Press), "Early Modern Witches and Demonic Sexual Fantasies: An Evolutionary Perspective" in *Mankind Quarterly.*

Edward Dutton
April 25th, 2021
Oulu, Finland

Witches,

Feminism,

and

The Fall of the West

Witchcraft, and Witches, have been, and are, the former part is clearly proved by the Scriptures, and the last by daily experience . . .

King James VI of Scotland
Demonology, 1597.

Chapter 1

Once Upon a Time...

Introduction

We begin with a folktale. *Once upon a time*, there were peoples known as the Europeans. We inhabited a world that was cold and harsh, and our various bands battled for survival and dominance. The groups that won out were the best suited to the struggle: bonded to one another and hostile towards outsiders. We were spirited, fertile, and hardy, as this was God's will. Soundness of body and soundness of mind went together. We lived lives of toil, even tragedy, but we reached the pinnacle of health, intelligence, and organization. We spun a connecting thread between ancestor and offspring.

Sometimes, though, the witches would come around. When they did, they were persecuted with a vengeance. The witches poisoned everything they touched. They formed communities apart. They disobeyed God with their spells, magic healing, and lives away from men. These women bore marks that announced them as unholy. A person's face can tell you quite a bit about her soul: *Monstrum in fronte, monstrum in animo*. Witches were at the bottom of society because that is where they belonged. Upright people rose to the top.

The Industrial Revolution, with all its marvels, changed everything. In 1800, half of all those born died as children; two centuries later, almost none did. More and more people who would not have survived in the old times walked among us. They were mistakes made flesh. They no longer uplifted the established rules; they endlessly criticized and undermined them, like the witches of yore. Unwell in body and mind, they were, at best, selfish and impulsive; at worst, they promoted depression and despair.

Some of these villains were born into society's highest ranks, or rose there due to their cleverness. The really spiteful ones advocated for ideas that were catastrophic. Worse still, people listened to them, since most are born to obey. The nature of our communities changed, including our outposts and colonies around the world. We all went mad, you could say—everyone, except those who were naturally resistant or too slow to conform. Deviancy became the norm; patriarchy was overturned. Those who were brightest were the first to accept the new religion, as they could talk themselves into anything. They even talked themselves into having small families or no children at all.

These new witches lived out in the open and were even celebrated. So many women were taken in by their spells: they behaved like men; they cared about careers more than children; they raised boys as girls. Even men listened to the witches. Our societies were feminized, though that didn't mean they became kinder and gentler. The persecuted became the persecutors, the judged became judges, the last came first. Everything was out of joint.

These are dizzying times . . . but nothing lasts forever. Those susceptible to the witches' spells are cursed with barrenness; those who are religious still multiply. We Europeans thus stand at a fork in the road. Some say that the children will bring about a revival of the old ways, though in a population that is much dimmer than in previous times. Some see a civil war or breakdown over the horizon. Others warn of a return to the harsh conditions of the past. Whichever way destiny takes us, the witches, and those under their spell, are not long for this world.

☾

This book, I'm afraid, won't answer the question of whether we will live happily—or unhappily—ever after. That will be the subject of future writing. But it is an attempt to tell a story about European evolution, how it was affected by religion, climate change, and the industrial revolution. In particular, it's a story of how the figure of the "witch" fits in to all this—how she went from being persecuted and despised to acting as a leader and "bad conscience" of postmodern society. In both cases, witches were not the stuff of nightmare or fantasy; they were *all too real*. And they impacted people and society in ways that have previously been misunderstood.

The Wicked Witch

The archetype of the "witch" is burnt deep into the European psyche, recurring again and again in folklore, fairytale, and fantasy. The old hag who lives alone in a spooky cottage on the edge of the village with a black cat: she is wicked, uses magic spells to achieve her diabolical ends, and she is to be avoided at all costs. Until the 18th century, many adults, in rural England for example, genuinely believed in the power of witches, to the extent that people accused of witchcraft could be put on trial and executed. Between 1482 and 1782, up to 50,000 people were executed for witchcraft across Europe.[1] This last happened in Britain, in Dornoch, in the Scottish Highlands, in 1722. Janet Horne, an elderly woman, was found guilty of having used her deformed daughter as a pony upon which to ride to the Devil. Horne was stripped, covered in tar, paraded down the High Street in a barrel, garroted, and burnt.[2]

Western adults do not generally believe in witches anymore. But the historical significance of witches is attested

1: Suzannah Lipscomb, "A Very Brief History of Witches," *History Extra*, 2015, https://www.historyextra.com/period/history-witches-facts-burned-hanged/.

2: W.N. Neill, "The Last Execution for Witchcraft in Scotland, 1722," *Scottish Historical Review*, 20 (1923): 218–21.

to by the way in which adults pass on the folk memory of them to their children through fairytales: *Hansel and Gretel, Sleeping Beauty*, *Snow White*, and many more. This is significant, because fairytales are more than just interesting bedtime stories. Evolutionary psychologists, those who study the evolution of the human mind, generally agree with American evolution-focused literary scholar Joseph Carroll that a vital component of fairytales is "transmitting practical information on such adaptively important matters as resource acquisition, predator avoidance, and social interaction."[3] According to American evolutionary psychologist Michelle Scalise Sugiyama, literature of this kind, as well as the oral tradition that precedes it, should be understood as an "information acquisition strategy." *Little Red Riding Hood*, for instance, "packs a double emotional wallop by combining our evolved fear of being harmed by animals with our evolved fear of being harmed by strangers."[4] Critics of this theory have asked how fairytales can possibly be more adaptive than simply telling children to stay away from strangers.[5] Presumably, the child is better able to absorb this crucial, adaptive information due to the information being presented as an escapist tale, with its assorted surreal elements. This is consistent with evidence that children are better able to imbibe information (that is, better able to learn) if it is presented together with imagination-stimulating fantasy elements than if it is simply explained in a matter-of-fact way.[6] Also, these stories have been vetted across generations to be maximally informative and engaging, meaning they are likely to be very useful guides to life, including guides to how to deal with strangers. And this

---

3: Joseph Carroll, "Violence in Literature: An Evolutionary Perspective," in *The Evolution of Violence*, eds. Todd Shackelford and Ranald Hansen (New York: Springer, 2014), 38.

4: Quoted in Carroll, *ibid.*

5: Stephen K. Sanderson, *Human Nature and the Evolution of Society* (Boulder: Westview Press, 2014).

6: Deena Weisberg, Hande Ilgaz, Kathy Hirsch-Pasek, *et al.*, "Shovels and Swords: How Realistic and Fantastical Themes Affect Children's Word Learning," *Cognitive Development*, 35 (2015): 1-14.

raises the question of what kinds of strangers, in particular, you should avoid. Fairy tales consistently provide children with the answer: Witches.

Roald Dahl: The Sage of Great Missenden

As children grow older, their parents stop reading them fairy tales, and place them in the hands of children's authors, whom the children eventually start reading themselves. The witch archetype in fairy tales has been developed by children's authors, and most obviously by Roald Dahl (1916-1990) in his 1983 novel *The Witches*. In this novel, the Norwegian grandmother of the unnamed boy, who is the eye of the story, stresses that witches are nothing like the portrayal in books:

> *"In fairytales, witches always wear silly black hats and black cloaks, and they ride on broom sticks.*
>
> *But this is not a fairytale. This is about REAL WITCHES.*
>
> *The most important thing you should know about REAL WITCHES is this. Listen very carefully. Never forget what is coming next.*
>
> *REAL WITCHES dress in ordinary clothes, and look very much like ordinary women. They live in ordinary houses and they work in ORDINARY JOBS.*
>
> *That is why they are so hard to catch"*[7]

Dahl, who was raised in Wales but had Norwegian parents, presents his child readers with the tantalizing possibility that real witches—who despise children with "a red-hot sizzling hatred" and who constantly plot to "do away with them, one by one"[8]—are *real* and live among us. There is a kind

7: Roald Dahl, *The Witches* (London: Jonathan Cape, 1983), 7.

8: *Ibid.*

of witch-led conspiracy to destroy children—and thus wipe out humanity itself—and Dahl offers these youngsters a dose of truth, such that they can be aware of the conspiracy and fight against it with every ounce of courage within them. They are like the character in the film *The Matrix* (1999), who eschews the comfortable "Blue Pill" and instead takes the "Red Pill," permitting him to see reality as it really is.[9] And it's a very good thing that they do take Roald Dahl's "Red Pill," because as we will see, he was right. Witches are *real*. Witches do indeed wear "ordinary clothes and look very much like ordinary women." It is true that witches live in ordinary houses and do ordinary jobs. And they are focused on wiping out children, and thus wiping out humanity itself.

Roald Dahl—who wrote most of his books in his shed in Great Missenden in Buckinghamshire in southern England—was known for his frequent re-working of fairytales.[10] Literary scholars have argued that Dahl's novels, such as *BFG*, *James and the Giant Peach*, and *Matilda*, tend to have very similar themes to those found in fairytales: children who are abused by their step-families or children who struggle due to lack of food.[11] Indeed, Dahl's fascination with fairytales was such that one of his books was a comical and macabre reworking of them entitled *Revolting Rhymes*.[12] There are also frequent allusions to fairytale imagery in Dahl's descriptions of characters. Miss Trunchbull, Matilda's demonic headmistress, is described as the "Prince of Darkness, the foul serpent, the fiery dragon." Matilda even seems to better understand herself—a precocious, sensitive schoolgirl with degenerate parents—through reading fairytales. Fairy

9: Jennifer McMahon, "Popping a Bitter Pill: Existential Authenticity in *The Matrix* and *Nausea*," in *The Matrix and Philosophy: Welcome to the Desert of the Real*, ed. William Irwin (Chicago: Open Court, 2002), 166.

10: Laura Vinãs Valle, *De-Constructing Roald Dahl* (Newcastle-Upon-Tyne: Cambridge Scholars Publishing, 2016), 132.

11: Roald Dahl, *BFG* (London: Jonathan Cape, 1982); Dahl, *James and the Giant Peach* (New York: Alfred A. Knopf, 1961); Dahl, *Matilda* (London: Jonathan Cape, 1988).

12: Roald Dahl, *Revolting Rhymes* (London: Jonathan Cape, 1982).

tales help Matilda recognize things about her own situation in life and crystallize in her mind that it is up to her to rescue her beloved teacher, Miss Honey, from the perilous situation she finds herself in.[13]

Perhaps Dahl's focus on the fairytale explains his success. It means that Dahl's books strike a chord in a way in which they otherwise would not. Beneath the humor and surrealism, Dahl's novels deal with cutting, poignant, and serious issues. And surely, there could be nothing more serious than the presence in Western countries of an intricate coven of witches, who aim to hurt children physically and mentally, and ultimately to persuade society as a whole to go barren. For, as we will see, this is exactly the situation we find ourselves in today.

The Rise of the Witch

We are living in a society that is increasingly dominated by witches. These witches do not fly on broom sticks, nor do they wear pointed hats. They also do not conform to all five of the specific components of the European witch, as set out by English historian Ronald Hutton.[14] In this taxonomy, witches who harmed their neighbors were part of a witching tradition via inheritance, initiation, or spontaneous manifestation. They were despised by the public, had made a pact with the Devil, and incited violent resistance from the community. They are, however, quite like witches in far deeper and more important ways. Witches were, in a sense, proto-feminists: they indirectly promoted greater equality between the sexes, by being financially independent, practicing folk magic, and thus competing with the patriarchal religion, or acting in ways which

13: Deborah Thacker, "Fairy Tale and Anti-Fairy Tale: Roald Dahl and the Telling of Power Stories," in *Roald Dahl*, eds. Ann Alston and Catherine Butler (Basingstoke, Hants: Palgrave Macmillan, 2019), 23-24.

14: Ronald Hutton, *The Witch: A History of Fear, from Ancient Times to the Present* (New Haven: Yale University Press, 2017).

were not consistent with patriarchal norms.[15] And they have ideological descendants today, in the form of actual feminists.

I will show that, in general, the kind of people who were executed for witchcraft in Europe up until the 18th century were of a very specific type. They were unmarried old women who acted to undermine the patriarchal religion of the period. In doing so, they acted to undermine a key aspect of that religion, which was to promote the genetic fitness of the population in order to maximize the probability that the population would pass on its genes. As I will show, modern feminists do the same. The religion these witches undermined was focused on ensuring that its adherents won the battle of what is called "group selection" with other rival groups under pre-Industrial conditions of harsh, Darwinian selection. "Group selection," which we will explore in more detail below, refers to two or more groups, members of which are genetically related to each other, fighting it out for limited resources. The group that is more adapted to this wins the struggle. Religion, we will see, was trying to ensure that its adherents were optimally adapted to the conditions they faced, such that they were successful in procreating. It did this, as all surviving religions have done, by identifying adaptive behavior and prescribing that behavior as the will of God, such that it was even more likely to be pursued. Groups that were highly internally cooperative and that fought valiantly against outsiders were more likely to triumph in the battle of group selection, so religion promoted such behavior as the will of God. Crucially, groups were more likely to be internally cooperative if they were patriarchal, if females were under male control. This is because if females were controlled by males, then males could be more certain that they weren't being cuckolded, reducing paternity anxiety. This would, in turn, reduce the need to invest energy in mate-guarding and it would lessen inter-male conflict, thus elevating the cooperativeness

15: I appreciate that there is much debate over precisely what constitutes "feminism." See Noelle McAfee, "Feminist Philosophy," *The Stanford Encyclopedia of Philosophy*, ed. Edward Zalta, 2018, https://plato.stanford.edu/archives/fall2018/entries/feminist-philosophy.

necessary to win the battle of group selection. Accordingly, a patriarchal system was also made the will of God. In conditions of intense group selection, of the kind that were seen in Europe in the 17th century when the continent was increasingly cold and over-populated, religiousness, and thus patriarchal religiousness, were strongly selected for.

The result was a period in which supposed witches were intensely persecuted. They were persecuted because, as widowed or unmarried old women, they implicitly undermine systems of male control. And those who were targeted combined this with other traits, such as being physically unattractive and even having a "Witch's Mark," such as a superfluous nipple or some other birth defect. I will show that such traits are more common among feminists than among non-feminists. This was important because religion also promoted physiognomy—the idea that you can infer psychology from a person's appearance—as the will of God. And, incredible as it may seem to some readers, they seemingly did this because it was adaptive to believe in physiognomy. There is a considerable body of empirical evidence behind it, as I will demonstrate. Those who have mutations of the body are very likely to have mutations of the mind, leading to ways of thinking that are fitness-damaging. Depression, for example, can spread, contagiously, from one person to another, making even those who are not genetically disposed to depression more likely to be depressed and thus act maladaptively, such as by committing suicide.[16] Consequently, the removal of witches, based on what they looked like, was for the good of the group.

We will also see that witches tended to be anti-social, undermining group cohesion under conditions in which group cohesion was vital, and this will also be demonstrated to be true of modern feminists. Witches were often accused of abusing children and particularly of infanticide and carrying out abortions. Many of them worked as healers and, in doing

16: T. E. Joiner, "Contagious depression: Existence, specificity to depressed symptoms, and the role of reassurance seeking," *Journal of Personal and Social Psychology*, 67 (1994): 287-296.

so, actually practiced "folk magic," establishing themselves as a direct rival to the adaptive, patriarchal religion. So, witches were persecuted, I will show, in order to ensure that the group triumphed in the war of group selection.

What is Patriarchy?

Terms such as "religion" and "patriarchy" are often poorly defined, so it is important to be clear what we mean by them. By "religion" I mean the belief in and collective worship of a moral god, or gods, as part of a religious community of practice. This specific definition is particularly relevant because, as we will see, it appears that this has been specifically selected for in evolution. This kind of religiousness is positively correlated with mental health, physical health, fertility and is partly genetic. (A "correlation" is a relationship between two variables). By "atheism" I mean those who do not believe in or collectively worship a moral god. This, as we will see, is associated with opposite life outcomes to religiosity.[17]

With regard to the concept of "patriarchy," in their fascinating study "It's a Man's World': Mate Guarding and the Evolution of Patriarchy,"[18] British biologists Rachel Grant and Tamara Montrose observe that there is no single, accepted definition of "patriarchy." It has been defined as "a hierarchical social system that functions in such a way to uphold men and their needs while subordinating and oppressing women according to male desires,"[19] or, more neutrally, as "a system of kin relations which is organized in terms of the rule of the father and which

17: See, Rüdiger Vaas, "God, Gains and Genes," in *The Biological Evolution of Religious Mind and Behavior*, eds. Eckhart Voland and Wulf Schiefenhövel (New York: Springer, 2009) and below.

18: Rachael Grant and V. Tamara Montrose, "It's a Man's World: Mate Guarding and the Evolution of Patriarchy," *Mankind Quarterly*, 58 (2018): 384-418.

19: Michelle Friedman, Jo Metelerkamp and Ros Posel, "What is Feminism?" *Agenda: A Journal About Women and Gender*, 1 (1987): 3-24, p.8.

endorses a set of social and economic values which promote young motherhood and large families."[20] Grant and Montrose, however, focus on an evolutionary definition of patriarchy: "... the control by males of female sexuality in the form of a system of implicit and explicit rules of conduct, of power structures, and of belief systems that support male control over women's reproduction."[21] They stress, however, that patriarchy developed, as we will see in more detail below, due to the way in which females have evolved to demand investment in return for sexual access. To ensure they are not cuckolded and that their resources are not wasted, males, therefore, moved to control female sexuality. I will employ Grant and Montrose's definition of "patriarchy" in this book.

Witches and Feminists

Having demonstrated why Early Modern witches were persecuted, I will then show, in depth, the central parallels between witches and modern feminists, permitting modern witches to be identified. As with "patriarchy," there is no agreed definition of a "feminist." In October 2018, I was at an Irish pub in Oulu in northern Finland, where I live. I got talking to a bright British architecture student who was on a work placement in Oulu. This 24-year-old informed me that she was *not* a feminist, though had she been born a century earlier than she may have been. She was rejecting what educationalist Joanna Williams has summarized as "Not Your Grandmother's Feminism," otherwise known as "Second Wave Feminism." "Feminism," argues Williams, had been motivated by a desire for greater personal freedom for women and greater equality before the law, such as the right to vote or own property.[22]

20: Mathias Lerch, "Patriarchy and Fertility in Albania," *Demographic Research,* 29 (2013): 133-166, p.135.

21: Grant and Montrose, "It's a Man's World," *op cit.,* 388,

22: Joanna Williams, *Women vs Feminism: Why We All Need Liberating from the Gender Wars* (Bingley, West Yorks: Emerald Publishing, 2017), 265.

Second Wave Feminism, argues Williams, was something very different, and it is often what people now mean by "feminism." Firstly, it is strongly related to other left-wing ideologies such as multiculturalism and other moves for "equality" for supposedly disempowered groups. Secondly, instead of giving women choice, it is motivated by a desire to enforce sexual equality in terms not merely of opportunity but also outcome: sex quotas in prestigious jobs and in politics, for example. It promotes, in effect, the empowerment of women over men. This was satirized by British comedians *The Two Ronnies* in a series of sketches in 1980 called "The Worm that Turned," in which there is a totalitarian society of feminists in England, and men are simply housewives. New Wave Feminism portrays males as inferior to females: violent, aggressive, and, almost, deserving of discrimination due to the sins of their fathers, and women as morally superior. For Second Wave Feminist Kate Millett (1934-2017), there is a battle for power between males and females, and Marxist notions of class-conflict are a distraction designed to "set one woman against another."[23] These people and their followers are modern-day witches, though they will often have influenced, if only through their power in society, many other women to think and behave against their genetic interests.

In this book I will demonstrate that, like witches, the most ardent feminists undermine the adaptive traditions of their society—as espoused by traditional religion—and thus render the society less adaptive. Indeed, they promote the antithesis of traditional religion; they literally encourage fitness-reducing ways of behaving, such as not having children, placing the interests of other ethnic groups over those of your own (and thus damaging your own genetic interests, as we will see), and even the mutilation of young boys so that they become infertile and appear outwardly, though rarely convincingly, as "girls." Moreover, they also promote abortion, something with which Early Modern witches were associated, and to some extent,

23: Williams, *Women vs Feminism, op cit.*, 197.

the abuse of children. In addition, I will present evidence that such feminists, like witches, are in comparison to non-feminist women, more likely to be single, childless, low in pro-social personality traits, irreligious, and physically unattractive, which is consistent with the relationship between physical and mental mutation. Like witches, they also tend to be shunned by males, as well as by many females, so there is a sense in which they are themselves subject to social exclusion.

Of course, modern feminists are not exactly witches. However, I am not simply attempting to better understand feminists via witches through a process of metaphor. A metaphor involves elucidating one concept by means of another, which may be superficially completely different but which is the same in key and profound ways.[24] My argument is that modern-day feminists perform the same functions witches once did and accordingly are psychologically and even physically extremely similar. This is akin to the way in which Polish social anthropologist Bronisław Malinowski (1884-1942) argued that modern-day cultural institutions perform the same essential societal functions as tribal ones and are likewise comparable in salient respects.[25] Differences between witches and feminists exist not due to the limitations of metaphor but because of fundamental changes in Darwinian selection pressures. In presenting this argument, I am not engaging in *infrahumanization*.[26] This is a tactic often employed by religious groups in which the out-group is portrayed as somehow "less human" than the religious in-group.[27] This, once more, involves the use of metaphor. It is similar to the way in which, in 1582, a

24: See, Deidre Gentner, "Are Scientific Analogies Metaphors?" in *Metaphor: Problems and Perspectives,* ed. David Miall (Brighton: Harvester Press, 1982).

25: Adam Kuper, *Anthropology and Anthropologists: The British School in the Twentieth Century* (London: Routledge, 2014), 21-22.

26: Jacques-Philippe Leyens, Paola Paladino, Ramon Rodriguez *et al.* "The emotional side of prejudice: The attribution of secondary emotions to ingroups and outgroups," *Personality and Social Psychology Review*, 4 (2000): 186–197.

27: Hector Garcia, *Alpha God: The Psychology of Religious Violence and Oppression* (New York: Prometheus Books, 2015), 175.

German Lutheran pastor called Nivander wrote a tract showing that Calvinists were like wolves in forty different ways.[28] I, by contrast, am simply highlighting an empirical fact.

Misogyny, Cognitive Dissonance, and Low Self-Esteem

"*How can you claim patriarchy can ever be a good thing?! This is just sexist, offensive and misogynistic!*" American social psychologist Kristin Anderson has written that even to state the empirical facts that women have been very successful in achieving equality and that, in some countries, men are subject to reverse discrimination via quotas[29] is an example of "modern misogyny."[30] I am simply making a reasonable assessment that, as we will see, is based on a large body of scientific and historical evidence. Those who would dismiss this out of hand, and especially those who would do so with insults such as "misogynist," should ask themselves why they are reacting in this emotional way. Such a reaction is an example of "cognitive dissonance." This occurs when a person's fervently believed worldview, which is important to their sense of identity and self-worth, is challenged and they recognize, on some level, that their worldview might be wrong. This will often "trigger" them. It will cause them to react in an emotional and aggressive fashion in order to suppress the person, and the ideas, which are making them feel uncomfortable.[31] This kind of reaction—of "taking offense"—

28: John Matusiak, *Europe in Flames: The Crisis of the Thirty Years War* (Stroud, Glos: The History Press, 2018).

29: See Guy Madison, "Explicating Politicians' Arguments for Sex Quotas in Sweden: Increasing Power and Influence Rather than Increasing Quality and Productivity," *Frontiers in Communication* (2019).

30: Kristen Anderson, *Modern Misogyny: Anti-Feminism in a Post-Feminist Era* (Oxford: Oxford University Press, 2014), xii.

31: Leon Festinger, *A Theory of Cognitive Dissonance* (Stanford: Stanford University Press, 1957).

has been found to be associated with having low self-esteem; a sense that you are not really of value and do not really matter.[32]

Modern feminists are functionally latter-day witches and, in this book, I will set out in detail precisely how this is the case. We will discover exactly who modern witches are, how we can identify them, and why their power will not last forever. In Chapter Two, we will explore the history of witchcraft, specifically in Western Europe, with a particular emphasis on understanding why people became more convinced of the reality of witches across the Medieval period. In Chapter Three, we will learn that humans are evolved to be religious under Darwinian conditions and that they are specifically evolved to forms of religiousness that promote ethnocentric behavior, and patriarchy, as the will of God. This is because these are the kinds of groups that survive the battle of group selection, where ethnic groups battle for space and resources. In Chapter Four, we will explore what the witch is, from an evolutionary perspective, and I will demonstrate that witches, implicitly or explicitly, undermined religious patriarchy and thus the cooperative society that survives under harsh Darwinian conditions and that they also displayed evidence of other maladaptive mutations. Chapter Five will look in detail at three case studies that are illustrative of the nature of English "witch crazes" and of the women hanged for witchcraft. In Chapter Six, we will see that with the collapse of Darwinian selection since the Industrial Revolution, there has been a growth in people adopting fitness-damaging ways of thinking and in "spiteful mutants," who persuasively advocate these ways of thinking, damaging the genetic interests of the entire society. This has taken place because of low child mortality. High child mortality, which existed until the 19th century, purged those with physical mutations from the population every generation. We will see that these physical mutations correlate with mental

32: Isabella Poggi and Francesca D'Errico, "Feeling Offended: A Blow to Our Image and Our Social Relationships," *Frontiers in Psychology* (2018). https://doi.org/10.3389/fpsyg.2017.02221.

mutations, which are associated with psychological conditions and viewpoints that would have been strongly maladaptive, if adopted by a group, under Darwinian conditions, and which remain maladaptive. We will see that witches are examples of "spiteful mutants," and we will explore why they tend to emanate from higher social classes. In Chapter Seven, I argue that feminism is ultimately a product of latter-day witches and explore the many ways in which feminism undermines group and individual fitness in the ways witches once did, contributing to the decline of civilization in the form of reducing ethnocentrism and undermining academia and even the potential for male scientific genius. We also explore the parallels between many transsexuals and witches. In Chapter Eight, we look at the life and work of American "Second Wave" feminist philosopher Andrea Dworkin (1946-2005), who fits the archetype of a witch. Finally, in Chapter Nine, we examine what happened in Finland in December 2019, when four young, left-wing females took on the four most senior positions in the government. They are not archetypal witches, though they are clearly influenced by "witchcraft." We see, however, that the power of the witch in Western countries will not last forever. A combination of factors—and in particular the tendency for witches and those influenced by them to not have children—means that the traditional religious society, with its focus on limiting the damage that witches do to society and genetic interests, will arise once again.

But, first of all, if we want to understand the influence of witches in the Western world, it is useful to begin with a brief overview of the history of witchcraft in this region. Writing in English as I am, I will focus on the history of witchcraft in England and Scotland, but I will also explore the issue in America and Continental Europe.

Chapter 2

Long, Long Ago...

A Brief History of Witchcraft

To understand how the idea of witches developed, we have to understand the religious context in which they were found. This was a world in which evil spirits were assumed to exist. In all such pre-industrial cultures, witches are marked out by two key factors. First, they are inherently evil, partly because they serve these evil spirits; second, they are empowered by these evil spirits and perform magic that harms people.[1]

The Anthropology of Witches

Many anthropological studies of primitive tribes, such as those in Sub-Saharan Africa, have found that such people, often women, are frequently believed to exist.[2] Some African groups, such as modern-day Yoruba, tend to be far more fervent in their belief in witches than do the Bushmen or the Maasai, as belief in witchcraft seems to rise and fall over time.[3] In India,

1: Steven Rasmussen, "Sickness and Witches in Northwestern Tanzania: Listening to Pentecostal Ministers" in *Communities of Faith in Africa and the African Diaspora: In Honor of Dr. Tite Tiénou with Additional Essays on World Christianity*, eds. Casely Essamuah and David Ngaruiya (Eugene, OR: Pickwick Publications, 2013).

2: C.M.N. White, "Witchcraft Divination and Magic Among the Balovale Tribes," *Africa*, 8 (1948): 2.

3: Rasmussen, "Sickness and Witches in Northern Tanzania," *op. cit.*, 111.

the Dakkans are, in effect, witches. According to Indian researchers: "These women are supposed to cause harm to all persons who come under their sway; when children begin to vomit, turn pale and thin, or go on weeping for the whole night without reason, it is believed to be due to the influence of a local Dakkan." They are believed to receive their powers, in part, by communing with Kali, the goddess of destruction, in cremation grounds.[4] A similar concept to the witch exists among shamanistic tribes—such as those in Siberia—where the tribe's spiritual leader is believed to enter the spirit world during a trance and negotiate with the spirits on behalf of the tribe.[5] In Siberia, it is believed that certain wicked shamans have been trained by witches rather than by other shamans.[6] The Romans, at various points, also believed in the power of witches. The targets of witchcraft allegations tended to be childless elderly women, who were specifically believed to want to do harm to children. Christian Rome also believed in witches, but by the Dark Ages, the educated classes no longer took witchcraft very seriously.[7]

Medieval Europe: Jews, Gnostics, Muslims, and Homosexuals

Until the Middle Ages, the Church was inclined to dismiss witchcraft as superstition, although technically illegal. But

4: A.K. Sinha and B.G. Banjeree, "Tribal Witchcraft and Personalistic [*sic.*] Disease Theory: Concepts and Issues," in *Tribal Health and Medicines*, eds. A.K. Kalla and P.C. Joshi (New Delhi: Concept Publishing, 2004), 197.

5: See, I.M. Lewis, *Ecstatic Religion: An Anthropological Study of Spirit Possession and Shamanism* (London: Penguin, 1971).

6: Andrei Znamenski, *Shamanism in Siberia: Russian Records of Indigenous Spirituality* (Dordrecht: Springer Verlag, 2013).

7: Debbie Felton, "Witches, Disgust, and Anti-Abortion Propaganda in Imperial Rome," in *The Ancient Emotion of Disgust*, eds. Donald Lateiner and Dimos Spatharas (Oxford: Oxford University Press, 2016).

as the Middle Ages progressed feelings began to change. As historian Joseph Klaits has put it:

> *Beginning in the twelfth century, religion seemed to take on a heightened sense of immediacy for many people.... There was, however, an ugly side to this upsurge in religious emotion. It ended the traditions of pluralism that had characterized the medieval world before the twelfth century. . . . A more personal spiritual style made it harder to accept the presence of nonbelievers and nonconformists.*[8]

This manifested itself, argues Klaits, firstly in the persecution of Jews. As evolutionary psychologist Kevin MacDonald has observed, this made a great deal of sense in evolutionary terms.[9] As we will explore in more detail below, ethnic groups constitute distinct genetic clusters, meaning that if you act in the interests of your ethnic group, you are ultimately indirectly passing on your own genes.[10] Thus, if two ethnic groups come into conflict or are competing for scarce resources, we would expect one group to persecute the other.

A little later, the Church turned to pursuing a war against the Islamic world with missionary zeal.[11] The Church then turned to persecuting gnostic heretical sects, such as the Waldensians, of which there were entire communities of believers in France, the Low Countries, Germany, Switzerland, and Italy. They then focused on the Cathars, another gnostic split from the mainstream Catholic Church.[12] Gnostic sects were characterized by a personal search for spiritual knowledge over accepting orthodox Catholic teaching, a belief in salvation

---

8: Joseph Klaits, *Servants of Satan: The Age of Witch-Hunts* (Bloomington: Indiana University Press, 1985), 20.

9: Kevin MacDonald, *Separation and Its Discontents: Towards An Evolutionary Theory of Anti-Semitism* (Bloomington: 1st Books, 2004).

10: Frank Salter, *On Genetic Interests: Family, Ethnicity and Humanity in an Age of Mass Migration* (New Brunswick: Transaction Publishers, 2007).

11: Klaits, *Servants of Satan, op cit.*, 21.

12: *Ibid.*, 21-22.

via knowledge of the Divine, and a strongly dualistic theology.[13] The Church also turned to persecuting male homosexuals. According to Klaits: "Homosexuality, widely accepted and apparently widely practiced in twelfth century Europe, was regularly condemned by theologians" but it was not legally penalized until the late Middle Ages.[14]

It *is* possible to understand all of these persecutions in terms of group selection, which had intensified as the climate became colder as we moved towards the Maunder Minimum of extreme cold in the 17th century. Heretical sects could be understood to undermine group cohesiveness. Muslims tended to be of a different "race," with "races" being even more distinct from each other, in genetic terms, than ethnic groups.[15] There is much debate over the environmental and genetic reasons for homosexuality. However, it could be argued that, at the level of group selection, it might be beneficial to have a celibate caste, with people who invest their energies into the good of the group; this could happen via religiously inspiring them as priests or monks. Persecuting homosexuals would, therefore, be beneficial, because it would force them to repress their sexuality and sublimate this

---

13: Roelof van der Broek, *Studies in Gnosticism and Alexandrian Christianity* (Leiden: BRILL, 1996).

14: Klaits, *Servants of Satan, op cit.*, 21.

15: See Salter, *On Genetic Interests, op cit.*: "Race," it should be noted, only suffers from the same inherent problems as any system of categories. Race is clearly important because people are much more likely to accept organs transplanted from others of their own race. The most persistent fallacious criticism is that "there are more differences within races than there are between them." But the number of differences is less important than the *direction* of the differences. If a number of small differences all push in the same direction—which they will in the case of subspecies evolved to different ecologies—then this can add up to significant overall differences. Also, this conclusion was only reached by looking at genetic loci that differ very little between races. When genetic loci are employed that do differ between races, the finding is reversed. For a detailed refutation of the criticisms of "race," see Edward Dutton, *Making Sense of Race* (Whitefish, Washington Summit, 2020).

into work that was useful to the group.[16] Alternatively, it could be argued that homosexuality is associated with elevated levels of mental illness.[17] People who associate with the mentally ill are more likely to become mentally ill, therefore it would be for the good of group selection, under increasingly intense conditions, to persecute homosexuals.[18]

Medieval Christianity and Pagan Syncretism

The Church's persecutory fervor only moved on to witches towards the end of the Middle Ages. There were two key elements to the witch at this stage. She performed harmful magic and she had some kind of connection to Satan. Any kind of magic was associated, in the Christian mind, with demons and thus with Satan. In the Early Church, there was a clear belief in the power of demons and in witches, worshippers of whom were simply examples of pagans. For members of the Early Church, there was a simple dichotomy: Christians were good, Pagans were evil.[19] Saint Paul (c.5-c.67 AD) asserted, "No, but the sacrifices of pagans are offered to demons, not to God, and I do not want you to be participants with demons" (I Corinthians, 10:20). Saint Augustine of Hippo (354-430) proclaimed that all superstitious practices were ultimately associated with demons. *The Theodosian Code*, adopted in 438

16: Edward Dutton, "Why are Non-Heterosexual Males Attracted to Religious Celibacy? A Case for the 'Gay Shaman' Theory," *Mankind Quarterly*, 59 (2018): 197-215.

17: Ray Blanchard, "Review and Theory of Handedness, Birth Order, and Homosexuality in Men," *Laterality*, 13 (2008): 51-70.

18: T.E. Joiner, "Contagious depression: existence, specificity to depressed symptoms, and the role of reassurance seeking," *Journal of Personal and Social Psychology*, 67 (1994): 287-296.

19: Kirsten Birkett, *The Essence of the Reformation* (Leicester: Inter-Varsity Press, 2009), 16.

AD, asserted that all witches, whether they used harmful magic or simply foretold the future, should be put to death.[20]

But as we move into the Medieval period, two things have happened. Firstly, in becoming Christian, Europe had syncretized its traditional pagan beliefs with those of Christianity, meaning that mainstream religiosity reflected this mix of the two. Thus, monks would wash the bones of saints and then give their patients the water to drink, because it had supposedly taken on magic powers. Magical incantations, which were considered sinful, would actually include the Lord's Prayer.[21] Thus, the antagonism between "Christian" and "pagan" was defused, creating a tolerance of remnant pagan practices and beliefs as aspects of Christianity. Biblical emphasis on anything pagan being associated with Satan was less pronounced than it had been during the time of the Early Church. Moreover, there was a Medieval Warm Period, leading to milder environments and reducing the intensity of group selection for extreme social cohesion.

The Crusades and Changes in Attitudes to Witches

A tension developed, by the Middle Ages, whereby the religious authorities increasingly believed that witchcraft was a false belief—and even that it should be a crime to accuse someone of witchcraft or for a woman to claim she had magical powers—while many ordinary people still passionately believed in the reality of witchcraft. We can only speculate on why, but it's a general rule that people of low socioeconomic status tend to be more conservative and nostalgic for the "old ways." Hence, in religiously plural societies worldwide, low levels of education predict adhering to the oldest of a country's religions or denominations; in South Korea, for instance, the least

20: Klaits, *Servants of Satan*, *op. cit.*

21: Birkett, *The Essence of the Reformation*, *op. cit.*, 16-17.

educated tend to be Buddhist.[22] For many authorities, it was obvious that demons, and thus witches, had no real power at all. These were childish beliefs held by foolish rustics and over-excited townsmen. In 1075, a mob threw a woman off the city walls of Cologne for being a witch. In 1128, the people of Ghent disemboweled a woman whom they had accused of witchcraft. But this was mob violence, rather than official justice enacted by the sovereign authority. Witchcraft was illegal, and it carried the death penalty to cast evil spells on people or commune with Satan, but the ruling class was skeptical about such things even being possible. Some authorities specifically denounced popular superstitions that witches could cause storms, sink ships, or make people ill.[23] Others took the view that Christ gave his disciples the power to summon and do battle with demons, so it could not possibly be a crime to summon demons.[24]

In the wake of the Crusades, ancient Christian texts with Arabic commentaries were discovered that presented evidence of a highly intellectual form of magic. This had been practiced by educated people and the intellectuals of the Early Church had taken it very seriously. In a sense, there was a revival of the viewpoints of the Early Church. As a consequence, educated churchmen such as Saint Thomas Aquinas (1224-1274), began to seriously believe in witchcraft, promulgating the view that humans could, indeed, enter into pacts with demons. In 1320, Pope John XXII (1244-1334), who believed his Avignon court was bewitched, demanded that it be clearly established precisely what behavior was to be regarded as demonic and how this could be tested.[25] Although her execution was politically motivated,

22: Gerhard Meisenberg, Heiner Rindermann, Hardik Patel, and Michael A. Woodley, "Is it Smart to Believe in God? The Relationship of Religiosity with Education and Intelligence," *Temas em Psicologia*, 20 (2012): 101-120.

23: Michael Bailey, "Witchcraft and Demonology in the Middle Ages" in *The Routledge History of Witchcraft*, ed. Johannes Dillinger (London: Routledge, 2019).

24: Richard Kieckhefer, *Magic in the Middle Ages* (Cambridge: Cambridge University Press, 2000).

25: Bailey, "Witchcraft and Demonology," *op cit.*

Joan of Arc (c.1412-1431) was burnt as a witch in 1431. By that time, there was also an upsurge in the burning of individuals for having espoused heretical beliefs, consistent with the society becoming more religious.[26] Also by this time, the world was becoming colder—intensifying group-selection pressure for religiousness, as we will explore in more detail below.

In 1484, Pope Innocent VIII (1432-1492) issued a papal bull condemning to punishment those who slay infants, by which he seemingly meant witches. By this time, attitudes had gradually changed into a more dualistic theology—more in line with the views of the Early Church—whereby the Devil was the source of all evil and anything pagan was demonic. This was particularly pronounced in Protestant theology, as this reflected a "Reformation" of the Church, more closely resembling the Early Church. Accordingly, witch persecution became even more intense with the rise of Protestantism, as well as the Counter-Reformation, in which the Catholic Church adopted aspects of Protestantism. It should be pointed out, however, that there were respects in which the rational aspects of Protestantism made people more skeptical of certain kinds of accusations of witchcraft.[27] These views combined with the growing belief, even among educated people, that you could make pacts with and serve the Devil, and that this is what witches did.

In 1487, German Dominican prior Heinrich Kramer (c.1430-1505) published his widely-read *Malleus Malificarum*, which set out his views on precisely what constituted a witch and how witches should be persecuted.[28] The book, reprinted in 1520, became extremely influential in secular courts.[29] Another

---

26: Kathryn Harrison, *Joan of Arc: A Life Transfigured* (New York: Doubleday, 2014).

27: Brian Levack, *The Witch-Hunt in Early Modern Europe* (Harlow, Essex: Pearson Education, 2006), 130.

28: Heinrich Kramer and Jacob Sprenger, *The Malleus Malificarum of Heinrich Kramer and James Sprenger*, trans. Montague Summers (New York: Dover Publications, 1971).

29: Levack, *The Witch-Hunt in Early Modern Europe*, *op cit.*

prior, James Sprenger (1436-1495) was named as co-author of the second edition, though it has been suggested that this was a falsehood, perpetuated to give the book greater authority.[30]

Why Were 16th-Century Witch Crazes So Mild?

By the mid-16th century, witchcraft finally carried the death penalty in England, this being one of the last Western European countries to take witchcraft seriously. Witch-hunting was less severe in Britain, it has been argued, because of the jury system. In Continental Europe, the accused would be subject to an inquisition, where they might be tortured to extract a confession. In Britain, torture could only be used with the permission of the Privy Council, and it would only grant permission in very serious cases. As a result, witch-hysteria was suppressed in Britain. Confessions to flying through the night and other surreal activities—as were extracted through torture in mainland Europe—were rarer in Britain, since torture was used only sparingly. It might be averred that the court records should not be used as evidence of what witches believed, because the courts were so biased in favor of convicting these women of witchcraft, and also due to the fact that confessions made under severe duress are dubious to say the least. But this reasonable assumption would simply be inaccurate in an English context. In general, English courts acquitted people who were put on trial for witchcraft. For example, in the assizes held in England's home circuit between 1560 and 1600, only 23 percent of those tried for witchcraft were found guilty. Even in the following century, during the "witch craze," more than half

30: Hans Broedel, *The* Malleus Malificarum *and the Construction of Witchcraft: Theology and Popular Belief* (Manchester: Manchester University Press, 2003), 19.

of English witchcraft trials culminated in acquittal.[31] Again, the use of torture was extremely rare in English witchcraft cases. It has been proposed that this explains why the more bizarre confessions by witches—such as nighttime flights to gather and lick Satan's anus—are not found in English cases. Moreover, the use of sleep deprivation on English witches was "exceptional," limited to the case of the corrupt "Witch-Finder General" Matthew Hopkins (c.1620-1647) during the heights of the witch craze.[32] English witches, therefore, confessed to forms of sexual congress with Satan, for example, without torture and as part of a legal system that was skeptical of witchcraft and tended to acquit defendants of witchcraft. The use of torture would often lead to accused witches denouncing many other people as witches, in a chain reaction, resulting in mass executions. The lack of torture in Britain meant that this was relatively rare as well, reducing the incidence of widespread panics.

Central authorities were less powerful in Scotland, allowing the illegal use of torture, confessions extracted under torture, and thus a more intense witch-craze than in England, though it was nowhere as pronounced as on the Continent.[33] Other factors which made witch persecution worse in Scotland included that local lay magistrates were granted greater powers to investigate witchcraft allegations without the supervision of judges, whereas in England almost all witchcraft cases were heard before professional lawyers. In Scotland, juries could convict on majority verdicts, and the death penalty was automatic for witchcraft by 1563, which it was not in England for a first offence. Scotland was also, in some ways, more religious than England. We can only speculate on why this might be, but one possibility is that as Scotland was colder than England,

31: Frances Dolan, *True Relations: Reading, Literature, and Evidence in Seventeenth-Century England* (Philadelphia: University of Pennsylvania Press, 2013), 265, note 26.

32: Gilbert Geis and Ivan Bunn, *A Trial of Witches: A Seventeenth Century Witchcraft Prosecution* (London: Routledge, 1997), 53.

33: Levack, *The Witch-Hunt in Early Modern Europe*, *op cit.*, 219.

Darwinian pressures were harsher, and religiousness was more strongly selected for. But whatever the reason, by 1563, Scotland was predominantly Calvinist, and its ministers wanted to turn Scotland into a pure theocracy, rendering it vital to drive out the witches.[34] Witches were unequivocally condemned in the Bible—"Thou shalt not suffer a witch to live" (Exodus 22:18.)—and Calvinists were very strongly focused on the need for specific Biblical warrant as a sign of how to live their lives.[35] By contrast, the Anglican Church was more of a syncretisation of Protestant and Catholic dimensions.[36]

Witchcraft in 16th Century Scotland and the Attempted Murder of the King

The other factor in the intensity of witch persecution in Scotland was King James VI (1566-1625, r.1567-1625). He later became King James I of England (r.1603-1625), as when Elizabeth I died childless, he was next in line, as the great-great grandson of England's King Henry VII. James had reigned in Scotland from the age of 13 months, after his mother, Mary Queen of Scots (1542-1587, r.1542-1567)—who had also ascended to the throne as a baby (as had Mary's own father)—was forced to abdicate in his favor. James was so concerned about witchcraft that he had suspected witches brought before him personally, presided over witch trials, and wrote learned tracts on demonology.[37] James penned two short books on the subject:

34: *Ibid.*, 220.

35: Brian Pavlac, *Witch Hunts in the Western World: Persecution and Punishment from the Inquisition through the Salem Trials* (Westport: Greenwood Press, 2009), 90.

36: See Kelvin Randall, *Evangelicals Etcetera: Conflict and Conviction in the Church of England's Parties* (London: Routledge, 2017).

37: Jim Sharpe, "Witching-hunting and Witch Historiography: Some Anglo-Scottish Comparisons," in *The Scottish Witch-Hunt in Context*, ed. Julian Goodacre (Manchester: Manchester University Press, 2002), 188.

News from Scotland in 1591 and *Demonology* in 1597.[38] The seeds of the Scottish witch craze were sown in August 1589, when James had, by proxy, married Princess Anne, daughter of the Danish king. In September, Anne duly sailed to Scotland to join her husband. But during the voyage, there was a terrible storm, and the fleet had to shelter in Norway for several weeks to fix the ships and wait until the storm passed. The Danish admiral in charge of the returning fleet was Peder Munk (1534-1623), who was extremely unhappy about the condition of the ships. Hearing what had happened, James set sail from Leith, near Edinburgh, with his 300-strong retinue to personally bring his new queen back to Scotland.[39] They married again, in Oslo, and returned to Scotland, stopping in Copenhagen, on 1st May 1590. They had to wait this long because earlier attempts were battered by storms, with one of the fleet's ships being lost.

Peder Munk was on this voyage as well, in his capacity as a Danish ambassador. He criticised Christopher Valkendorff (1525-1601), the governor of Copenhagen, for the perilous nature of the crossing, blaming him for the condition of the ships. Witchcraft was taken far more seriously in Continental Europe than it was in Britain, as noted above. Valkendorff blamed a supposed witch in Copenhagen, Karen the Weaver, for sabotaging the ships and raising the storms. Karen was arrested in July 1590. She confessed and named one Anne Koldings as an accomplice. Under torture, Koldings named five other accomplices, including the wife of the Mayor of Copenhagen. Ultimately, 12 women were burned at the stake for bewitching Anne of Denmark's ships and raising storms against them. James took a keen interest in these trials and information about what had happened was widely reported in Scotland.[40]

38: Donald Tyson, *The Demonology of King James I* (Woodbury: Llewellyn Publications, 2011).

39: David Harris Wilson, *James VI and I* (London: Jonathan Cape, 1963), 85.

40: P. Maxwell-Stuart, "The Fear of the King is Death: James VI and the Witches of East Lothian," in *Witchcraft in the British Isles and New England: New Perspectives on Witchcraft, Magic, and Demonology*, ed. Brian Levack (London: Routledge, 2001), 210.

The North Berwick Witch Trials

Witchcraft trials continued in Scotland as normal. On April 28th, 1590, Meg Dow was tried for infanticide and witchcraft. She was found guilty and executed. On May 7th, there was an investigation into a complaint of witchcraft against Agnes Sampson. In November. David Seton, the Bailiff Depute of Trenent in East Lothian, became suspicious that his maid, Gellie Duncan, was a witch. He tortured her and after the discovery of a witch's mark, she confessed and was imprisoned. James himself wrote in *News from Scotland* that she was brutally tortured:

> *Yet would she not confess any thing, whereupon they suspecting that she had been marked by the Devil (as commonly witches are) made diligent search about her, and found the enemy's mark to be in her forecrag or forepart of her throat: which being found, she confessed that all her doings was done by the wicked allurements and enticements of the Devil, and that she did them by witchcraft.*[41]

In prison, Duncan began to tell a chilling story, naming a large number of other witches in the process. She alleged that a group of Scottish witches had conspired to delay or kill the King and Queen on their homeward voyage and that they had made subsequent attempts to kill the King by use of witchcraft and poisoning. She also stated that Frances Stewart, Earl of Bothwell (1562-1612) had requested that they do this. Bothwell was James's half-cousin via an illegitimate son of King James V (1512-1542, r.1513-1542). Bothwell was arrested and accused of treason, though he managed to escape and flee into exile.

The result of Duncan's confession was the North Berwick Witch trials between 1590 and 1591.[42] Roughly 70 people were accused, though the exact number burnt at the stake is not clear. They would all have been garroted—strangled as a spike

41: King James VI, *News From Scotland* (Edinburgh, William Wright, 1591).

42: Maxwell-Stuart, "The Fear of the King is Death," *op cit.*

was driven through their necks—before being burned.[43] One of those executed was a poor elderly widow and healer called Agnes Sampson, mentioned above. She was named by Duncan; however, even under torture, Sampson would not confess. James was so obsessed with witchcraft by this stage that, in January 1591, he had Sampson personally brought before him, where she *did* confess to raising a storm to kill the king, as well as to many other diabolical activities, such as meeting the Devil, who had appeared to her as a black man and as a dog. James became convinced of her guilt when she told him words that had passed between himself and his wife on their wedding night. It is quite possible, it should be added, that these were overheard by nearby courtiers, who started rumors that Agnes had somehow heard.

Between 1560 and 1707, roughly 4,000 people were burnt as witches in Scotland.[44] In England, between 1560 and 1707, fewer than 2,000 people were hanged for witchcraft. In 1700, the Scottish population was 1 million, compared to 5 million in England, so the witch persecution was clearly far fiercer in Scotland. The witch craze began slowly in England in the 1590s, picking up speed after King James I came to the throne in 1603. The peak of witch persecutions, as we will explore in more detail, was in the 1640s during the reign of James' son, Charles I (1600-1649). After this, witch-fervor gradually died down, as fewer and fewer educated people accepted the reality of witchcraft.[45] But, clearly, the nature of the society's religion is central to understanding any witch craze. And it is to understanding the nature of religion that we will now turn.

43: Brian Levack, *The Witch-Hunt in Early Modern Europe* (Harlow, Essex: Pearson Education, 2006), 94.

44: T.C. Smout, *A History of the Scottish People, 1560-1830* (London: Fontana Press, 1969).

45: It has been suggested that outbreaks of the mold ergot may have been responsible for some cases of witch hysteria, such as at Salem, Massachusetts. This has been disputed, not least because many of the relevant symptoms were not observed during witch crazes and also because ergot poisoning was already understood even at the time. See Homayun Sidky, *Witchcraft, Lycanthropy, Drugs and Disease: An Anthropological Study of the European Witch Hunts* (New York: Peter Lang, 1997).

Chapter 3

Fairy Godmothers

Religion, Patriarchy, and Physiognomy

Religion—generally understood as the collective worship of metaphysical beings, such as gods, spirits or ancestors—can take many forms. But the phenomenon is a human universal. It is an evolved cognitive bias or, you could say, "instinct." Strong religious feelings get elevated at times of stress, as are all cognitive biases.[1] Among other things, religion offers a sense of order and direction to our lives—and we are evolved to seek that out in the world. For example, we perceive causation in our surroundings and tend to over-detect agency. There are good reasons for this. If we assume the cause of that twig snapping in the woods is a wolf, then we'll prepare or run away. If we're wrong about that, we have lost very little. But if we assume that the sound it just the wind, and we're wrong, we have lost everything. This over-detection of agency leaves us with a cognitive bias whereby we are prone to find evidence of a "hidden hand" behind the workings of the world itself.[2] This is one of the reasons why people are inclined towards "conspiracy theories" at times of stress, and people who suffer from neuroticism—which involves constant strong negative feelings and stress—are prone to believing in such things (we will

1: Ara Norenzayan and Azim Shariff, "The Origin and Evolution of Religious Pro-sociality," *Science*, 322 (2008): 58-62.

2: Pascal Boyer, *Religion Explained: The Human Instincts that Fashion Gods, Spirits and Ancestors* (London: William Heinemann, 2001).

look at the nature of personality traits in more detail below).[3] Conspiracy theorists are, in effect, over-detecting agency and causation: "There is no such thing as a coincidence" and there are shadowy "agents" behind everything that takes place.

Further evidence for religiousness having been selected for in prehistory is that individual variation in this regard is influenced by genes. "Heritability" refers to the proportion of this variation that is accounted for by genes in a certain population at a certain time, and it can assume values between zero and 1. Religiousness is about 0.4 heritable, based on twin studies.[4] In addition, higher religiousness is associated with higher fertility[5] and with better physical and mental health.[6] Religiousness, specifically involving religious belief combined with collective worship, is correlated with overall health at about 0.3. The correlation is relatively modest because schizophrenia and bipolar disorder predict extreme religiosity. Nevertheless, it is clear that religiousness is robustly associated with health.[7] What is notable is that these associations are partly genetically influenced, meaning that the same genes (or genes that tend to

3: Emily Charlton, "Conspiracy Theories and Dissociative Experiences: The Role of Personality and Paranormal Beliefs," *MMU Psychology Journal* (2014), https://e-space.mmu.ac.uk/576580/.

4: Matt Bradshaw and Christopher Ellison, "Do Genetic Factors Influence Religious Life? Findings from a Behavior Genetic Analysis of Twin Siblings," *Journal for the Scientific Study of Religion*, 47 (2008): 529-544.

5: Lee Ellis, Anthony Hoskin, Edward Dutton, and Helmuth Nyborg, "The Future of Secularism: A Biologically Informed Theory Supplemented With Cross-Cultural Evidence," *Evolutionary Psychological Science*, 3 (2017): 224-242.

6: See Edward Dutton, Guy Madison, and Curtis Dunkel, "The Mutant Says in His Heart, 'There Is No God': The Rejection of Collective Religiosity Centred Around the Worship of Moral Gods is Associated with High Mutational Load," *Evolutionary Psychological Science,* 4 (2018): 233-244; Rachel Dew and Harold Koenig, "Religious Involvement, the Serotonin Transporter Promoter Polymorphism, and Drug Use in Young Adults," *International Journal of Social Sciences*, 2 (2014): 1.

7: Harold Koenig, "Religion, Spirituality, and Health: The Research and Clinical Implications," *ISRN Psychiatry*, 2012, http://dx.doi.org/10.5402/2012/278730.

be selected together) influence religiousness and health, rather than it being the religious lifestyle that causes better health. In other words, you involve yourself with collective worship because you are physically and mentally healthy; you don't become physically and mentally healthy simply because you attend church, though attending church does seem to help with mental health. Finally, religious behaviors are associated with activity in specific areas of the brain (as we will explore in more detail below). Taken together, all these factors strongly indicate that religiousness has been specifically selected for. Under harsh Darwinian conditions, humans evolved to be religious.[8]

Why Was Religiousness Adaptive?

There are a number of non-competing reasons that would potentially explain why religiousness has been selected for. Firstly, as mentioned, religiousness seems to hit in at times of stress and uncertainty and also during periods in which people are feeling excluded.[9] Religiousness would, therefore, allow people to feel that their life had meaning, calm them down such that they could act adaptively, stop them from becoming depressed and anxious, and reduce the negative health effects associated with being depressed and anxious.

Secondly, those who believed they are being watched over by a moral god would be less likely to get into fights, would be more pro-social, and would thus be less likely to be cast out by the band. Accordingly, believing in the same moral god

8: See Rüdiger Vaas, "God, Gains and Genes," in *The Biological Evolution of Religious Mind and Behavior*, eds. Eckhart Voland and Wulf Schiefenhövel (New York: Springer, 2009).

9: Norenzayan and Shariff, "The Origin and Evolution of Religious Pro-sociality," *op. cit.*

would cause people to be more pro-social.[10] In addition, people who are high in empathy are very concerned with identifying external signals of internal states. It would follow that this could be carried over to the world itself, meaning that they might feel that the world provided external signals of the feelings of a "mind" behind it. Seemingly for this reason, autism (blindness to social cues) and also low empathy predict atheism.[11]

Consistent with this hypothesis regarding how religiousness developed, religiousness has been found to be associated with the personality traits of Agreeableness (altruism) and Conscientiousness (rule following) in both religious and non-religious cultures.[12] Atheists have been shown to be higher in psychopathic personality (a condition that we will explore in more detail below) than religious people and also more willing to engage in deceptive activities such as tax fraud.[13] "Liberalism" and "conservatism" strongly parallel atheism and religiousness. For example, according to the Pew Research Center, 78 percent of Americans who identify as "conservative" claim to be "absolutely

10: Edward Dutton and Guy Madison, "Execution, Violent Punishment and Selection for Religiousness in Medieval England," *Evolutionary Psychological Science*, 4 (2018): 83-89 and Norenzayan and Shariff, "The Origin and Evolution of Religious Pro-sociality," *op. cit.*

11: Edward Dutton, Jan te Nijenhuis, Guy Madison, *et al.*, "The Myth of the Stupid Believer: The Negative Religiousness-IQ Nexus is not on General Intelligence (*g*)," *Journal of Religion and Health*, 59 (2020): 1567-1579; C. Caldwell-Harris, C. Fox Murphy, T. Velazquez, *et al.*, "Religious Belief Systems of Persons with High Functioning Autism" in *Proceedings of the 33rd Annual Meeting of the Cognitive Science Society*, Austin, TX: Cognitive Science Society, (2011): 3362-3366; Kirsten Barnes and Nicholas Gibson, "Supernatural Agency: Individual Difference Predictors and Situational Correlates," *International Journal for the Psychology of Religion*, 23 (2013): 42-52.

12: Jochen Gebauer, Wiebke Bleidorn, Samuel Gosling *et al.*, "Cross-Cultural variations in Big Five relationships with religiosity: A sociocultural motives perspective," *Journal of Personality and Social Psychology*, 107 (2014): 1064-1091.

13: Matthew Sarraf, Michael A. Woodley of Menie, and Colin Feltham, *Modernity and Cultural Decline: A Biobehavioral Perspective* (Basingstoke, Hants: Palgrave Macmillan, 2019), 167.

certain" that God exists, compared to 45 percent of liberals.[14] "Liberals" are primarily concerned with the individualizing values of "equality" and "harm avoidance," while "conservatives," though also concerned with these, also prize the binding values of group-loyalty, authority, and sanctity. These differences reflect the human's dual role as a pack animal, who will work for the good of his group, but also as an individual, who wishes to ascend the hierarchy of his pack.[15] Those with "liberal" values have been shown to be more aggressive than those with "conservative" values.[16] This further demonstrates that religiousness, in its current form, was selected for, in part, because it made you more pro-social and so less likely to make enemies and be killed. Religiousness both created and reflected a personality that was adaptive in the context of a highly group-oriented species.

It should be emphasized, however, that these are weak relationships. Thus, we would expect to find many "liberals" who were low in mutational load. Moreover, it should be emphasized that we are using the word "liberal" to describe those who are generally left-wing today, in a context in which being pro-equality and anti-traditionalism is associated with anti-natalism, atheism, nihilism, and multiculturalism. This has not always been the case. As we will see below, liberalism—if defined as challenging tradition and promoting equality—has long been a means via which members of the "middle class" have played for status—meaning it was adaptive, within certain boundaries, to be "liberal." The problem is that those boundaries—in essence, group selection for ethnocentric groups—have collapsed. This permits the virtue-signaling of liberalism to run away unchecked into signaling ideas that are extremely damaging to group and individual fitness, such as prizing another ethnic group over your own or prizing anti-natalism. In addition, we would expect

14: Pew Research Center, *Religious Landscape Study: Liberals*, 2020: https://www.pewforum.org/religious-landscape-study/political-ideology/liberal/.

15: Jonathan Haidt, *The Righteous Mind: Why Good People Are Divided By Politics and Religion* (London: Penguin, 2012).

16: Sarraf, Woodley, and Feltham, *Modernity and Cultural Decline*, *op. cit.*, 168.

the "spiteful mutants" I mentioned in Chapter 1—previously smaller in number and more easily suppressed—to innovate the more extreme forms of these ideas, and that these ideas would be accepted and employed as means of virtue-signaling for status. Thus, it is only in modern times that the "liberal" perspective has become clearly maladaptive. We will expand on this in more detail below.

Personality and Religiousness

What we call "personality" can be understood as behavioral and social tendencies, which recur in individuals. You probably know a few people who are "neurotic" to various degrees, some who are "open-minded" and "agreeable"; some who are "hot tempered," etc. There are many ways in which these traits can be compartmentalized, but for the purpose of the present discussion, we will use the five-factor or "Big Five" model. These factors are clusters of more specific facets—such as warmth or gregariousness—which tend to "go together" in the same individual. They are heritable in the region of 0.5[17] and can be described as:

1. *Extraversion*. Those who are outgoing, enthusiastic, and active; they seek novelty and excitement and experience positive emotions strongly. Those who score low on this express Introversion and are aloof, quiet, independent, cautious, and enjoy being alone.

2. *Neuroticism*. Those who are prone to stress, worry, and negative emotions and who require order. The opposite is those who are Emotionally Stable and who are better at taking risks.

3. *Conscientiousness*. Organized, directed, hardworking, but controlling. The opposite types are spontaneous, careless, and prone to addiction.

17: Daniel Nettle, *Personality: What Makes You Who You Are* (Oxford: Oxford University Press, 2007).

4. *Agreeableness*. Trusting, cooperative, altruistic, and slow to anger, such people can be contrasted with those who are uncooperative and hostile. There are two larger sub-dimensions to Agreeableness: altruism and empathy ("theory of mind," that is, the ability to intuit what others are thinking and feel what they feel). These positively correlate, but they are not the same.

5. *Openness to experience*. Those who are creative, imaginative, aesthetic, artistic, and open to new ideas. They can be contrasted with those who are practical, conventional, and tend to be set in their ways. The traits that compose Openness, such as "unusual thought patterns," "impulsive non-conformity," or "aestheticism," are often only weakly correlated.

Each factor is conceived as a dimension that is independent from the others, which means that together they form a more or less unique spectrum for each individual. The factors are named after one of their extremes. They are considered useful because they allow successful predictions to be made about life outcomes. Extraversion, independent of any other factor, is a predictor of early death. It increases the risk threefold, probably because Extraversion encourages you to take risks in pursuit of the high positive emotional reward.[18] Low Agreeableness predicts criminality and divorce. High Conscientiousness predicts doing well in the worlds of education and work, while low Conscientiousness predicts criminality, low socioeconomic status, and addiction. High Neuroticism predicts depression, anxiety, marital breakdown, and aspects of creativity. It is also associated with being a religious seeker and having periodic phases of religious fervor,[19]

18: Howard Friedman, Joan Tucker, Carol Tomlinson-Keasey, *et al.*, "Does Childhood Personality Predict Longevity?" *Journal of Personality and Social Psychology*, 65 (1993): 176-185.

19: Peter Hills, Leslie Francis, Michael Argyle, *et al.*, "Primary Personality Trait Correlates of Religious Practice and Orientation," *Personality and Individual Differences*, 36 (2004): 61-73.

as well as, very specifically, with heart disease,[20] possibly because constant stress puts pressure on the heart. Interestingly, being continuously religious—as opposed to going through phases of religiousness when stressed—correlates with *low* Neuroticism.[21] This means that mentally stable people tend to be, to some degree, religious. As we will explore in more detail below, this is seemingly because we have been under Darwinian selection to be religious and also to be mentally stable, because mentally unstable people not only become depressed and anxious but also angry and jealous, and they are prone to fights and dysfunction. Accordingly, religiousness and mental stability—selected for at the same time—have become bundled together.[22] An optimally high level of Openness is associated with artistic success.[23]

As mentioned, there are also sub-dimensions of the five factors that tend to be correlated with each other in most individuals. But it is also the case that what we might call the socially positive facets of each factor are correlated across factors. These are the aspects that make you a socially effective person—friendly, diligent, cooperative, reliable, open-minded—meaning that you "get on in life." As such, personality can be reduced down to a "General Factor of Personality," which involves being, in essence, high in most aspects of Agreeableness, Conscientiousness, Extraversion, and Openness, and low in most aspects of Neuroticism.

In much the same way, intelligence can be reduced down to the so-called "*g*-factor." Intelligence refers to the ability to solve cognitive problems and also how quickly you can solve them. The faster you can solve a problem, and the

---

20: Iva Cukic and Timothy Bates, "The Association Between Neuroticism and Heart Rate Variability is not Fully Explained by Cardiovascular Disease and Depression," *PLoS One*, 10 (2015): e0125882.

21: Hills, Francis, Argyle, *et al.*, "Primary Personality Trait Correlates of Religious Practice and Orientation," *op cit.*

22: Dutton, Madison, and Dunkel, "The Mutant Says in His Heart, 'There Is No God,'" *op cit.*

23: Nettle, *Personality*, *op. cit.*

harder it must be before you are stumped, then, generally, the more intelligent you are. There are three key kinds of intelligence: verbal, mathematical, and spatial. People differ in their abilities in tasks that measure each of these but, overall, people who score highly in one form of intelligence (such as verbal) also score highly in the other two. As such, there is a "general factor of intelligence" —known as *g*— which underpins these three different kinds of intelligence.[24] The same is true of the Big 5 personality factors and "General Factor of Personality."

People can be positioned higher or lower on a spectrum measuring this General Factor of Personality (GFP). GFP is associated with socioeconomic success.[25] It is also associated with religiousness.[26] This may be because a number of elements of the GFP—high Conscientiousness, high Agreeableness and low Neuroticism—predict religiousness. It may also be because, under Darwinian conditions, socioeconomic status predicted fertility,[27] and so did religiousness, as we will see in more detail below.

Certain unusual and socially problematic combinations of personality traits are known as personality disorders. Two such disorders will be germane to this exploration of witches, and so it would be useful to explore them at this point. The

---

24: See Arthur Jensen, *The* g *Factor: The Science of Mental Ability* (Westport, CT: Praeger, 1998); Edward Dutton and Michael A. Woodley of Menie, *At Our Wits' End: Why We're Becoming Less Intelligent and What It Means for the Future* (Exeter: Imprint Academic, 2018).

25: Dimitri van der Linden, Jan te Nijenhuis, and Arnold Bakker, "The General Factor of Personality: A Meta-analysis of Big Five Inter-correlations and a Criterion Related Validity Study," *Journal of Research in Personality*, 44 (2010): 315–327.

26: Curtis Dunkel, Charlie Reeve, Michael A. Woodley of Menie and Dimitri van der Linden, "A comparative study of the general factor of personality in Jewish and non-Jewish populations," *Personality and Individual Differences,* 78 (2015): 63-67.

27: Gregory Clark, *A Farewell to Alms: A Brief Economic History of the World* (Princeton: Princeton University Press, 2007).

first is Psychopathic Personality, now officially known as "Anti-Social Behavioral Disorder." As we noted earlier, this is higher among the non-religious than among the religious.[28] Anti-Social Behavioral Disorder is characterized by

1. Inability to sustain consistent work behavior;
2. Non-conformity, irritability and aggressivity;
3. Failure to honor financial obligations;
4. Frequent lying, failure to plan ahead and impulsivity;
5. Reckless behavior;
6. Inability to function as a responsible parent;
7. Failure to maintain long-term monogamous relationships;
8. Lack of remorse;
9. Conduct disorder in childhood.[29]

The other personality disorder that will become relevant is Narcissistic Personality Disorder. The term "narcissist," rather like "psychopath," has been popularized in recent years and has become something of a cheap insult, sometimes for a person who stands out or is willing to go against the grain. So we need to be clear what we mean by it. Narcissistic Personality Disorder is characterized by:

1. Grandiosity, with expectations of superior treatment from other people;
2. Fixation on fantasies of power, success, intelligence or attractiveness;
3. Self-perception of being unique, superior, and associated with high-status people and institutions;

28: Sarraf, Woodley of Menie, and Feltham, *Modernity and Cultural Decline*, *op cit.*, 167.

29: See Richard Lynn, "Racial and Ethnic Differences in Psychopathic Personality," *Personality and Individual Differences*, 32 (2002): 273-316.

4. Needing continual admiration from others;
5. A sense of entitlement to special treatment and to obedience from others;
6. Being exploitative of others to achieve personal gain;
7. Unwilling to empathize with the feelings, wishes, and needs of other people;
8. Being intensely envious of others, and the belief that others are equally envious of them;
9. A pompous and arrogant demeanor.[30]

It can be seen that psychopathic personality and Narcissistic personality crossover, but they are not exactly the same. Evidently, however, they involve aspects of low Agreeableness and low Conscientiousness.

Group Selection, Genetic Interests, and Altruism

So we can see how religiousness has been selected for in terms of individual selection, but this is not the only form of selection. Another is "group selection," something which is highly relevant because, as we will see below, this concept presents a likely explanation for the persecution of witches. Australian psychologist Frank Salter has demonstrated that people indirectly pass on their genes by aiding their kin, such as their cousins, as they share 12.5 percent more of their genes with a cousin than they do with a random member of their ethnic group.[31] Thus, "kin selection" explains why the childless

30: Hiram Caton, "The Exalted Self: Derek Freeman's Quest for the Perfect Identity," *Identity: An International Journal of Theory and Research*, 5 (2005): 359-384.

31: Frank Salter, *On Genetic Interests: Family, Ethnicity and Humanity in an Age of Mass Migration* (New Brunswick: Transaction Publishers, 2007).

spinster might be inclined to invest her resources in her nieces and nephews by giving them money at Christmas. They share, on average, a quarter of her genes and investing in them allows her to pass on her legacy.

We can move beyond "kin selection" to "group selection," a concept which we briefly explored earlier. An "ethnic group" is, in essence, a highly extended kinship group. Salter has demonstrated, using genetic data, that two random members of the same ethnic group, such as two native Englishmen, are, on average, more genetically similar to each other than they would be to a random Frenchman. It will be in your genetic interests to cooperate with kin over non-kin, helping your kin pass on their genes and thus, indirectly, yours. In much the same way, especially in a situation of conflict between two ethnic groups, it will be in your genetic interests to cooperate with members of your own ethnic group. Indeed, when there is the possibility of large numbers of your own ethnic group being killed by the other group, it may be in your genetic interests to *fight* that group, to the extent of sacrificing your own life. Using genetic assay data, Salter has calculated how related different races are, and thus how many members of a particular race would have to invade another race's territory for it to significantly damage the genetic interests of the native population. Such an invasion would damage the native population's genetic interests because if the invading population outcompeted or outbred the native population, then there would be fewer people carrying an individual native's genes, and thus fewer of his genes would survive.

To put this in perspective, if the world were composed solely of English people, then two random English people would have zero kinship. However, if the world were composed of English people and Danes, then two random English people would be the equivalent of seventh cousins: they would share a set of six great-grandparents. An enormous Danish invasion of England would be necessary for it to be the genetic equivalent, in terms of loss of genetic interests, of an English person having their nephew killed. This is because the English and the Danes are so genetically similar. If, however, England were invaded by Bantu people, then two random English people would be the equivalent of half-siblings or uncle and nephew in relation to these Bantu. This is because they would, in comparison to the Bantu, be so closely genetically related. Accordingly, a serious loss of the English person's genetic interests would be reached with far fewer Bantu invaders, due to the larger genetic distance between English people and Bantu people. In such a situation, it would potentially be in the genetic interests of a random English person to promote the genetic interests of their group, such as by sacrificing their life to repel even a small number of Bantu invaders. And, as we know, this is precisely what soldiers are expected to do. Heroism, praised in legend and verse by every people on Earth, is an example of group selection in action.[32]

So, once cooperative groups develop within a species, selection will act to promote those groups that possess the optimum level of certain qualities that permit them to out-compete other groups. Thus, selection will still operate on individuals within a group, but can also be seen to operate on groups themselves, as collections of individuals. This model helps to explain, for example, the development of altruistic tendencies: you behave altruistically towards people, in general, because it is a way of indirectly passing on your genes; hence people tend to be increasingly altruistic to others the more closely related they are to them. This has been found even within families and helps to explain why some siblings get on better with each other than others.[33]

British-Canadian psychologist J. Philippe Rushton (1943-2012) amassed a substantial body of work in favor of his "Genetic Similarity Theory." This is the idea that people act to maximize their indirect genetic interests, thus engaging in kin selection and group selection. Rushton found that we tend to

---

32: *Ibid.*

33: See J. Philippe Rushton, "Ethnic Nationalism, Evolutionary Psychology, and Genetic Similarity Theory," *Nations and Nationalism*, 11 (2005): 489-507.

be attracted to opposite sex photographs when our own faces are subtly morphed into them. Most couples are more similar than two random people from the same culture on numerous physical characteristics, particularly on the more genetic characteristics. We find people who are genetically similar to us attractive because by mating with somebody relatively—though not overly—similar to us, we pass on more of our genes. To a lesser extent, this is true of best friends. This operates even within families. Parents and grandparents invest more resources and emotional energy in children and grandchildren who are more genetically similar to themselves.[34] In terms of group selection, all else being equal, academics will cite other academics who are more ethnically similar to themselves,[35] people will be more inclined to give money to beggars from ethnic groups that are genetically closer to their own,[36] and single young people tend to live with other young people from their own race.[37] Kin selection involves making sacrifices for and investing in your kin. Group selection is a logical extension of this, as ethnic groups are extended genetic kinship groups.

Some researchers are skeptical of group selection being possible. In an essay entitled "The False Allure of Group Selection," Canadian psychologist Steven Pinker has criticized the concept by arguing that it deviates from the traditional model of Darwinian selection. According to Pinker, humans are surely not going to be evolved to do anything that damages their individual genetic interests.[38] It can be responded that, as an

---

34: *Ibid.*

35: Anthony Greenwald and Eric Schuh, "An Ethnic Bias in Scientific Citations," *European Journal of Social Psychology*, 24 (1994): 623-39.

36: Rushton, "Ethnic Nationalism, Evolutionary Psychology and Genetic Similarity Theory," *op cit.*

37: Vicky Clark and Keith Tuffin, "Choosing Housemates and Justifying Age, Gender, and Ethnic Discrimination," *Australian Journal of Psychology*, 67 (2015): 20-28.

38: Steven Pinker, "The False Allure of Group Selection," *The Edge*, June 18, 2012, https://www.edge.org/conversation/the-false-allure-of-group-selection.

extension of Darwin's model, by definition group selection will deviate, as does kin selection. By sacrificing themselves for their group, humans can indirectly benefit their genetic interests and, clearly, history is replete with humans engaging in self-sacrificial behavior for the group. The self-sacrifice of drone bees in a hive offer a useful analogy—clearly something beyond individual selection is occurring. It has also been proposed that early human groups were too small and sparse for group selection to take place, but this has been comprehensively refuted by abundant evidence of genocide among such groups. Genocide levels have increased with adoption of agriculture, and separated clans seem to form large groups with the express intent of repelling invaders from different tribes.[39] Moreover, detailed modeling has proffered that group selection is a reality, with researchers concluding: "If culturally transmitted systems of rules (institutions) that limit individual deviance organize cooperation in human societies, then it is not clear that any extant alternative to cultural group selection can be a complete explanation."[40]

Accordingly, if witches somehow damaged group selection, we can start to understand why they might be persecuted. Group-selected behavior, then, is effectively ethnocentric behavior. Religiousness is also associated with ethnocentric behavior, with being prepared to make sacrifices for your group, and with being apprehensive towards members of other groups: so-called positive and negative ethnocentrism.[41] Indeed, there is direct neurological evidence of the relationship between religiousness and ethnocentrism. In one study, an area of the brain called the posterior medial frontal cortex was rendered less active by trans-cranial magnetic stimulation. As a consequence, the subjects became both less negatively

---

39: See Brian Kiernan, *Blood and Soil: A World History of Genocide and Extermination from Sparta to Darfur* (New Haven: Yale University Press, 2007).

40: Peter Richerson, Ryan Baldini, Adrian Bell, *et al.*, "Cultural Group Selection Plays an Essential Role in Explaining Human Cooperation: A Sketch of the Evidence," *Brain and Behavioral Sciences*, 39 (2016): e30.

41: Edward Dutton, *Race Differences in Ethnocentrism* (London: Arktos, 2019).

ethnocentric and less likely to believe in God.[42] So, religiousness elevates ethnocentrism. Many computer models have shown that the group that is highest in positive and negative ethnocentrism is most likely to dominate other groups, all else controlled for, and thus win the battle of group selection.[43] Thus, religiousness is selected for in this way as well.

The religions that have survived the process of evolution—or, rather, the religious groups that have done so—are those that turn evolutionary imperatives into the "will of God." These groups believe that they are a special people, "chosen," while other groups are, in extreme cases of conflict, in league with the Devil or, at least, in some way inherently bad. As has been documented, they all have in common the fact that they render evolutionarily adaptive behavior—having many children, eating healthily, avoiding sources of disease, being ethnocentric, even disciplining your children in specific ways—divinely inspired and thus more likely to be followed.[44]

The Bounds of Patriarchy

Religion, which we know is adaptive, tends to reinforce a patriarchal society. This would imply that a patriarchal society is somehow more evolutionarily adaptive than a non-patriarchal one. It would potentially mean, for example, that a patriarchal society would be more conducive to high positive and negative

---

42: Colin Holbrook, Keise Izuma, Choi Deblieck, *et al.*, "Neuromodulation of Group Prejudice and Religious Belief," *Social Cognitive and Affective Neuroscience*, 11 (2016): 387-394.

43: Ross Hammond and Robert Axelrod, "The Evolution of Ethnocentric Behavior," *Journal of Conflict Resolution*, 50 (2006): 1-11.

44: Yael Sela, Todd Shackelford, and James Liddle, "When Religion Makes it Worse: Religiously Motivated Violence as a Sexual Selection Weapon," in *The Attraction of Religion: A New Evolutionary Psychology of Religion*, eds. David Slone and James Slyke (London: Bloomsbury, 2015).

ethnocentrism than a non-patriarchal society would be. Could this be the case? I would suggest that there is a persuasive argument that it may well be.

Islamic societies tend to be highly patriarchal. This is most obvious in the practice of "Purdah," the veiling of females once they reach puberty. In a society that is low in trust, females' wearing of the veil ensures that they are less likely to be raped, because they will not be able to sexually arouse men other than their husbands, as only they, along with very close male relatives, will see their hair or even their faces. This means that the veil is a kind of "insurance policy," allowing the husband to be relatively certain that the children in whom he is investing his resources are genuinely his own. It may be easy to infer that there is a fertile young woman behind the veil, but even so, the fact that she is covered will render her less arousing. The result of this, indirectly, is a more cooperative society. Males are better able to trust each other; they are less likely to get into jealous fights over females; and it is less necessary for males to invest their resources in mate-guarding. This has important implications for ethnocentrism—and thus for group selection—because it means that the whole society will become more internally cooperative and so more positively ethnocentric. The whole system of Purdah—which includes many other restrictions on female behavior—can be understood as an example of patriarchy.[45]

Rachel Grant and Tamara Montrose have made the important point that the evolution of patriarchy becomes fairly likely once males start investing in their female partners and offspring.[46] Central to this thesis is the Life History Strategy model. A fast Life History Strategy (LHS) is a suite of physical and mental traits that develop in an easy but unstable ecology, in which you must respond to sudden

45: For a discussion of Purdah and the evolutionary psychology of Islam, see Edward Dutton, *Islam: An Evolutionary Perspective*, Second Edition (Whitefish: Washington Summit Publishers, 2021).

46: Rachael Grant and V. Tamara Montrose, "It's a Man's World: Mate Guarding and the Evolution of Patriarchy," *Mankind Quarterly*, 58 (2018): 384-418.

unpredictable challenges by being extremely aggressive. A fast LHS is called an r-strategy, while a slow LHS is known as a *K*-strategy.[47] People who follow an r-strategy "live for the now." They live fast and die young, because they could be wiped out at any moment. Therefore, they invest energy in copulation but invest little energy in their partners nor in nurturing any offspring. *K*-strategists are adapted to a predictable yet harsh (and thus competitive) ecology, in which offspring who are insufficiently nurtured could all simply die. Thus, they "live slow and die old" and direct energy away from copulation and towards nurture, of both their partner and offspring.[48]

If husbands are extreme r-strategists, investing very little resources in a wife or children, then it doesn't really matter how a female behaves. The male simply seeks out sex and avoids investing in sexual partners or their offspring. Let the chips fall as they may. However, as we move towards a slower Life History Strategy, and females select for males who are prepared to invest in them, paternity certainty becomes increasingly relevant, because the male must avoid wasting bio-energetic resources. The male can try to achieve this goal by carefully selecting the kind of female in whom he invests, such as by trading looks for a seemingly trustworthy and cooperative personality, or by selecting based on markers of this, such as religiosity. But if the society is lawless and most people are relatively untrustworthy, he can gain an advantage by insisting on a highly patriarchal system. In the most extreme versions of this, Islamic societies being an example, only he can see his wife's face and her genitals might even be mutilated, meaning she can't enjoy sex and is less likely to be tempted to commit adultery. It is to the husband's advantage, if the wife demands investment in return for sexual access, to say, effectively, "*I will*

47: Michael A. Woodley, "The Cognitive Differentiation-Integration Effort Hypothesis: A Synthesis Between the Fitness Indicator and Life History Models of Human Intelligence," *Review of General Psychology*, 15 (2011): 228-245.

48: For a discussion of Life History Strategy, see Edward Dutton, *Making Sense of Race* (Whitefish: 2020), Chapter 6.

only give you that investment if I am in control, and thus can ensure I don't end up cuckolded." In other words, the husband must ensure that his investment is not wasted, genetically speaking. Thus, paternal control of females—and female sexuality especially—is the essence of patriarchy.

This is how Purdah, and patriarchal religion more generally, would be of evolutionary benefit in a relatively unstable society low in trust. Patriarchy would mean that males could be sure that their genes would be passed on. In its absence, with females being relatively free, they could more easily be raped by hostile bands of strongmen, perhaps even foreigners, or engage in frequent sexual liaisons. This type of station would greatly elevate paternity anxiety and inter-male conflict; there would be fierce competition to either guard mates or capture new ones. Such an internally warring and chaotic society would present itself as an easy target for a more unified tribe to dominate or conquer. Societies that have not developed patriarchy exist today, such as the Yanomamö of Venezuela and an abundance of tribes in Papua New Guinea, all of which maintain Stone Age levels of development. In these intensely violent and unstable cultures, females walk around naked, wield considerable power—including killing their own babies if they don't want them—and jealous males frequently fight over the best mates.[49] The primitive quality of these groups has a great deal to do with their failure to foster patriarchy.

In addition, as British researcher Steve Moxon has summarized: "Islamic garb, like other phenomena such as foot-binding and female circumcision, is as much to do with female–female competition as it is with men jealously guarding their women."[50] Wishing to reduce paternity anxiety, males are likely to sexually select for females who display evidence of being obedient to patriarchal norms. Thus, females, in order to gain

49: Napoleon Chagnon, *Yanomamö: The Fierce People* (New York: Holt, Rinehart and Winston, 1968).

50: Steve Moxon, *The Woman Racket: The New Science Explaining How the Sexes Relate at Work, at Play and in Society* (Exeter: Imprint Academic, 2008).

high-status males (as is their evolved desire), will compete to signal their religiousness and acceptance of patriarchal norms.[51] Religiousness tends to be higher in females, as it has been selected for repeatedly throughout human history.[52] And females will attempt to out-compete each other in displays of their acceptance of patriarchal norms.

Among the Maasai of Kenya, for example, girls are ritualistically circumcised just after they reach puberty. This takes place in front of a large number of witnesses, such as members of the initiates' family and their friends. Maasai females display great eagerness to be circumcised.[53] Among the Hamner of Ethiopia, boys graduate into manhood by stripping naked and jumping over a line of cattle. When a young unmarried woman's brother is about to undergo his cattle jumping ordeal, she enters a trance in which she allows herself to be severely whipped, by male members of the tribe, on her back, legs, and arms, such that there are permanent scars. These scars are proudly displayed as evidence of her loyalty to her brother and to her broader family. She will ask to be whipped as brutally as possible, until she is streaming with blood, and, often, senior males in the Hamar intervene to prevent the process from going too far. In doing so, she is competing with other women to show her loyalty to the patriarchal system.[54]

Certainly, most critics of patriarchy, feminist and otherwise, do not stress its evolutionary logic, particularly a

---

51: David Buss, *The Evolution of Desire: Strategies of Human Mating* (New York: Basic Books, 1989).

52: Darren Sherkat, "Sexuality and Religious Commitment in the United States: An Empirical Examination," *Journal for the Scientific Study of Religion*, 41 (2002): 313-323.

53: William Kladky, "Maasai Circumcision Ceremony," in *They Do What? A Cultural Encyclopedia of Extraordinary and Exotic Customs from around the World*, ed. Javier Galvan (Santa Barbara: ABC-Clio, 2014).

54: Bruce Parry and Mark McCrum, *Tribe: Adventures in a Changing World* (London: Penguin, 2007).

logic that would promote social cohesion. At best patriarchy is viewed as a grave historical mistake, or perhaps merely a product of the fact that human males are stronger and more aggressive than females (which is itself, of course, an evolved phenomena). At worst, critics of patriarchy view it as an enormous "conspiracy theory," in which females are effectively suppressed for the sake of it, with no evolutionary logic to it at all. In response, it can be argued that there is abundant evidence that ethnic groups are extended genotypes. Patriarchy would reduce inter-male conflict at the expense of female freedom—but this would lead to greater cooperation and positive ethnocentrism. Regarding witches—who can be seen as a particularly vehement attempt to undermine patriarchy—the groups that persecuted them the most effectively would have elevated their evolutionary fitness.

A second objection to Grant and Montrose's model is that a simpler explanation for witch persecution is at hand. Witches were unpleasant old women who, for whatever reason, antagonized their neighbors. So, in the most obnoxious cases, they were persecuted and killed as a result. Certainly, witches' unpleasantness may have been a part of why they were targeted, but again, the evolutionary logic to this would be that their ultimate crime was undermining in-group cooperation. Moreover, such a proposal begs the question of why it was specifically women who were targeted, when there were surely plenty of unpleasant old men as well. It also makes one wonder why witchcraft was tolerated for long periods of English history, for example, with the witch craze only manifesting in earnest in the 17th century, as we will see later. It has been demonstrated that there was genetic selection for religiousness over time in England between the Middle Ages and the 16th century and thus selection for patriarchy.[55] As Grant and Montrose note, this religiousness was tightly linked to patriarchy, which was upheld as God's will.

55: Edward Dutton and Guy Madison, "Execution, Violent Punishment and Selection for Religiousness in Medieval England," *Evolutionary Psychological Science*, 4 (2018): 83-89.

A third argument is that witchcraft—with its belief in Satanic sex, which we will explore later—is a highly convoluted way of repressing females, and there are surely simpler means.[56] It can be countered that many forms of patriarchal repression might be regarded as extremely elaborate compared to others, but they are still accepted as such. There are surely easier ways to repress women than foot-binding or circumcision. In an evolutionary power battle between males and females, imposing patriarchy can be expected to lead to a kind of arms race between male and female interests, in which methods become evermore elaborate and complicated, and, from an outside perspective, bizarre. Moreover, there is good reason to believe that males did not simply concoct the basic components of "witchcraft," so the entire argument is based on a highly questionable premise. The idea of the "incubus"—a night devil that copulates with females—is extremely ancient, being recorded in ancient Near Eastern texts.[57] This would imply that the incubus is an interpretation, by religious people, of some psychological event.

A fourth argument is to aver that as most of the women accused of witchcraft were old, they could not possibly create the "paternity anxiety" that might be understood as undermining the patriarchal system. The rejoinder to this is that the witches themselves might not be creating paternity anxiety, but their survival as independent females might induce others to question the need for patriarchal controls, and thus obedience to the social system in general. In that females would have evolved to a system of patriarchy, it could be assumed that, in its absence, females might behave in ways that are socially problematic, and thus damaging to the good of the group.[58] Grant and Montrose's model is overall more

---

56: Stuart Clark, *Thinking with Demons: The Idea of Witchcraft in Early Modern Europe* (Oxford: Oxford University Press, 1999).

57: See Raphael Patai, *The Hebrew Goddess* (Detroit: Wayne State University Press, 1990).

58: Apostolou, *Sexual Selection Under Parental Choice, op cit.*

parsimonious than the alternatives. It explains more and is less question-begging.

Patriarchy in World Religions

Put simply, at the level of group selection, patriarchy is adaptive. We would, therefore, expect successful religions to promote patriarchy as divine will, and this is exactly what they do. Saint Paul tells the Corinthians: "But I want you to realize that the head of every man is Christ, and the head of the woman is man, and the head of Christ is God" (1 Corinthians 11:3). He later added,

> *Let your women keep silence in the churches: for it is not permitted unto them to speak; but they are commanded to be under obedience as also saith the law. And if they will learn any thing, let them ask their husbands at home: for it is a shame for women to speak in the church. (1 Corinthians 14: 34-35)*

Women are to be subjugated by men as God's will—Saint Paul was absolutely explicit: "Wives, submit yourselves unto your own husbands, as it is fit in the Lord" (Colossians, 3:18). In the Old Testament, God Himself is clear that patriarchy is His divine will: "Unto the woman He said, 'I will greatly multiply thy sorrow and thy conception; in sorrow thou shalt bring forth children; and thy desire shall be to thy husband, and he shall rule over thee'" (Genesis, 3: 16). God also punishes Adam specifically because he listened to his wife, who told him to eat the fruit from the Tree of Knowledge of Good and Evil, fruit God had told them not to eat but which Eve had been tempted to partake in by the Serpent (Genesis, 3:17). Those who fail to believe in or fear God will be miserable. But it could also mean that you should not tolerate females in positions of authority, and if you do, then there will be terrible consequences. Indeed, this interpretation would be consistent with the previous verse, in which Eve is punished for disobeying her husband.

During the period in which the Old Testament texts were written, the Jews had already seen civilizations, including their own, rise and fall. The prophetic literature was written during the period of Exile, when Israel and Judea had been invaded by other peoples, meaning that Jewish power and civilization had collapsed. This was blamed on the Jews losing their fear of Yahweh and adopting decadent, pagan practices, including worshipping assorted pagan gods. However, it was also implicitly blamed on the collapse of patriarchy: "As for my people, children are their oppressors, and women rule over them. O my people, they which lead thee cause thee to err, and destroy the way of thy paths" (Isaiah, 3: 12).

Islam is equally clear about the place of females. Women must obey their husbands, and if they are particularly problematic, the husband has the right to kill his wife:

> *He sat before the Prophet (peace be upon him) and said: Apostle of Allah! I am her master; she used to abuse you and disparage you. I forbade her, but she did not stop, and I rebuked her, but she did not abandon her habit. I have two sons like pearls from her, and she was my companion. Last night she began to abuse and disparage you. So I took a dagger, put it on her belly and pressed it till I killed her. Thereupon the Prophet (peace be upon him) said: Oh be witness, no retaliation is payable for her blood. (Sunan Abu Dawud, 38:4348)*

Hinduism is similarly patriarchal. It is stated in the Sanskrit legal text *Manusmriti*: "A virtuous wife should constantly serve her husband like a god, even if he behaves badly, freely indulges his lust, and is devoid of any good qualities."[59] Devout Hindu women must be obedient to their male relatives: "When her father, or her brother with her father's permission, gives her to someone, she should obey that man while he is alive and

59: *Manu's Code of Law: A Critical Edition and Translation of the Manava-Dharmasatra*, trans. Patrick Olivelle (Oxford: Oxford University Press, 2005), Chapter 5.

not violate her vow to him when he is dead."[60] Indeed, in some respects, Hinduism is the most extreme patriarchal religion.

> *For a woman, there is no independent sacrifice, vow or fast; she will be exalted in Heaven by the mere fact that she has obediently served her husband. A good woman, desiring to go to the same world as her husband, should never do anything displeasing to the man who took her hand, whether he is alive or dead. After her husband is dead, she may voluntarily emaciate her body by eating pure flower, roots, and fruits, but she must never mention even the name of another man. Aspiring to that unsurpassed Law of women devoted to a single husband, she should remain patient, controlled, and celibate until her death.*[61]

In effect, the Hindu wife is encouraged to commit "Sati," allowing herself to be burned alive on her husband's funeral pyre. It is as if when her husband dies, she does as well. She is nothing without him. The British banned this practice in 1861, but it persisted in rural areas of India for over a hundred years.[62] The last known case of Sati was in Rajastan, in northern India, in 1987, when an 18-year-old widow was burned alive on her husband's funeral pyre.[63]

In Hinduism there are three main gods who manifest themselves in different stages of the universe. Universes come into existence as "Brahma," they follow the life cycle of "Vishnu," and they are ultimately destroyed by "Shiva," the goddess of destruction. Then Brahma breathes new life into the universe, and the process

---

60: *Ibid.*, Chapter 4.

61: *Ibid.*, Chapter 5.

62: Sukeshi Karma, *Bearing Witness: Partition, Independence, End of the Raj* (Calgary: University of Calgary Press, 2002), 41.

63: Hamza Khan, "India's Last Known Case of Sati" *The Indian Express*, September 22, 2019, https://indianexpress.com/article/india/she-ceased-to-be-a-woman-was-a-goddess-6016915/.

begins anew.[64] Like the Prophet Isaiah, Hindu scriptures associate female empowerment with this collapse of civilization. Each "universe" or cosmic life span ("Kalpa") is divided into four ages, known as "Yugas." In each of the ages, the metaphorical "bull of dharma" loses one of his legs, meaning that by the fourth age, he has lost all of his legs. The fourth stage is known as Kali Yuga. It is a period of irreligious chaos, after which the world is destroyed by a great flood and the cosmos re-emerges from this, purified, such that the cycle can begin all over again.[65] According to the *Manusmriti*:

> *In the Kaliyuga . . . everyone will delight in evil. . . . The Brahmans will neglect the Vedas, hanker after presents, and be lustful and cruel. . . . They will despise the scriptures, gamble, steal and desire intercourse with widows. . . . In this Yuga, men will be under the sway of women, and women will be excessively fickle. . . . In the first twilight of the Kaliyuga, people will disregard Vishnu; and in the middle of it, no one will mention his name.*[66]

Put simply, religions that have survived tend to be patriarchal, because it is patriarchal societies that are more likely to survive the battle of group selection. Accordingly, anything that questioned patriarchy or traditional religious values more broadly, such as the spiteful mutant, would have been purged or viewed as a sign of the apocalypse.

Judging People by What They Look Like

Many of these evolutionarily adaptive ideas are, essentially, openly expressed in religious texts, such as the instruction

64: See Gavin Flood, *An Introduction to Hinduism* (Cambridge: Cambridge University Press, 1996).

65: See Devdutt Pattanaik, *The Man Who Was a Woman and Other Queer Tales from Hindu Lore* (London: Routledge, 2014).

66: Quoted in William Chambers and Robert Chambers, "Hinduism," in *Chambers' Miscellany of Instructive and Entertaining Facts*, Vol. 8, (1870), 179.

to "Be fruitful and multiply" (Genesis 1:28). However, others are conveyed more subtly, though it is quite obvious that the religious society accepts them and that they are adaptive. One of these is physiognomy: the ancient art of judging a person's psychology—the kind of personality they have and how intelligent they are—from what they look like, and particularly from their face. The Ancient Greeks accepted the utility of physiognomy. Aristotle (384-322 BC) wrote in *Prior Analytics*, "It is possible to infer character from features," and many other Ancient Greek thinkers were of the same opinion.[67] This belief in physiognomy manifested itself in the view that it was possible to discern whether or not a woman was a witch by her appearance. She would tend to be unsightly and deformed, and she might even possess a "Witch's Mark." This would likely have been a birth defect but, as already discussed, physical mutations generally correlate with mental mutations, for reasons we will explore in greater depth below.

Belief in physiognomy is also reflected in Christian texts. Biblical scholar Chad Hartsock has noted that, "the use of the physical body to indicate one's character is very much practiced in the Hebrew Bible" and, also, that the belief in physiognomy was "widespread throughout the cultures of Mesopotamia."[68] For example, Hartsock analyses the rather "sinister" story of Ehud the Benjaminite, found in Judges 3 (12-30). Ehud is a devious man, and left-handed, and Hartsock explains that the early readers of this text would have immediately picked up on this fact. Ehud was sent by Israel to the Moabite King, Eglon. Ehud was able to smuggle a dagger into Eglon's court precisely because he stashes it in his right thigh, where it wouldn't be noticed. After arranging a private meeting with the King, Ehud stabs Eglon and "filth" flows out of his body. The author of the story conveys a great deal of meaning through these descriptions.

67: Aristotle, *Prior Analytics*, trans. Robin Smith (Indianapolis: Hackett Publishing, 1989).

68: Chad Hartsock, *Sight and Blindness in Luke-Acts: The Use of Physical Features in Characterization* (Leiden: BRILL, 2008), 83.

Eglon was not just an adversary of Israel but morally repugnant, deserving of his ignoble end. Ehud is a dangerous assassin—but one useful to Israel—and his left-handedness is not incidental.[69]

"Sinistrality" is, in fact, indicative of abnormality. Since the norm is to be right-handed, left-handed people have asymmetrical brains and tend to have been subject to some kind of developmental instability.[70] Consistent with this, left-handedness is associated with elevated levels of depression and autism, as well as with moderately reduced IQ.[71] Higher levels of psychopathic personality are correlated with being ambidextrous, that is, non-right-handed.[72] This makes sense because left-handedness, or non-right-handedness, reflects the fact that something has gone wrong in development due to mutant genes or a suboptimal environment; so we would expect it to be associated with other things going wrong, such as the development of a personality disorder.[73] It has also been found that though left-handed people have lower average IQ than right-handed people, they are over-represented among those who have outlier *high* IQ. Having outlier high IQ could itself be caused by (albeit positive) mutation, which would correlate with other (likely negative) mutations, as most mutations are maladaptive. Deviousness is a function, in part, of psychopathic personality and high intelligence.

Analyzing Leviticus, which deals with Jewish purity laws, Hartsock also notes that priests must be without physical

69: Hartsock, *Sight and Blindness in Luke-Acts, op. cit.*, 90.

70: Michael A. Woodley of Menie, Heitor Fernandes, Satoshi Kanazawa, and Edward Dutton, "Sinistrality is Associated with (Slightly) Lower General Intelligence: A Data Synthesis and Consideration of Secular Trend Data in Handedness," *HOMO: Journal of Comparative Human Biology*, 69 (2018): 118-126.

71: Dutton, Madison and Dunkel, "The Mutant Says in His Heart, 'There Is No God,' *op cit.*

72: A.R. Mayer and David Kosson, "Handedness and psychopathology," *Cognitive and Behavioral Neurology*, 13 (2000): 233-238.

73: Woodley of Menie, Fernandes, Kanazawa, and Dutton, "Sinistrality is Associated with (Slightly) Lower General Intelligence," *op cit.*

"blemish" (Leviticus 21: 16-18).[74] In other words, they mustn't have physically unattractive markers. This is because, he explains, physical blemishes are assumed to reflect "moral blemishes." This assumption is not inaccurate and, indeed, it is consistent with belief in the Witch's Mark.

"Blemishes" are quite significant features in light of Darwin's conception of "sexual selection," as he lays it out in *The Descent of Man* (1871). This is the idea that, within a species, one sex selects mating partners from the other sex on the basis of traits that do not have direct survival value, but nevertheless signal superior genetic health. These are called sexual ornaments. An obvious example of such sexual ornaments is the peacock's tail, which is conspicuous to predators and cumbersome when out-running them. The tail is, however, a "fitness indicator," in the sense that only a healthy and well-fed animal could grow such an outlandish ornament and also stay alive while carrying it around. A peacock with poor genotypic fitness, or many deleterious mutations, would have to invest more of its resources in simply staying alive, and would not be able to grow or maintain as impressive a tail. The tail of a less fit peacock would be smaller, duller, less ornate, and more asymmetrical. As such, the peacock is advertising the fact that his genes are so fantastic that he can handicap himself with a large tail and still have the resources left over to make it colorful and ornate. It's rather like a human male openly giving money to charity and, in so doing, stressing just how successful he is. He has cash to burn. American evolutionary psychologist Geoffrey Miller argues that sexual dimorphism in humans—men and women looking different—can therefore partly be explained by sexual selection.[75]

This has obvious consequences in terms of physiognomy. The brain is an extremely complex organ and 84 percent of our genes relate to the brain, rendering it quite susceptible

---

74: Hartsock, *Sight and Blindness in Luke-Acts*, *op cit.*, 98.

75: Geoffrey Miller, *The Mating Mind: How Sexual Choice Shaped the Evolution of Human Nature* (New York: Anchor Books, 2000).

to deleterious mutations.[76] This means that an individual whose body exhibits signs of deleterious mutations will almost certainly have a brain that is also negatively affected. These can be personality disorders, mental illnesses, ways of thinking that are fitness-damaging (such as not wanting to have children), or anything else of this kind, even to a very minor degree. In this way, your maladaptive body will, even in only a small way, be a reflection of your maladaptive mind.

We can extend this to anything that people find attractive, even "unblemished skin." If you have a skin condition, it either means that you have a poor immune system—meaning you cannot fight off pathogens and so maintain attractive skin—or you carry mutations that cause your skin to develop maladaptively. In essence, you have high "mutational load." Consistent with this, it has been found that psychiatric conditions, depression, and anxiety are elevated among patients with acne; the more severe their acne is, the more pronounced these symptoms are.[77] One might counter that suffering from acne triggers depression or anxiety. But another study has dealt with this very question, finding that greater acne severity is not simply causally related to worse quality of life. Acne sufferers, independent of their acne, are prone to poorer social outcomes and poorer quality of life, and this is more pronounced the more severe the acne is.[78]

More broadly in line with the model examined above, it has been found that the faces of criminals are less symmetrical

---

76: Michael A. Woodley of Menie, Matthew Sarraf, Radomir Pestow, and Heitor Fernandes, "Social Epistasis Amplifies the Fitness Costs of Deleterious Mutations, Engendering Rapid Fitness Decline Among Modernized Populations," *Evolutionary Psychological Science*, 3 (2017): 181-191.

77: Ali Gul and Emine Colgecen, "Personality Traits and Common Psychiatric Conditions in Adult Patients with Acne Vulgaris," *Annals of Dermatology*, 27 (2015): 48-52.

78: Jennifer Krejci-Manwaring, Katherine Kerchner, Steven Feldman, *et al.*, "Social Sensitivity and Acne: The Role of Personality in Negative Social Consequences and Quality of Life," *International Journal of Psychiatry in Medicine*, 36 (2006): 121-130.

than the faces of non-criminals.[79] This is just as we would expect. Criminality is associated with low Agreeableness, low Conscientiousness, psychopathic personality, and, accordingly, low levels of cooperativeness. Under harsh Darwinian conditions of group selection, there would be strong evolutionary pressure for cooperative societies, meaning that societies high in criminality would have been wiped out. There would also be a strong tendency for criminals to be cast out or executed, preventing them from passing on their genes. Indeed, it has been argued that the fact that many European societies executed almost all criminals across the Medieval and Early Modern eras—these being overwhelmingly young men—acted to "pacify" Europe, by reducing the fertility of those low in Conscientiousness and Agreeableness and high in psychopathic personality, a point made by Peter Frost and Henry Harpending (1944-2016).[80] We are selected to be genetically non-criminal, so we would expect criminality to be associated with mutations relating to the mind, and these, in turn, would be associated with mutations of the body, leading to criminals being more likely to have asymmetrical faces. As already noted, this helps to explain why witches were judged by what they looked like.

A parallel explanation for the shunning of those with poor skin from the Jewish priesthood relates to those who tended to pass on their genes in pre-industrial societies. It was the rich who passed on more of their genes; priests would be rich; so it had to be ensured that priests were not genetically maladapted. The heritability of personality traits is around 0.5,[81] and Jewish priests (unlike Catholic ones) were permitted to have children.[82]

79: Xiaolin Wu and Xi Zhang, "Automated Inference on Criminality Using Face Images," *arXiv* (2016): 1611.04135.

80: Peter Frost and Henry Harpending, "Western Europe, State Formation, and Genetic Pacification," *Evolutionary Psychology*, 13 (2015), https://doi.org/10.1177/147470491501300114.

81: Nettle *Personality*, *op cit.*

82: Karl Skoreki, Sara Salig, Shraga Blazer, *et al.*, "Y Chromosomes of Jewish Priests," *Nature*, 385 (1997).

We know from wills and parish records that in Early Modern Europe, the richer 50 percent of the population had between 40 and 100 percent more surviving children compared to the poorer 50 percent.[83] This was because wealthier parents had, on average, genotypes that entailed better health and ability to care for themselves and their children, at the same time as these favorable traits also entailed their higher wealth. This wealth, in turn, provided them with better living conditions in general and better access to more nutritious food in particular. Thus, while the average child mortality rate was about 50 percent in pre-industrial England, it was much lower among the wealthier and much higher among the poor, many of whom would find that all their children died before reaching fertile age.

The result of this was that traits that predicted attaining socioeconomic status increased, and those of low IQ and poor impulse control, occupying the lowest rung of the socioeconomic ladder, died out across generations. Intelligence is about 0.8 heritable and personality traits such as Conscientiousness are about 0.5 heritable, and both strongly predict socioeconomic status.[84] This created "downward mobility," in which people had to move down the social ladder to fill the spaces left open by the death of the previous generation's lowest rung. Accordingly, most Early Modern males occupied a lower social rank than that of their father: the sons of gentlemen became yeomen (doing some farm work themselves); the sons of yeomen became husbandmen (taking to the plough themselves); the sons of husbandmen mixed a smallholding with doing labor for husbandmen or yeomen; and so on.[85]

83: Dutton and Woodley of Menie, *At Our Wits' End*, *op cit.*; Clark, *A Farewell to Alms*, *op. cit.*; Richard Lynn, *Dysgenics: Genetic Deterioration in Modern Populations* (London: Ulster Institute for Social Research, 2011), 45.

84: Mathilde Almlund, Angela Duckworth, James Heckman, and Tim Kautz, "Personality, Psychology and Economics" in *Handbook of the Economics of Education*, eds. Eric Hanushek, Stephen Machin, and Ludger Woesmann (Amsterdam: Elsevier, 2011).

85: See Clark, *A Farwell to Alms*, *op cit.*

We know that this process of social descent and increasing intelligence was occurring in all pre-industrial societies much of the time, though there were periods in which it weakened tremendously. Even so, in all such societies, to varying degrees, socioeconomic status predicted the number of surviving children.[86] According to Jewish scholars Alexander Carlebach and Judith Baskin, there was a specific commandment for all Jewish males to be as fertile as possible.[87] God specifically blessed those who feared him with "the absence of barrenness" (Exodus 23: 26), to the extent that the Egyptians were worried about how fertile their Hebrew slave population were (Exodus 1: 7-12). Barrenness was often regarded as a specific curse from an angry God (Jeremiah 22: 30). So intense is the Jewish focus on fertility that "Rachel preferred death to childlessness" (Genesis 20: 17-18). A childless scholar is not eligible to sit on the Sanhedrin. And a priest who "hath his stones crushed" is unfit for Temple service (Leviticus 21:20). It has been demonstrated that Jewish priests, at least in later periods, had particularly high completed fertility, in part due to eugenic customs that rendered them wealthy and thus able to have large families.[88] In a society in which priests were extremely fertile, it would thus be imperative that only the highly intelligent and highly conscientious be allowed to enter this profession: their offspring would be the leaders of the future. It would be adaptive to judge people's psychology by their appearance and exclude the physically unattractive from the priesthood, due to the elevated likelihood that they would be mentally maladaptive as well.

Fascinatingly, it has been documented that Karl Marx (1818-1883) suffered from a skin condition, whereby he would

---

86: *Ibid.*

87: Alexander Carlebach and Judith Baskin, "Barrenness and Fertility," in *Encyclopedia Judaica,* 2008, https://www.jewishvirtuallibrary.org/barrenness-and-fertility.

88: Kevin MacDonald, *A People That Shall Dwell Alone: Judaism as an Evolutionary Strategy* (Westport: Praeger, 1994).

regularly erupt with boils all over his face and body.[89] Marx advocated atheism. As we will see in more detail below, atheism can be understood, in evolutionary terms, as a "spiteful mutation," which is associated with being maladaptive. Indeed, it could be argued that Marx's poor physical and mental health was clearly manifested in his children. Three died as infants; two committed suicide; and one died of bladder cancer at the age of just 38.[90]

Belief in physiognomy continued well beyond ancient times. Michael Scot (1175-1232), a Scottish mathematician at the court of the Holy Roman Emperor, wrote an entire thesis on the subject.[91] In *The Canterbury Tales* from the late 14th century, Geoffrey Chaucer (c.1343-1400) gave the Wife of Bath a gap in her front teeth to imply that she was highly sexual. The Reeve is of slim build, suggesting he is "choleric" (bad-tempered and irritable), while the Summoner is unattractive, because he's an unpleasant person.[92] Physiognomy was taught as an academic subject at English universities until it was outlawed by Henry VIII (r.1509-1547) for having become associated with fortune-telling.[93] Even so, educated people carried on openly believing in it right up until the beginning of the 20th century.[94] It was the British writer Oscar Wilde (1854-1900) who famously noted, in his 1891 novel *The Picture of Dorian Gray*, "It is only shallow people who do not judge by appearances."[95]

89: Matthew Sarraf, Michael A. Woodley of Menie, and Colin Feltham, *Modernity and Cultural Decline: A Biobehavioral Perspective* (Basingstoke, Hants: Palgrave Macmillan, 2019), 255.

90: Michael Evans, *Karl Marx*, Part I (London: Routledge, 1975), 5.

91: Martin Porter, *Windows of the Soul: Physiognomy in European Culture 1470-1780* (Oxford: Clarendon Press, 2005), 122.

92: See Margaret Hallissy, *A Companion to Chaucer's Canterbury Tales* (Boulder: Greenwood Publishing, 1995).

93: Porter, *Windows of the Soul, op cit.*, 134.

94: See *Physiognomy in Profile: Lavater's Impact on European Culture*, eds. Melissa Percival and Graeme Tytler (Newark: University of Delaware Press, 2005).

95: Oscar Wilde, *The Picture of Dorian Gray* (London: Simpkin, Marshall, Hamilton, Kent and Co., 1891), 29.

The Victorians were right to believe in physiognomy. I have explored the evidence for physiognomy in an earlier book entitled *How to Judge People By What They Look Like*.[96] The evidence for the veracity of physiognomy is substantial. It was first scientifically tested in 1878. In that year, gentleman scientist Sir Francis Galton (1822-1911) published an article in the journal *Nature* in which he presented his findings. He developed a system of composite photographs, whereby he superimposed a variety of faces onto each other using multiple exposures. This allowed him to create photographic representations of those with certain qualities, such as being beautiful, criminal, or ill. These led to distinct photographs, implying, for example, that there is a degree to which criminals have distinct faces from the rest of the population.[97]

Since then, many studies have shown weak but statistically significant correlations between physical and mental traits. ("Statistical significance" tests whether results are flukes, based on the sample size and the strength of the correlation. If we can be 95 percent or more certain that results are not flukes, then they have attained statistical significance). Obviously, this does not mean that you can observe that a person has a small nose and thus conclude that, therefore, they have low IQ, though, within race, there is a weak positive association between nose size and IQ.[98] However, if this is found alongside other markers of low IQ—such as a wide face and small eyes—then such a judgment becomes rather more reasonable. In understanding why this is the case, researchers who unearthed similar findings proposed that having a small nose, for example, is associated with Down's Syndrome and Fetal Alcohol Syndrome. Both of these maladies result from major disruptions of developmental

---

96: Edward Dutton, *How to Judge People By What They Look Like* (Oulu: Thomas Edward Press, 2018).

97: Francis Galton, "Composite Portraits," *Nature*, May 23, 1878: 97-100.

98: Karel Kleisner, Veronika Chvátalová, and Jaroslav Flegr, "Perceived Intelligence is Associated with Measured Intelligence in Men but not Women," *PLoS ONE* 9 (2014): e81237.

pathways, and they lead to very low intelligence and a very small nose. Thus, even minor disruptions would lead to slightly reduced intelligence and a slightly smaller nose. The same could be said for distance between pupils and face height, which reached significance in terms of a relationship with objective intelligence.[99] Facial symmetry is also weakly associated with intelligence, possibly because high mutational load will render you both less physically attractive and will lead to sub-optimal brain function.[100]

Evidence that believing in physiognomy is adaptive can be seen in the fact that we are evolved to be able to engage in it. Without even meaning to do so, we correctly judge people's psychology from their physical appearance, even if we are brought up being told not to. Experimental evidence has shown that people regularly judge others' personalities by their facial features,[101] these judgments are concurred with by others,[102] and people do so cross-culturally, strongly implying that this is an evolved behavior. Indeed, experiments indicate that the judgments are actually correct, as set out in a *New Scientist* article in 2009.[103] In 1966, the article reported, psychologists at the University of Michigan conducted an experiment on 84 undergraduates who had never met. They had to sit in complete silence with each other for 15 minutes and rate each other on the Big 5 personality traits, simply by appearance. Each participant also sat a personality test. For three of these

99: Anthony Lee, Courtney Hibbs, Margaret Wright, *et al.*, "Assessing the Accuracy of Perceptions of Intelligence Based on Heritable Facial Features," *Intelligence*, 64 (2017): 1-8.

100: George Banks, John Batchelor and Michael Mcdaniel, "Smarter People Are (a Bit) More Symmetrical: A Meta-analysis of the Relationship Between Intelligence and Fluctuating Asymmetry," *Intelligence,* 38 (2010): 393-401.

101: Janine Willis and Alexander Todorov, "First Impressions: Making Up Your Mind After a 100-Ms Exposure to a Face," *Psychological Science*, 17 (2006): 592-598.

102: Richard Highfield, Roger Wiseman, and Robb Jenkins, "How Your Looks Betray Your Personality," *New Scientist*, February 11, 2009.

103: *Ibid.*

traits—Extraversion, Conscientiousness and Openness—the students' appearance-based judgments significantly positively correlated with the actual personality scores.[104] Clearly, it would have been a better experiment if sociological factors, such as clothing and hair style were rigorously controlled for, but the result is certainly eye-opening. Accordingly, the experiment was repeated using mug shots and the results for Extraversion and Conscientiousness were replicated.[105]

So, there is an extent to which certain world religions, under Darwinian conditions, accepted and promoted physiognomy, and they were empirically correct to do so. Accordingly, beliefs about witches were, to an extent, empirically accurate and thus adaptive. Witch crazes removed spiteful mutants who, even if they could have no children, might, and often did, act to undermine societal cohesion and thus group selection, from the society.

The Story So Far

In this chapter we have found a number of key things. Firstly, traditional religiousness tends to be evolutionarily adaptive, by virtue of taking adaptive behavior and transforming it into God's will. Secondly, religiousness tends to promote positive and negative ethnocentrism—indeed, it is associated with these behaviors—and, all else being equal, the most ethnocentric group will triumph in the battle of group selection. Thirdly, a system of patriarchy helps to elevate ethnocentrism, and thus group-selectedness, explaining why world religions promote patriarchy as divinely ordained. Fourthly, these religions also promote, usually implicitly, physiognomy as being real,

104: Frank Passini and Norman Warren, "A Universal Conception of Personality Structure?" *Journal of Personality and Social Psychology*, 4 (1966): 44-49.

105: Anthony Little and David Perrett, "Using Composite Images to Assess Accuracy in Personality Attribution to Faces," *British Journal of Psychology*, 98 (2007): 111-126.

to the extent of, in effect, trying to limit the fertility of the physically unattractive. And they are right to do so because physiognomy is empirically justifiable. It is adaptive to judge psychology from appearance; we are adapted to be able to do so; and thus, once more, religions are effectively taking something that is adaptive and giving it the divine stamp of approval. In this sense, religious people are the products of selection for individual and group fitness, meaning that they would be strongly selected to reject anything that might damage this fitness in any given set of circumstances, because their fitness-proneness would be strongly genetic. Thus, they would be adapted to conform to group norms, but only when these ultimately promoted genetic fitness, meaning that deeply religious people can sometimes be highly counter-cultural, at least when societal religiosity declines.

With these conclusions in mind, we can turn, in more detail, to the nature of witches.

Chapter 4

She Laughed Wickedly

The Nature of Witches

We have seen that patriarchy is adaptive at the group level, meaning that anything, or anyone, that undermines patriarchy is likely to be maladaptive. Religiousness, historically at least, promoted what was adaptive as the will of God or the gods and cast what was maladaptive as blasphemous, or even inspired by the Devil or an evil god. This would lead us to make three predictions. Firstly, under the intense Darwinian conditions that existed until the Industrial Revolution, those who undermined patriarchy would be accused of being in league with the Devil and thus of being witches. Secondly, those people would tend to be physically unattractive, due to the relationship between physical and mental maladaptation. Thirdly, accusations of witchcraft would intensify during periods of particularly harsh Darwinian selection, because people would be selected to be highly religious during these periods. And they would also become more religious due to the elevated stress and "morality salience" (that is, awareness of death) associated with a period of want and conflict.

To begin our examination of the nature of witchcraft, let us look at the historical variability in the persecution of witches. I will take England as a case study.

Execution and the Civilizing of Medieval Europe

When people think of witchcraft in England, they may be put in mind of the scene in the 1975 film *Monty Python and the Holy Grail*, where "Sir Bedevere the Wise," played by Terry Jones (1942-2020), is approached by a mob of excited villagers who believe they have apprehended a witch, played by Connie Booth. They demand the right to "burn her," and Sir Bedevere explains to them that there are ingenious ways of testing whether or not she is really a witch. Hilarious though the scene is (I won't ruin it for you), nothing like it could ever have happened. Nobody was ever burned at the stake for witchcraft in England. This occurred in Scotland, as we saw earlier, as well as in much of Continental Europe. In England, however, witches were hanged because witchcraft was defined as a "felony," for which hanging was almost always the punishment. More importantly, *The Holy Grail* was set in the year 932 AD. Witchcraft wasn't a criminal offence in England until the passing of the Witchcraft Act of 1542.[1]

How could this be? How could the English possibly have become *more* superstitious across time? There are two related reasons for this. Firstly, there is considerable evidence that up until the Reformation, we were becoming more and more religious, mainly for genetic reasons.[2] Religiousness is associated with fertility, so for that reason we would expect English people to have been becoming more religious across time, assuming that levels of mortality—in terms of how frequently people came into contact with human death due to child mortality, for example—remained substantially constant,

1: Carson Hudson, *Witchcraft in Colonial Virginia* (Charleston, SC: The History Press, 2019).

2: Edward Dutton and Guy Madison, "Execution, Violent Punishment and Selection for Religiousness in Medieval England," *Evolutionary Psychological Science*, 4 (2018): 83-89.

which they did until the Industrial Revolution. Child mortality was between 40 percent and 50 percent in England in 1800; today it is 1 percent. This means that a child born in 1800 was at least 40 times more likely to die before reaching maturity than a child born today. Accordingly, it has been argued that the collapse of child mortality has had a very significant impact on human evolution, because child mortality was, until relatively recently, the key reason why people failed to pass on their genes. It could even be conceived of as "the Crucible of Human Evolution."[3]

In 18th-century rural Sweden, life-expectancy—once you survived childhood—was 72 years and only around 15 percent of the adult population failed to breed, either due to infertility (2-4 percent) or simply failure to find a mate.[4] Other studies, such as in 17th-century England, have found that 20 percent of marriages were childless, partly due to high child mortality.[5] By the end of the 17th century, roughly 20 percent of males and females over the age of 40 were unmarried, this being a relatively high point of not marrying in pre-Industrial England.[6] But the key point is that these data only serve to highlight the importance of child mortality to human evolution in pre-Industrial societies. Its impact is far higher than any other factor that might influence human evolution. The above estimates, it should be noted, imply that in England, by the end of the 17th century, as many as 90 percent of people who were born did not pass on their genes. Using computer modeling, it has been found that for a population to maintain optimum genetic health, based on the frequency of genetic mutations,

---

3: Tony Volk and Jeremy Atkinson, "Is Child Death the Crucible of Human Evolution?" *Journal of Social, Evolutionary, and Cultural Psychology*, 2 (2008): 103-116, 106-107.

4: *Ibid*, 104, 106-107.

5: Richard Grassby, *The Business Community of Seventeenth-Century England* (Cambridge: Cambridge University Press, 2002), 132.

6: E.A. Wrigley and R.S. Schofield, *The Population History of England, 1541-1871* (Cambridge: Cambridge University Press, 1989), 264.

approximately 88 percent of that population in any given generation should fail to breed.[7]

A second reason why Medieval people were becoming more religious is that Conscientiousness is associated with religiousness[8] *and* socioeconomic status.[9] In Medieval England, socioeconomic status was positively correlated with completed fertility.[10] So, for this reason as well, they would have become more religious over time. English evolutionary psychologist Bruce Charlton has argued that one mechanism that might increase intelligence across time would be that more intelligent mothers would be better able to ensure the survival of their offspring, such as through successfully pre-empting accidents for example.[11] But equally, it has been shown that infants are more likely to survive if the maternal bond is strong,[12] and those who are high in Agreeableness, in effect, create stronger bonds.[13] Agreeableness is associated with religiousness, so the selection for strong maternal bonds would indirectly select for religiousness and also help to explain, in part, why females

---

7: Yann Lesecque, Peter Keightley, and Adam Eyre-Walker, "A Resolution of the Mutation Load Paradox in Humans," *Genetics*, 191 (2012): 1321-1330.

8: Jochen Gebauer, Wiebke Bleidorn, Samuel Gosling, *et al.*, "Cross-Cultural Variations in Big Five Relationships with Religiosity: A Sociocultural Motives Perspective," *Journal of Personality and Social Psychology*, 107 (2014): 1064-1091.

9: Mathilde Almlund, Angela Duckworth, James Heckman, and Tim Kautz, "Personality, Psychology and Economics" in *Handbook of the Economics of Education*, eds. Eric Hanushek, Stephen Machin, and Ludger Woesmann (Amsterdam: Elsevier, 2011).

10: Gregory Clark, *A Farewell to Alms: A Brief Economic History of the World* (Princeton: Princeton University Press, 2007).

11: Bruce Charlton, "Why are Women so Intelligent? The Effect of Maternal IQ on Childhood Mortality May be a Relevant Evolutionary Factor," *Medical Hypotheses*, 74 (2009): 401-402.

12: See Volk and Atkinson, "Is Child Death the Crucible of Human Evolution?" *op cit.*

13: See Daniel Nettle, *Personality: What Makes You Who You Are* (Oxford, Oxford University Press, 2007).

tend to be more religious than males.[14] The collapse of child mortality would mean the collapse of selection pressure for such mothers and the collapse of the need to strongly bond with your offspring. This is important because it has been shown that a weak maternal bond is associated with pathological outcomes, such as anti-social behavior and mental illness.[15]

Thirdly, and perhaps surprisingly, widespread execution likely elevated religiousness in England. As we discussed briefly earlier, Canadian anthropologist Peter Frost and American anthropologist Henry Harpending have examined the way in which judicial violence acted as a selection pressure in pre-industrial Europe.[16] Until the 11th century, they show, execution was not widely employed in Europe. This was because the Church was opposed to it, law enforcement was rudimentary, and it was believed that people should have the right to settle their own disputes—such as through duels—though these would often result in death. But as the Medieval Era progressed, the Church accepted that the "wicked" should be executed so that the "good" could live in peace.

By the Early Modern Era, all felonies carried the death penalty. This was religiously justified, drawing upon the dictates of the Old Testament: "But if there is any further injury, then you shall appoint as a penalty life for life" (Exodus 21: 23). Simply put, those who behave in a violent manner are to be discouraged from doing so through agonizing punishment and mutilation, while those who take another life are themselves to be killed. From an evolutionary perspective, note Frost and Harpending, these kinds of punishments would likely prevent a certain number of anti-social, violent young men from passing

---

14: See Darren Sherkat, "Sexuality and Religious Commitment in the United States: An Empirical Examination," *Journal for the Scientific Study of Religion*, 41 (2002): 313-323.

15: Volk and Atkinson, "Is Child Death the Crucible of Human Evolution?" *op cit.*

16: Peter Frost and Henry Harpending, "Western Europe, State Formation, and Genetic Pacification," *Evolutionary Psychology*, 13 (2015), https://doi.org/10.1177/147470491501300114.

on their genes or influencing the gene pool as much as they otherwise would have done.

Frost and Harpending calculated that this meant that up to 1 percent of the male population of Europe was executed each generation, with approximately another 1 percent dying at the scene of the crime or in prison while awaiting trial. Most of these felons, Frost and Harpending demonstrate, were *young* men, who could have gone on to have children. Frost and Harpending argue that this process would have altered the nature of Western personality, by preventing those with high psychopathic personality from passing on their genes. Indeed, they find that the actual decrease in violence is consistent with the prevalence of execution, according to the so-called Breeder's Equation. Their model also has implications for intelligence. Those who were executed or died in prison were overwhelmingly poor and uneducated. In England, those who were of high social status could fund relatively luxurious conditions in prison and, unless their crime was treason or heresy, they could avoid execution by pleading "Benefit of the Clergy." This meant that if they could read, they would avoid execution.

As an aside, which will become relevant below to understanding the dynamics of witch crazes, it should be noted that any kind of environmental harshness—including widespread execution—will select for intelligence. Intelligence is negatively associated with criminality and positively associated with the ability to solve social problems, something which tends to make intelligent people empathetic, altruistic, and civic-minded. They are also more trusting, open to new ideas, less conservative, less religious, less negatively ethnocentric, and more acquiescent (prone to accept things without always consenting to them). Intelligence is associated with planning for the future, long time horizons, impulse control, and, of course, the ability to solve all kinds of problems.[17] There is

17: Edward Dutton and Michael A. Woodley of Menie, *At Our Wits' End: Why We're Becoming Less Intelligent and What It Means for the Future* (Exeter, Imprint Academic, 2018), 11.

also evidence that intelligence is negatively associated with strongly feeling "instincts" or "cognitive biases" that humans have evolved. In order to logically solve problems, one has to be able to rise above these. Thus, intelligence is associated with being attracted to non-instinctive possibilities and with not simply reacting in an instinctive way. This may be one reason why intelligence is associated with being open-minded.[18]

Accordingly, when an environment becomes both predictable (meaning a payoff for future-orientation) and harsh (meaning more problems to solve of greater difficulty), there tends to be increased selection for intelligence. This dimension to selection for intelligence is known as Cold Winters Theory.[19] It explains why alleles (forms of a gene) associated with very high levels of educational attainment (and thus very high intelligence) become less common in populations the closer you get to the equator.[20] It also explains why IQs tend to get higher the further you move away from the equator, although exceptions exist.[21] Agriculture tends to select in favor of intelligence by selecting against those who lack the future-orientation to pursue it.[22] Thus, populations that did not adopt agriculture, such as the Inuit, are less intelligent than might be predicted by their distance from the equator.

18: Edward Dutton and Dimitri van der Linden, "Why is Intelligence Negatively Associated with Religiousness?" *Evolutionary Psychological Science*, 3 (2017): 392-403.

19: Richard Lynn and Tatu Vanhanen, *Intelligence: A Unifying Construct for the Social Sciences* (London: Ulster Institute for Social Research, 2012).

20: Davide Piffer, "Correlation Between PGS and Environmental Variables," *RPubs* (2018), https://rpubs.com/Daxide/377423.

21: It is beyond the scope of this book to look at the assorted criticisms of national IQs. For a detailed refutation of them, see Richard Lynn and David Becker, *The Intelligence of Nations* (London: Ulster Institute for Social Research, 2019).

22: Gregory Cochran and Henry Harpending, *The 10,000 Year Explosion: How Civilization Accelerated Human Evolution* (New York: Basic Books, 2009).

Returning to the issue of execution and its impact on religiousness, the widespread use of execution in Medieval England should have increased levels of religiousness, in addition to the decreasing levels of violence noted above. Religiousness significantly increased between 1400 and 1500, as evidenced by a large rise in the per-capita numbers of people joining religious orders. Comparing genetic correlation data for traits predicting religiousness with the heritability of religiousness, the high level of execution seems to have played a role in selecting for the religious minded in England. Exploring the mechanisms by which it would have done so, Swedish psychologist Guy Madison and I argue that religiousness is associated with low General Factor of Personality, low levels of autism (autism is characterized by an inability to empathize), low levels of suffering from stress, and with a feeling of being watched.[23] All of these crucial dimensions to religiousness are negatively associated with rule-breaking and criminality. So, in Medieval England, there was an extent to which the government was, through its policy of widespread execution, preventing the relatively irreligious from passing on their genes. It was acting in such a way as to make the society more religious and thus even more law-abiding.

Witchcraft, Climate Change, and Group Selection

The Medieval Warm Period lasted from around 900 to about 1300 AD. During this period, it was considerably warmer even than today. It was possible to grow grapes in parts of England,[24] something preserved in road names such as Vine

23: Dutton and Madison, "Execution, Violent Punishment and Selection for Religiousness in Medieval England," *op cit.*

24: Colin Platt, *Medieval England: A Social History and Archaeology from the Conquest to 1600 AD* (London: Routledge, 1994), Chapter 1.

Street in London.[25] Accordingly, Darwinian selection (for traits such as intelligence, pro-social personality, and religiousness) would not have been especially intense, though it still would have been taking place. Indeed, we know it was taking place from around 1100 onwards, when we left the chaos of the Dark Ages, before which a previous civilization had collapsed. Between around 1100 and 1870, per-capita major innovations continuously increased, consistent with rising intelligence. Interest rates decreased (implying the longer time horizons, which are associated with intelligence); literacy and numeracy increased; and the size of people's heads actually increased (with brain size being associated with intelligence).[26] With the end of this warm period, and the beginning of a cold period that reached its nadir in the Maunder Minimum between 1645 and 1715, selection for these traits would have become increasingly savage, as people competed for fewer resources. Most obviously, the same amount of land would have yielded less food in a year, the colder it was.[27]

A harsh climate also increases the intensity of group selection. Groups are more likely to survive if they are internally cooperative and externally harsh, that is, if they are positively and negatively ethnocentric, something associated with religiousness. Thus, within certain boundaries, ecological harshness selects for pro-social personality traits such as Conscientiousness, Agreeableness, mental stability, and social anxiety. This will create a smaller gene pool, in which the people are highly intelligent and highly ethnocentric. In conditions of ecological harshness, group selection will intensify, because there won't be sufficient resources to feed the entire human population, which would have expanded enormously during the

---

25: Alicia Amherst, *London Parks and Gardens* (Cambridge: Cambridge University Press, 2014), 303.

26: Dutton and Woodley of Menie, *At Our Wits' End*, *op cit.*, Chapter 4.

27: See Michael Woodley of Menie, A.J. Figueredo, Matthew Sarraf, *et al.*, *The Rhythm of the West: A Biohistory of the Modern Era, AD 1600 to the Present* (Washington, DC: Scott Townsend Publishing, 2017).

Medieval Warm Period. This will lead to unrest and war, which will disproportionately impact the less well off (and thus the less intelligent) because they are less likely to have the resources to escape its effects and they are less likely to be sufficiently forward-thinking to escape its effects.[28]

Such a change will also lead to mass starvation and many people, weakened by hunger, succumbing to disease. The result will be a population collapse. This is exactly what happened in Medieval Europe. Adding to the devastation, the Black Death swept across Europe between about 1347 and 1351. As Michael Woodley of Menie and I have argued, this, too, was a selection event. Between a third and half on the English population were killed by the plague, but among the serfs and free laborers, those of the lowest socioeconomic status, the death rate was roughly 80 percent.[29] It has been demonstrated by Gregory Clark that the heritability of socioeconomic status (SES) was about 0.7 across three generations in Medieval England, the same as it was in the 1950s.[30] Accordingly, there's every reason to conclude that SES would have robustly correlated with intelligence in the Middle Ages. It follows that the Black Death would have heavily disproportionately killed those of low IQ, low GFP and, following our analysis of execution, low religiousness. It would have made Europe much more religious and much more intelligent very quickly, likely helping to explain why both the Renaissance and the Reformation took place when they did.

Why did these changes parallel a rise in the persecution of witches? By the end of the Medieval Period, and continuing beyond this right up to the early 19th century, people were

28: See Dutton and Woodley of Menie, *At Our Wits' End*, *op cit.*

29: Ben Dodds, "Patterns of Decline: Arable Production in England, France and Castile, 1370–1450," in *Agriculture and Rural Society After the Black Death: Common Themes and Regional Variations*, eds. Ben Dodds and Richard Britnell, (Hatfield: University of Hertfordshire Press, 2008).

30: Gregory Clark, *The Son Also Rises: Surnames and the History of Social Mobility* (Princeton: Princeton University Press, 2014).

under extremely intense selection for both religiousness and intelligence. Intelligence might tell you that witchcraft is mere superstition, but religious impulses—deeply concerned about a spirit world and pleasing a moral God who is in battle with the Devil—would tell you quite the opposite.

These conditions would also have elevated inter-group conflict, both within and between countries, something most obvious in England's Civil War which culminated in the execution of Charles I in 1649, during the Maunder Minimum. Indeed, it has been argued that the Civil War was the height of England's witch craze,[31] though it is likely that the stress of the Civil War contributed to the intensity of this craze. This kind of group selection would have favored the more ethnocentric, and thus more religious group, which it duly did in the form of Oliver Cromwell's (1599-1658) strongly Puritanical Roundheads. Thus, England would have become more and more religious and so more and more likely to be strongly negatively ethnocentric, and to treat those perceived as enemies to all that is holy in brutal ways. Consistent with this, by the mid 1400s, we see the widespread burning of heretics, something that was particularly intense under the reign of zealous Catholic Queen Mary I (1516-1558, reigned: 1553-1558): approximately 300 Protestants who would not recant were burned alive.[32]

We have seen that an adaptive aspect of religiousness, in terms of group selection, is the promotion of patriarchy. So, if witches undermined patriarchy, a core aspect of religiousness, we would expect them to be cast as in league with the Devil and to be persecuted with increased harshness. In line with this, in 1542, witchcraft became a felony, punishable by hanging. In 1563, a new Act of Parliament specified that a witch needed to have caused "harm" to be hanged, rather than merely have practiced witchcraft, for which she would merely be jailed. Even so, the witch craze began in England around this time. In 1604, a new

31: Gary Jensen, *The Path of the Devil: Early Modern Witch Hunts* (New York: Rowman & Littlefield, 2007), 27.

32: See Jasper Ridley, *The Tudor Age* (London: Constable, 1988).

act broadened the definition of witchcraft to include those who communed with spirits or invoked evil spirits. Serious penalties for witchcraft were finally abolished in 1736.[33]

This leads us to the question of who was accused of being a witch and why. Many historians have explored this issue in a British context. Between 1560 and 1600, "some eight thousand elderly women were burned as witches in Scotland, a country of less than one million people. . . . Within the two year period of England's Long Parliament (1645-1647), two hundred witches were burned at the stake."[34] The Long Parliament was during England's Civil War, when witch persecution was at its height. Approximately 85 percent of people convicted of witchcraft in England between 1566 and 1666 were women over the age of fifty. Roughly 40 percent of them were widows, and the rest never married at all.[35] No more than 20 percent of people were unmarried in their forties at the end of 1700s; at the beginning of the century, it was fewer than 10 percent; so singletons were certainly over-represented.[36] In many regions over half of convicted witches had never been married.[37] Witches tended to be of low socioeconomic status, with witch-hunters showing, according to researcher David Pickering, a "marked preference for elderly, ignorant women who lived as outcasts from the local community" and who displayed "odd ways and unfriendly behaviour." Witches also tended to be physically unattractive: "Anyone with a squint, with eyebrows that joined in the middle, or with a generally unattractive physical appearance" was more likely to be accused of being a witch. Similarly at risk were

33: See Hudson, *Witchcraft in Colonial Virginia*, *op cit*.

34: Ron Pahl, *Breaking Away from the Textbook: The Enlightenment through the 20th Century* (Plymouth: Rowman & Littlefield, 2002), 5.

35: David Pickering, "Witch," in *Cassell Dictionary of Witchcraft* (London: Cassell, 1998).

36: Volk and Atkinson, "Is Child Death the Crucible of Human Evolution?" *op cit.*

37: Brian Levack, *The Witch-Hunt in Early Modern Europe* (London: Routledge, 2016).

females who did not conform to gender norms, such as those who were old yet unmarried.[38]

There were regional exceptions to this. For various cultural reasons, in parts of France, and also in Finland as a whole, the majority of people convicted of witchcraft were male. However, even in Finland, in the Early Modern era, the percentage of women being convicted of witchcraft substantially rose.[39] In other areas, such as Carinthia in Austria, begging became associated with witchcraft, due to so-called "refusal guilt." People felt guilty for not giving alms to beggars, so they dealt with this guilt by deciding that the beggars were witches. In late 17th-century Carinthia, two thirds of beggars were male, leading to males being disproportionately accused of witchcraft in that region.[40] Thus, one possible interpretation is that witchcraft was an acceptable means of shunning and purging those at the very bottom of society. This would prevent them from being a drain on the community and, in that falling into penury is associated with anti-social personality traits, it would stop them undermining societal cohesion.[41] Accusing anti-social men of witchcraft would work in the same way. But this still leaves us asking why most of the persecution was focused on females.

Rachel Grant and Tamara Montrose, whom we discussed earlier, have presented a convincing argument to explain the sociological dynamics of these persecutions.[42] Not only can we argue that patriarchy elevates group selection, but also that it assists individual selection. The authors present data showing that even in developed societies, children who grow up with single

38: *Ibid.*

39: Marianne Hester, "Patriarchal Reconstruction and Witch Hunting," in *Witchcraft in Early Modern Europe: Studies in Culture and Belief*, eds. Jonathan Barry, Marianne Hester, and Gareth Roberts (Cambridge: Cambridge University Press, 1996), 288, footnote 1.

40: Julian Goodacre, *The European Witch-Hunt* (London: Routledge, 2016).

41: Nettle, *Personality*, *op cit.*

42: Rachael Grant and V. Tamara Montrose, "It's a Man's World: Mate Guarding and the Evolution of Patriarchy," *Mankind Quarterly*, 58 (2018): 384-418.

mothers are at an increased risk of mortality and poor health. In addition, until recently, females who did not conform to the patriarchal system would have been shunned and would have been unable to obtain a high-status male, in a context in which completed fertility was predicted by high status. Furthermore, the children of such women would have been more likely to be subject not just to poverty and neglect but also to infanticide and exposure, not uncommon practices among single mothers in Europe a few centuries ago.[43] Thus, argue Grant and Montrose, gene-forms that might have made females resistant to patriarchy would have been selected out, meaning that the vast majority of women would have accepted the patriarchal system. Those who didn't would, therefore, be likely to carry mutant genes relating to the mind, which, as discussed, we would expect to see reflected, to some extent, in the body.

Witches, or at least those witches who were single women, were undermining the system of patriarchy simply by being independent females, whether as spinsters or widows who chose not to remarry. Grant and Montrose's summary of these women's predicament is so trenchant that it is worth simply quoting verbatim.

> *One historical example of the consequences of resistance to patriarchy is the witch hunts which took place between the 11th and 17th centuries in Europe. Women who resisted patriarchal norms (marriage and child-bearing) were viewed with extreme suspicion, tortured to extract confession and usually killed. . . . Witch hunting targeted primarily single women. . . . Women could also be branded as witches and killed as scapegoats for misfortune occurring in communities or for the "crime" of being sexually abused and made pregnant outside marriage. . . . The persecution of females was legitimized by both the Church and the state and it is thought to be an example of sexual and social control of women by inducing fear of torture, imprisonment and death.*[44]

43: Lynn, *Dysgenics*, *op cit.*, 50-52.

44: Grant and Montrose, "It's a Man's World," *Mankind Quarterly*, *op cit.*

With regard to witchcraft allegations being leveled against females who had become pregnant out of wedlock, in witch trials in Essex in southeast England in 1582 and in 1589, the fact of having an illegitimate child was used as evidence against the accused. This was because popular superstition held that witches had an "excess of passion," which made them commit "sexually deviant acts."[45] One way of understanding this is that females who were "erotophiles"—who had strong sex drives and who thus broke the society's sexual rules—were accused of witchcraft as a result. There is evidence that "sexual guilt" in women—which would be imbued under a system of religious patriarchy—is negatively associated with erotophilia and being sexually experienced.[46] It would follow that perceiving such females as witches, and so removing them from the gene pool, would be adaptive at the group level. It would be removing women who were not adapted to the patriarchal system and whose behavior helped to undermine it. Nevertheless, such women could be expected to manifest each generation through mutation, unlikely gene combinations and/or environmental factors.

Sex with Satan

Witches frequently confessed to lying in sexual congress with Satan himself.[47] It is often assumed that these were manufactured and confessed to due to torture or hysteria. But in an English context, this is simply not the case, as we have already seen. These were voluntarily admissions. This implies that they might have been genuine sexual fantasies, which, as we will see below, independent, socially dominant females are

45: Alison Findlay, *Illegitimate Power: Bastards in Renaissance Drama* (Manchester: Manchester University Press, 1994), 52

46: Julie Schulman and Sharon Horne, "Guilty or Not? A Path Model of Women's Sexual Force Fantasies," *Journal of Sex Research*, 43 (2006): 368-377.

47: See Walter Stephens, *Demon Lovers: Witchcraft, Sex, and the Crisis of Belief* (Chicago: University of Chicago Press, 2003) and below.

particularly prone to having. In our day, feminist identification correlates with erotophilia, as does having "rape fantasies," in which a female fantasizes of being ravished and ultimately submitting.[48] We will discuss the evolutionary reasons for this in Chapter 8, but this would appear to be a clear point of commonality between witches and feminists.

In the religious society of 17th century, in which sexual guilt was paramount, women may have assumed that these intense fantasies actually involved the Devil. In 1680, Temperance Floyd, one of "Bideford Witches"—from Bideford in Devon in the southwest of England—confessed that the Devil appeared in her bedroom and sucked her nipples until she was extremely sexually aroused, after which they had sex for nine consecutive nights.[49] Another of the Bideford witches, Mary Trembles, confessed that the Devil "sucked her secret parts, and that his sucking was so hard which caused her to cry out for the pain thereof."[50] An English pamphlet from 1705 describes how witches confessed that the Devil appeared to them in the form of a "black man" and that they then endured extremely unpleasant and painful sex with him.[51]

Alternative models to explain witchcraft-copulation have been presented, but these are not congruous with the available data. For example, historian Walter Stephens has argued that the idea that witches had sex with devils was created in order to uphold religiosity.[52] According to Stephens, the authorities were not confident in their demonology, so they became fixated on demonic copulation as one efficient way of establishing the reality of the spirit realm, a reality that had been destabilized by Scholastic philosophers in the 13th and 14th centuries. It

48: Schulman and Horne, "Guilty or Not?" *op cit.*

49: Charlotte-Rose Millar, *Witchcraft, the Devil, and Emotions in Early Modern England* (London: Routledge, 2017), 138.

50: *Ibid.*, 139.

51: *Ibid.*

52: Stephens, *Demon Lovers*, *op cit.*

has been documented, however, that we were under intense selection for religiousness and people became more religious between the Middle Ages and the 17th century.[53] Also, why would devil-copulation, specifically, persuade the populace to be more religious? And most importantly, as already shown, the belief in devil-copulation was of ancient origin and found in different parts of the world.[54] This would be congruous with a psychological explanation rather than 17th-century religious men fabricating the idea.

Another possibility is that these were not fantasies but real experiences, with men stalking women and having sex with them and telling them that they were devils; or perhaps the women made sense of these encounters as the work of the devil. Sociosexual women would have been more likely to have received such attention. Nevertheless, this explanation seems unlikely for a variety of reasons. First, rapes occurred and were reported as such during this period, and women would surely recognize that a rape by a real person was taking place. Secondly, these women would have lived in small villages, where everyone knew everyone else, seeing them in church once a week, so would likely know who their rapists were. Finally, many witches were elderly, unattractive spinsters, and it seems most improbable that someone would want to stalk and rape them. Similarly, it might be averred that in a very repressive religious environment, persecuting a witch (a lone and unprotected female) was an excuse for particular males to indulge themselves in rape, torture and coercion—and get away with it. Again, this seems improbable—at least as a general explanation—considering that it was unattractive, old women who tended to be accused of witchcraft.

53: See Dutton and Madison, "Execution, Violent Punishment and Selection for Religiousness in Medieval England," *op cit.*

54: See Raphael Patai, *The Hebrew Goddess* (Detroit: Wayne State University Press, 1990).

Prostitution and Witchcraft

Regarding sexual deviance more broadly, there is evidence, from early 17th century German records, that two women who were found guilty of witchcraft in their 60s had been prostitutes when they were younger.[55] And this was far from the only example of crossover between prostitution and witchcraft. In 1637, in Venice, widow Marietta Battaglia (b.1599) worked both as a prostitute and a witch, casting "love spells" on men in return for money. She was tried for witchcraft in 1637, 1645, and 1649; on the final occasion, she was sentenced to "jail and perpetual banishment."[56] There was a case in Aragon in 1626 in which two elderly women confessed to witchcraft and sex with the Devil, for which they were jailed as prostitutes. In Arras in 1460, several witches were accused of having allowed the Devil to have anal intercourse with them.[57] In *Malleus Maleficarum*, witches are understood to "voluntarily prostitute themselves to Incubus devils."[58] The French judge Pierre de Lancre (1553-1631), who presided over many witchcraft trials, reported, in 1612, that up to 14,000 witches (both female and male) might meet at a nighttime Sabbath and dance together naked. They would engage in a parody of the mass, work on evil plots, have sex (including anal sex) with Satan (who would appear in the form of a goat), and enjoy a diabolical orgy with each other, which would include incest.[59]

It could be argued that prostitution questioned the patriarchal system, because it involved single women earning

---

55: Jonathan Durrant, *Witchcraft, Gender, and Society in Early Modern Germany* (Leiden: BRILL, 2007), 174.

56: Sally Scully, "Marriage or a Career? Witchcraft as an Alternative in Seventeenth-Century Venice," *Journal of Social History*, 28 (1995): 857-876, 859.

57: Goodacre, *The European Witch-hunt*, *op cit*.

58: Heinrich Kramer and Jacob Sprenger, *The Malleus Malificarum of Heinrich Kramer and James Sprenger*, Part II, trans. Montague Summers (New York: Dover Publications, 1971) Question 2, Ch. 1.

59: Joseph Klaits, *Servants of Satan: The Age of Witch-Hunts* (Bloomington: Indiana University Press, 1985), 53.

money independent of male control. These women were also flagrantly flouting Christian morality and were, in the view of the authorities, inducing males to do likewise. Indeed, prostitution began to become increasingly socially unacceptable at around the same time that witchcraft did, the 15th century. Prior to that time, prostitutes were even allowed to take part in church processions in many European cities.[60] "Municipal brothels" were established in Medieval Europe precisely because it was felt that the unmarried males required a sexual outlet. The use of prostitutes was "such an accepted activity that groups of young men often visited brothels together."[61] This system was tacitly endorsed by the Church. In Rome, as late as the early 16th century, prostitutes paid tithes and attended mass. Indeed, they were "assiduous churchgoers" because it was "an excellent form of publicity."[62] Interestingly, it has been found that females who are prepared to have sex without commitment tend to be relatively high in "Dark Triad" traits such as psychopathology.[63] Female sex workers have been found to score lower in the personality traits of Agreeableness and Conscientiousness than female controls.[64] In that men score lower than females on these traits,[65] prostitutes are thus more psychologically masculinized, and so less submissive to patriarchy than the average woman.

60: Maria Mies, *Patriarchy and Accumulation On A World Scale: Women in the International Division of Labour* (London: Zed Books, 1998), 81.

61: Ruth Karras, *Sexuality in Medieval Europe: Doing Unto Others* (London: Routledge, 2017), 169.

62: Georgina Masson, *Courtesans of the Italian Renaissance* (London: Secker & Warburg, 1975). 28.

63: Elena Fernandez del Rio, Pedro Ramos-Villagrasa, Angela Castro, *et al.*, "Sociosexuality and Bright and Dark Personality: The Prediction of Behavior, Attitude, and Desire to Engage in Casual Sex," *International Journal of Environmental Research and Public Health*, 16 (2019): 2731.

64: Nathaly Cabrera, *About the Nature of Prostitution: Personality and Individual Differences Between Sex Workers and a Cohort Sample* (Rochester: Rochester Institute of Technology, 2020).

65: Nettle, *Personality*, *op. cit.*

The Witch's Curse

It might be added that some of those who were accused of being witches were believed to actually practice witchcraft and might have actually done so, in the sense that they cast spells, cursed people, and so on. There was an extent to which they literally established an alternative to the patriarchal religion, with themselves as powerful members of the system. And they might have even hurt people. For example, in March 1612, a young woman called Alison Device (c.1593-1612), who believed herself to be a witch, and whose family were known to practice folk magic in return for money, was walking near her home village of Pendle in Lancashire, when she passed a pedlar from Halifax in Yorkshire called John Law. Alison asked Law to sell her some pins, but Law refused. So Device cursed him. Law promptly dropped to the ground, possibly having a stroke. The pedlar later accused Device of witchcraft, of which she voluntarily confessed to be guilty. Device was hanged later that year.[66]

The pedlar believed in the power of witchcraft, so, having been cursed by a girl from a family of suspected witches, he could have suffered a stroke by what's called the "nocebo" effect. The opposite of the placebo effect, this is where potent belief can make you seriously ill or even kill you.[67] According to American literary scholar Katy Stravreva, these kinds of witch's curses "hurled the enemy's body to the ground, racked it, burned or froze it, caused suffocation or bloating, crippled the legs and the arms" because people believed in the power of the witch's curse. Such women were often physically violent, and it was these kinds of women who would often be accused of witchcraft.[68]

66: See Philip Almond, *The Lancashire Witches: A Chronicle of Sorcery and Death on Pendle Hill* (London: I. B. Tauris, 2017) and below.

67: Shelly Adler, *Sleep Paralysis: Nightmares, Nocebos, and the Mind-Body Connection* (Piscataway: Rutgers University Press, 2010).

68: Katy Stravreva, *Words Like Daggers: Violent Female Speech in Early Modern England* (Lincoln: University of Nebraska Press, 2015).

Witches, Infanticide, and Abortion

Throughout Early Modern England, women who were found to have carried out abortions on other women would sometimes be accused, not merely of murder, but of witchcraft as well.[69] Female healers often seemed to know folk remedies for inducing abortion, as has been documented in Early Modern Ireland.[70] Historian Margaret Brannan Lewis notes that in 16th-century Germany, there was a strong belief that women who harmed children were witches and that witches specifically set out to harm children:

> *[W]itches specifically attacked reproduction. Attacks on reproduction were seen not just in fictional depictions of witches but also in actual witch trials, which reached their zenith in the late sixteenth and early seventeenth centuries. Witches were often accused of harming or killing children, frequently in the course of their work as healers and midwives. The death or injury of a child was in many situations the spark that ignited a witch trial or even a full-blown witch-craze. The focus of witchcraft accusations on attacks on children connects witchcraft closely with infanticide.*[71]

Lewis explains that the fact that witchcraft was associated with attacking children meant that it was closely connected to infanticide. The crimes—abortion and infanticide—were similar in the sense that the victims were infants and fetuses, the crimes were perpetrated by women, and they were highly secretive. In *Malleus Maleficarum,* the authors tell us:

> *For in the diocese of Basel at the town of Dann, a witch who was burned confessed that she had killed more than forty children, by sticking a needle through the crowns of their*

69: Joseph Dellapenna, *Dispelling the Myths of Abortion History* (Durham: Carolina Academic Press, 2006).

70: Pauline Jackson, "Abortion Trials and Tribulations," *Canadian Journal of Irish Studies*, 18 (1992): 112-120.

71: Margaret Brannan Lewis, *Infanticide and Abortion in Early Modern Germany* (London: Routledge, 2016), 92.

> *heads into their brains, as they came out from the womb . . . another woman in the diocese of Strasburg confessed that she had killed more children than she could count. And she was caught in this way. She had been called from one town to another to act as midwife to a certain woman, and, having performed her office, was going back home. But as she went out of the town gate, the arm of a newly born child fell out of the cloak she had wrapped around her, in whose folds the arm had been concealed. This was seen by those who were sitting in the gateway, and when she had gone on, they picked up from the ground what they took to be a piece of meat; but when they looked more closely and saw that it was not a piece of meat, but recognized it by its fingers as a child's arm, they reported it to the magistrates, and it was found that a child had died before baptism, lacking an arm. So the witch was taken and questioned, and confessed the crime, and that she had, as has been said, killed more children than she could count.*[72]

Abortion provides females with control over their own reproduction and, thus, can be seen to undermine aspects of the patriarchal system. It can also be regarded as an expression of the personality of the abortionist or the woman who voluntarily submits to an abortion. In the view of Early Modern people, there would be little in the world that was more "unnatural" than a woman who would want to kill her own child or assist in killing children, and they would have regarded the "victims" as the babies whether in utero or not.[73] In some cases, women who underwent abortions were accused of being witches.[74] In Ancient Rome, there were cases of women who procured abortions being characterized as witches.[75] Early Modern texts on witchcraft

---

72: Kramer and Sprenger, *The Malleus Malificarum of Heinrich Kramer and James Sprenger*, *op cit.*, Chapter 8.

73: Dellapenna, *Dispelling the Myths of Abortion History*, *op cit.*, 1034.

74: Stephen Mitchell, *Witchcraft in the Nordic Middle Ages* (Philadelphia: University of Pennsylvania Press, 2011), 188.

75: Debbie Felton, "Witches, Disgust, and Anti-Abortion Propaganda in Imperial Rome," in *The Ancient Emotion of Disgust*, eds. Donald Lateiner and Dimos Spatharas (Oxford: Oxford University Press, 2016), 199.

specifically argued that women who procured abortions were witches, as were those who carried them out. In *Malleus Maleficarum*, the authors note: "Another instance occurred hardly four years ago in Reichshofen. There was a most notorious witch, who could at all times and by a mere touch bewitch women and cause an abortion."[76] Dutch physician Johann Weyer (1515-1588), in his witchcraft tract *De Praestigiis Daemonum*, likewise argued that witches conducted abortions.[77] In Shakespeare's *Macbeth* (1606), the three witches refer to infanticide and other perceived evils in making their unholy brew.

Liver of blaspheming Jew,
Gall of goat, and slips of yew
Sliver'd in the moon's eclipse,
Nose of Turk and Tartar's lips,
Finger of birth-strangled babe
Ditch-deliver'd by a drab,
Make the gruel thick and slab.
Add thereto a tiger's chawdron,
For th' ingredience of our cau'dron. (IV, i)

Shakespeare's witch characters were inspired by confessions that Shakespeare had read, reported in *News from Scotland*.[78]

Modern research has found that women who undergo abortion have a markedly different personality compared to those who do not. Females who have had abortions score higher than controls in histrionic characteristics (attention-seeking), Narcissism (which includes low empathy and low altruism), and anti-social personality (which also includes low empathy and

76: Kramer and Sprenger, *The Malleus Malificarum of Heinrich Kramer and James Sprenger*, *op cit.*, Chapter 6.

77: Johann Weyer, *Witches, Devils, and Doctors in the Renaissance: Johann Weyer, De Praestigiis Daemonum* (Tempe, AZ: Medieval and Renaissance Texts and Studies, 1991), 52.

78: Tracy Borman, "Shakespeare's Macbeth and King James's Witch Hunts," *History Extra*, June 18, 2018, https://www.historyextra.com/period/stuart/shakespeares-macbeth-and-king-jamess-witch-hunts/.

low altruism).[79] So, females who have abortions are likely to be unpleasant, anti-social people. The practice of abortion will also damage group selection, all else being equal, by helping to create a smaller group, more likely to be overwhelmed by an out-group.

Witches and Mutation

All of this makes a great deal of sense in evolutionary terms. To the extent that younger females were executed for witchcraft, the witch craze was removing from society females who were physically and psychologically unattractive, so helping to maintain the highly group-selected nature of the polity. This might have had some kind of genetic effect, due to the fact that a key predictor of being accused of witchcraft was that a woman's mother had been a witch.[80] This effect would have been slight, as the numbers were quite small, but witch persecution would have prevented potentially or known anti-social people from undermining group cohesion. One might ask why unattractive males were not similarly removed. The reason seems to be, as obnoxious as they appeared, that they did not undermine the patriarchal system. The execution for witchcraft of women over 50 can also be understood as a religiously sanctioned form of group selection, even though such women would not be able to have any further children. These anti-social, uncooperative women were, so it seems, high in mutational load, as reflected in their appearance.

Furthermore, the witch craze could be explicable in terms of the "Social Epistasis Amplification Model" presented by Michael Woodley of Menie and his colleagues, to which we

---

79: Thomas Strahan, "Personality Characteristics of Women Who Had Induced Abortions," *Association for Interdisciplinary Research in Values and Social Change*, 4 (1992): 3.

80: Pickering, "Witch," *op cit.*

will now turn.[81] Woodley of Menie has observed that human society might be more usefully compared to a beehive than to a group of highly advanced chimpanzees.[82] This comparison works because, like bees, humans live in intensely social societies in which there are extremely clearly marked divisions of labor. In addition, human society, like a beehive, is in stark competition with other similar societies, meaning it is subject to a very high level of "group selection."

Woodley of Menie argues that cooperation is so central to humans and bees that, in many crucial respects, these societies can be conceived of as kinds of organisms, with each individual playing a small but important role in the optimum functioning, and thus survival, of the whole. Every individual is part of a profoundly interconnected network, wherein he relies on those with whom he interacts to behave in an adaptive fashion, such that his own genes are expressed, phenotypically, in the same optimally adaptive fashion. It follows that if a feeder bee (in charge of feeding the larvae) has a mutation that causes her to feed the larvae at random, rather than according to an instinctively "normal" pattern, she will damage the fitness of the entire hive, because there will be, for example, far too many queens and not enough workers.

Similarly, if a human carries a spiteful mutation, which makes him believe and strongly propagate the view that life has no meaning, his mutation will impact those around him, causing (as with the bees) their environment to be different from that to which their genes are optimally adapted. Humans are highly environmentally plastic. Less complex organisms are born ready to get on with life, following their instincts. More complex organisms, often evolved to a harsher but more predictable

---

81: Michael A. Woodley of Menie, Matthew Sarraf, Radomir Pestow, and Heitor Fernandes, "Social Epistasis Amplifies the Fitness Costs of Deleterious Mutations, Engendering Rapid Fitness Decline Among Modernized Populations," *Evolutionary Psychological Science*, 3 (2017): 181-191.

82: Quoted in Edward Dutton, *The Silent Rape Epidemic: How the Finns Were Groomed to Love Their Abusers* (Oulu: Thomas Edward Press, 2019).

ecology, benefit from having a "childhood," in which they are able to learn about their harsher, more difficult-to-survive-in environment, and so be more likely to thrive. Accordingly, they are born helpless, and relatively low in "instinct." They learn adaptive behaviors from their parents and from their broader group. They are socialized into the most adaptive possible ways to behave; directed to follow a road map of life that will make them the most likely to survive, to develop optimally and to pass on their genes. In addition, this "road map" directs them to optimally thrive in the very specific and narrow environment to which their species, or sub-species, has long been adapted, and any instincts they have will be optimally useful in that environment. Thus, if the environment rapidly changes, members of such a species may experience an "evolutionary mismatch," resulting in their behaving in maladaptive ways. And if the nature of the group changes – such that it ceases to be composed overwhelmingly of genetically healthy people – then it will cease to socialize its offspring properly, resulting in more and more offspring adopting fitness-reducing behaviors, especially as such a society will increasingly direct them towards these.

Woodley of Menie and his colleagues have presented a large amount of evidence that nihilism is fitness-damaging and a product of deleterious mutations, which would have been selected out under harsh conditions. Believing in nihilism is associated with psychopathology, with such people tending to be killed by the band under conditions of intense selection.[83] It is also associated with depression and schizophrenia, both of which are strongly genetic and lead to very bad life outcomes and reduced fertility. Thus, people who have nihilistic worldviews tend not to pass on their genes.[84] However, nihilists also spread their way of thinking to those with whom they associate and on whom they exert influence. This means

---

83: Matthew Sarraf, Michael A. Woodley of Menie and Colin Feltham, *Modernity and Cultural Decline: A Biobehavioral Perspective* (Basingstoke, Hants: Palgrave Macmillan, 2019), 15.

84: *Ibid.*, 16.

that their friends' and acquaintances' genes will be expressed differently—sub-optimally. These non-carriers of spiteful mutations may be somewhat genetically predisposed to be nihilists and abandon reproduction because they begin to be convinced that "life is pointless" due to certain environmental conditions.

If these conditions never occur, because the spiteful mutation carriers are not present in their society, they will not develop those destructive behaviors. But once the spiteful mutant manifests, he can undermine the societal culture (such as its religious rituals) and stop his genetically "normal" co-ethnics from being religious. In other words, his fitness-damaging worldview can spread like a virus, even to those who lack the spiteful mutation or who lack its most virulent form. And, so, this single mutant—and even more so if there are many of them—can help to undermine the extent to which the group is optimally group-selected.

If these spiteful mutants ascend to positions of power or influence, they will be able to influence those who do not carry the spiteful mutations—by persuading them, for example, that women who are dedicated wives and mothers are "losers." They will thus undermine the capacity of the group to engage in adaptive behavior and hold adaptive beliefs. In that religiousness was selected for under preindustrial conditions, we would, therefore, expect atheism to be correlated with evidence of mutation. We have shown that this is, indeed, the case in our study entitled "The Mutant Says in His Heart, 'There is No God.'"[85]

Atheism is predicted by autism, which is itself predicted by having an old father and thus by age-related poor sperm quality due to increasingly poor quality sperm with increasing numbers of *de novo* mutations. It is predicted by left-handedness; this is a marker of developmental instability and thus mutational load,

---

85: Dutton, Madison and Dunkel, "The Mutant Says in His Heart, 'There Is No God,'" *op cit.*

because we are evolved to be symmetrical, and symmetrical brains tend to result in right-handedness. Atheism is associated with poor physical health poor (genetic) mental health. Alleles which predict depression are less prevalent among religious people—even with fluctuating asymmetry—that is, not being physically symmetrical. By contrast, the collective worship of a moral god, which is what European societies overwhelmingly engaged in prior to the Industrial Revolution when they were experiencing heightened levels of group selection, is associated with optimum physical and mental health, low autism, and being right-handed.

Political conservatism crosses over with fundamentalism at about 0.75.[86] Political conservatives in the U.S. have more symmetrical faces than political liberals,[87] and, controlling for socioeconomic status, more attractive people are more likely to identify as conservative.[88] Controlling for socioeconomic status is important, because some people may have high mutational load, and thus be of low socioeconomic status, and yet still be conservative due to the relationship between being right-wing and having low IQ. This relationship may exist for a number of possible reasons, which we will examine later. One may be that more intelligent people are better able to notice that the dominant ideology is liberal, better able to appreciate the benefits of conforming to it, and have the self-control necessary to force themselves to believe it.[89] Another may be that IQ is negatively associated with openness to new

86: Brian Laythe, Deborah Finkel, and Lee Kirkpatrick, "Predicting Prejudice from Religious Fundamentalism and Right Wing Authoritarianism: A Multiple Regression Analysis," *Journal for the Scientific Study of Religion*, 40 (2001): 1-10.

87: Niklas Berggren, Henrik Jordahl, and Panu Poutvaara, "The Right Look: Conservative Politicians Look Better and Voters Reward It," *Journal of Public Economics*, 146 (2017): 79-86.

88: Rolfe Peterson and Carl Palmer, "Effects of Physical Attractiveness on Political Beliefs," *Politics and Life Sciences*, 36 (2017): 3-16.

89: Michael A. Woodley of Menie and Curtis Dunkel, "Beyond the Cultural Mediation Hypothesis: A Reply to Dutton (2013)," *Intelligence*, 49 (2015): 186-191.

possibilities. A central component of beauty is symmetry. As already noted, we are supposed to be symmetrical, so if we are not, this indicates that either mutations have made us less symmetrical, or they have compromised our immune system, so we have not maintained a symmetrical phenotype because we needed to dedicate too much of our bio-energetic resources to fighting off disease, especially in childhood.

The key point with regard to the witch craze is that witches can reasonably be regarded as spiteful mutants, who, through their behavior, rendered the entire community less group selected, as their anti-social behavior could potentially inspire others to be anti-social, spreading anti-social behavior contagiously. Further, it might be suggested that these woman, by rejecting "natalism" or simply by virtue of not being of sexual interest to men, were at best a burden on pre-Modern society and, at worst, likely to be the carriers of mutations.

Parallel Explanations for the Witch Craze

It might be countered that the problem with my argument (that witch crazes should be substantially understood in terms of promoting group selection and patriarchy) is that 20 percent of those executed for witchcraft in England between 1566 and 1666 were male and only a large minority of those executed were single women. I have emphasized that promoting patriarchy is not the sole explanation for witch crazes. Moreover, this does not undermine the argument that the witch craze is most parsimoniously understood as an evolutionary strategy ultimately grounded in group selection.

Ugliness

As already noted, physically unattractive women were acutely targeted because their features betokened damaging mutations. Consistent with this, ethnographic studies in Sub-Saharan

Africa have found that the key predictors of being accused of witchcraft are being ugly or deformed.[90] For example, British anthropologist Edward Evans-Pritchard (1902-1973) noted, in his ethnography of the Azande, who live in what is now the Democratic Republic of Congo and the Central African Republic, that those accused of witchcraft tended to be "spiteful, dirty, unmannerly or physically deformed."[91] Moreover, the Early Modern English rightly believed that physical repulsiveness was often a reflection of psychological repulsiveness; this had to be purged because maladaptive, anti-social behavior would undermine group cohesion and thus group selection. Such behavior can also spread. Depression, which is highly maladaptive as it is causally associated with infertility,[92] is literally contagious. Non-depressed people who spend a great deal of time with depressed people tend to become depressed themselves.[93]

Psychological Unattractiveness

Another key factor can be seen in Evans-Pritchard's use of the word "spiteful." People accused of witchcraft were frequently unpleasant people that nobody liked, even if there was a general tendency for them to be female. As already noted, one way an old woman could get herself accused of witchcraft was by "cursing" people, and this was a time in which people strongly believed in the power of curses. Due to the nocebo effect, mentioned earlier, being cursed could sometimes have devastating consequences. Thus, it would make sense that

---

90: For a summary, see Alan MacFarlane, *Witchcraft in Tudor and Stuart England: A Regional and Comparative Study* (London: Routledge, 2002).

91: E. E. Evans-Pritchard, *Witchcraft, Oracles and Magic Among the Azande* (Oxford: Clarendon Press, 1963), xvii.

92: Kristin Rooney and Alice Domar, "The Relationship Between Stress and Infertility," *Dialogues in Clinical Neuroscience*, 20 (2018): 41-47.

93: T.E. Joiner, "Contagious Depression: Existence, Specificity to Depressed Symptoms, and the Role of Reassurance Seeking," *Journal of Personal and Social Psychology*, 67 (1994): 287-296.

unpleasant, unpopular people would be accused of witchcraft. Removing them from the society would help ensure that it remained pro-social and positively ethnocentric. As historian Frederick Valletta has summarized, of England's 17th century witch craze:

> *External influences such as war and lack of religious toleration may have provided the catalyst necessary for persecutions of unpopular figures to take place . . . the heightened suspicion and distrust of unpopular neighbours prevalent in many communities could only be legitimised when similar suspicions existed among the elite.*[94]

Valletta speculates that the use of demonic imagery by members of the ruling elite to smear political opponents in the polarized England of the time may have, in part, inspired the witch craze, which was mainly a rural phenomenon. He may be right, though I would submit that the elevated stress and mortality salience caused by poor living conditions and a religiously polarized and internally warring society is a simpler explanation. But the key point is that it was unpopular people who were smeared as witches, and this makes evolutionary sense. In the 1640s, in Kent, in southern England, for example, an old woman called Joan Cariden was accused of witchcraft. It was written of her in 1635 that she "doth wraile against her neighbours and saith they shall never prosper, Because she hath curst them." She was "in some quarters at least—[an] unpopular figure," regarded as highly aggressive prior to the leveling of any witchcraft allegations.[95] Cariden also sold corn in the context of a grain shortage, and people were going hungry. In other words, summarizes historian Malcolm Gaskill, "Joan Cariden was probably resented as a creditor

94: Frederick Valletta, *Witchcraft, Magic and Superstition in England, 1640–70* (London: Routledge, 2017).

95: Malcolm Gaskill, "Witchcraft in Early Modern Kent: Stereotypes and Background to Accusations," in *Witchcraft in the British Isles and New England: New Perspectives on Witchcraft, Magic, and Demonology*, ed. Brian Levack (London: Routledge, 2001), 267.

and a retailer, as much as reviled as an evil curser and sower of discord."[96]

Burdens on the Community

Those targeted with allegations of witchcraft were often, very specifically, *poor* old women. Historian John Swain has summarized that "witches were often poor old women who were usually accused by more prosperous younger neighbours, following a refusal of charity."[97] By the 17th century, the Medieval idea of voluntary alms for the poor had been replaced by the Poor Law. This banned begging and forced landowners to pay a tax for the upkeep of paupers. As the population increased markedly throughout the 16th and 17th centuries, recovering from the collapse caused by the Black Death, society became poorer, there being more competition for increasingly limited resources combined with temperatures getting colder. This meant that "the poor felt the full force of unfavourable market forces."

> *A rejected beggar would often curse his uncharitable neighbour, and, should something then go wrong, the neighbour might attribute his misfortune to witchcraft. Also present is the notion that the victim, aware that he had failed in his social obligations, sought to exonerate himself by transferring the guilt he felt to the beggar.*[98]

In New England, this taxation was not restricted to the gentry, the large landowners who didn't do any physical labor. Many people in a parish had to pay income tax to support paupers, meaning that paupers were, effectively, parasites off the community. Paupers relied on the compulsory extraction of resources from their struggling neighbors in order to survive.

96: *Ibid.*, 268.

97: J.T. Swain, "The Lancashire Witch Trials of 1612 and 1634 and the Economics of Witchcraft," in *Witchcraft in the British Isles and New England, op cit.*

98: *Ibid.*

In times of extreme want, we can understand why this situation would be resented, potentially inclining unscrupulous people to make accusations of witchcraft, in order to eliminate the paupers in question. But from the perspective of group selection, such paupers really are parasites. They live off the community. In the battle of group selection, a group is more likely to survive if all members contribute to its common good. Thus, it would make sense, from an evolutionary perspective, if those who failed to do this were regarded as in league with the Devil and so accused of witchcraft. This would be especially adaptive if their parasitic behavior was combined with their being socially discordant people. An analysis of the witch craze in 17th-century Massachusetts has highlighted economic dependency on the community as being a significant factor in being accused of witchcraft. "Even before suspicions were generated," writes American historian Richard Weisman, "relations between the witches of pre-Salem Massachusetts and their neighbors were likely to be problematic, if only because of the witches' economic dependency."[99] The kind of people accused of witchcraft tended to be a drain on an already struggling society:

> *Accordingly, it may be noted that the characteristics of those who were both eligible and available for poor relief in colonial Massachusetts overlapped considerably with the characteristics of the malefic witch. The class of paupers who did not work because they diabled [sic] included such groups as orphans, widows, unwed mothers, and men and women incapacitated by age, sickness, and other infirmities. It is from this population of the "impotent poor"—as well as from the population of those who risked inclusion in this category—that the overwhelming majority of pre-Salem witches were drawn.*[100]

Thus, we can see why, from a Darwinian perspective, there was pressure to eliminate them.

99: Richard Weisman, *Witchcraft, Magic, and Religion in 17th-century Massachusetts* (Amherst: University of Massachusetts Press, 1984), 80

100: *Ibid.*

Even in England itself, where money for relief of the poor was usually via charitable donation from the gentry and aspirant gentry, and taxation of the gentry, these kinds of economic dependents were, in effect, taking resources that could have been distributed to socioeconomically useful villagers. English villages in the 17th century were based around social ranks, at the top of which was the gentry. The gentry were divided, usually in order of wealth, into knights, esquires, and gentlemen. Knights and esquires tended not only to be wealthier than "gentlemen" but they were also armigerous. They had the right to bear "coat armor," rendering them officially part of a kind of "lower nobility" in an intensely status-conscious society. Those who were "gentlemen" were either less wealthy armigers or non-armigers ("plebeians") who could "live like a gentleman." Such people were gentlemen by community acclamation, meaning that they might be able to successfully obtain a coat of arms if the College of Arms, in its regular visitations through the counties to prevent the misuse of "coat armor," concluded that they were, indeed, "gentlemen." A significant component to being accepted as a "gentleman" was that you spent lavishly and were generous to the community.[101] According to English social historian Mary Abbott, "In 1613, the church wardens of Great Burstead, Essex, rejected Edmund Blagge's claim to be a gentleman because 'the gates of his house were not greasey with giving alms to the poor.'"[102] These kinds of alms could have gone to someone who at least contributed something socioeconomically. Thus, we can understand why paupers were resented, even in England.

Heresy and Intolerance

It might be argued that the Medieval period heralded the beginning of a more general intolerance of anything that

---

101: See Edward Dutton, *The Ruler of Cheshire: Sir Piers Dutton, Tudor Gangland and the Violent Politics of the Palatine* (Northwich, Cheshire: Léonie Press, 2015), Chapter 2.

102: Mary Abbott, *Family Ties: English Families, 1540-1920* (London: Routledge, 1993), 72.

was "different." This included Jews, heretics, and witches, a point implied by Joseph Klaits, whom we met above. It can be countered, however, that such an explanation is inherently more convincing if it can be reduced down to hard science, because hard scientific explanations are quantitatively testable and allow correct predictions to be made.[103] Simply asserting that there is an increase in "intolerance" raises the question of why this is the case and, thus, what is happening from an evolutionary perspective. The simplest explanation for the increase in the persecution of Jews would be a society becoming more religious and thus more group selected and more negatively ethnocentric. As for heretics, who were also increasingly persecuted, they were, sociologically, very different from witches.

An examination of those executed for heresy makes it clear that they cannot easily be lumped together with witches. Whereas witches tended to be poor, uneducated, elderly ladies, those executed for heresy were, generally, quite different sociologically. According to English historian Jasper Ridley (1920-2004), with regard to those who were burned during the reign of Queen Mary I: "The Protestants and their martyrs came from every social class and age group, but chiefly from the young artisans of south-east England and the intellectuals, especially the Divinity students at Cambridge University."[104] The north of England was so overwhelmingly Catholic that only one heretic—out of at least 280 heretics burnt under Queen Mary—was executed north of the River Trent.[105] People act selflessly in the interests of their ethnic group because it is an extended kinship group. But they are also likely to do so in the interests of smaller-scale genetic clusters based around genetic similarity. The fact that most of the martyrs were young and male would imply that they

103: Edward O. Wilson, *Consilience: The Unity of Knowledge* (New York: Alfred A. Knopf, 1998).

104: Ridley, *The Tudor Age*, *op cit.*, 114,

105: *Ibid.*, 113.

were, in effect, soldiers, acting selflessly on behalf of whatever group they were fighting for or fighting to inspire with their incredible bravery in becoming martyrs.

In line with this theory, there are distinct sub-ethnic cleavages within England. Geneticists have found that the Southeast of England represents a relatively distinct genetic cluster of people whose ancestry overwhelmingly derives from Anglo-Saxon invaders, who began coming to the country just after the fall of Rome. As we move north and west of this area, the English become increasingly Celtic.[106] Similarly, if we move forward to England's Civil War, support for the Puritans was mainly in the southeast of England and far south west, as well as in East Anglia, while the north was mainly Royalist.[107] A similar cleavage can be found in England's earlier civil war, the Wars of the Roses, in which two rival groups vied for power. Put very simply, the north was Lancastrian and the south was Yorkist.[108] It may even be that the American Civil War is partly explicable in these terms, as immigrants to the north and south hailed from different parts of England.[109] In this regard, it may be worth noting that the chief persecutor of Protestants under Queen Mary I—Edmund Bonner, Bishop of London (c.1500-1569)—was "the illegitimate scion of the Savages," who were a gentry family from Cheshire in northern England.[110]

In addition, there are genetic dimensions to social class, meaning that those who were martyred for Protestant

---

106: Ross Byrne, Rui Martiniano, Lara Cassidy, *et al.*, "Insular Celtic Population Structure and Genomic Footprints of Migration," *PLOS Genetics* (2018), https://doi.org/10.1371/journal.pgen.1007152.

107: Linda Matthews, *Middling Folk: Three Seas, Three Centuries, One Scots-Irish Family* (Chicago: Chicago Review Press, 2010), 33.

108: Albert Makinson, "The Wars of the Roses: Who Fought and Why?" *History Today*, 9 (1959): 9.

109: David Hackett Fischer, *Albion's Seed: Four British Folkways in America* (Oxford: Oxford University Press, 1989).

110: Tim Thornton, *Cheshire and the Tudor State, 1480-1560* (Woodbridge, Suffolk: The Boydell Press, 2000), 204; Ridley, *The Tudor Age, op cit.*

heresy under Mary may have been fighting for their social class interests as well, in an environment in which being part of the higher "middling sort" (such as yeomen, husbandmen, merchants, and craftsmen) predicted completed fertility.[111] It was these middling "strivers" who disproportionately passed on their genes, while the nobility tended to die off in battle.[112] Dying for Protestantism can thus be regarded as a proxy for dying in order to inspire those with similar genetics to oneself and strike fear into those who are genetically dissimilar. As a group, sending martyrs to the flames is a way of saying: "*Look how brave we are! Look how many of us there are! We will never give up nor run out of fighters for our cause! We are that fanatical!*" One might argue that a similar model would contribute to making sense of the Islamic practice of suicide bombing or Japan's former use of Kamikaze pilots.

That said, there is a degree of psychological and sociological crossover in a minority of cases between witches and those who were burnt for heresy. Firstly, although those who were burnt for heresy and those who were hanged for witchcraft were, sociologically, noticeably distinct, it could be argued that both groups can be seen as undermining society's religion and, consequently, its unity and ethnocentrism. Secondly, we would expect those who were relatively low in altruism or empathy—that is anti-social people—to be prepared to question society's religiosity in this way. Accordingly, executing them, especially if they were young men, would remove anti-social people, who might potentially undermine group selection, from the gene pool. One example of such a person would be the Protestant Law student "Collins," who walked into his local church service with his dog, held it up by its legs, and imitated the acts performed by the priest with it. Another is one "Crowbridge," who was burnt by the Bishop of Lincoln as a heretic for claiming that Christ is the "future deceiver of the world" and that "all that

111: J. Philippe Rushton, "Genetic Similarity, Human Altruism, and Group Selection," *Behavioral and Brain Sciences*, 12 (1989): 503-559.

112: See Clark, *A Farwell to Alms*, *op cit.*

believe in Christ shall be damned."[113] In a religious society, it might be argued, both men were simply trying to be grotesquely offensive. Both ended up burned as heretics.

Thirdly, there were some cases in which heretic burning may have been motivated by removing people perceived as, in a sense, congenitally wicked or burdensome to society. For example, on the channel island of Guernsey, in July 1556, three women—a mother and her two daughters—were, together, burned for heresy. One of the daughters, Perotine Massey, the wife of a Calvinist minister who had fled to London, was heavily pregnant: "The belly of the woman burst asunder by the vehemence of the flame, the infant, being a fair man-child, fell into the fire."[114] The baby was rescued and taken to the island's lead citizen, the Bailiff of Guernsey, Hellier Gosselin (c.1500-1579). Gosselin ordered that the baby be thrown back into the fire, alive, which it duly was.[115] On 15th May 1556, Hugh Laverock, a 68-year-old "cripple" and John Aprice, who was blind, were burnt at Stratford in east London. The following day "Catharine Hut, of Bocking, widow; Joan Horns, spinster, of Billerica; Elizabeth Thackwel, spinster, of Great Burstead, suffered death in Smithfield."[116] Joan Waste a "poor, honest woman, blind from her birth, and unmarried, aged twenty-two," the daughter of a barber from Derby, was burnt on August 1st, 1556.[117] But these are all relatively unusual cases that run in contrast to the general pattern. Thus, it makes theoretical sense to separate "heretics" from "witches." Their persecution reflects different, though related, causes.

113: George Townsend, *The Acts and Monuments of John Fox: With A Life of the Martyrologists, and a Vindication of the Work*, Vol. I (London: Seeley, Burnside & Seeley, 1843), 214.

114: *Ibid.*, 934.

115: See William Berry, *The History of the Island of Guernsey* (London: Longman, Hurst, Rees, Orme and Brown, 1815), 242.

116: John Foxe, *Foxe's Book of Martyrs* (London: Knight and Son, 1856), 929.

117: *Ibid.*, 935.

So, we can see that in a society under intense Darwinian selection, including under group selection, witches were likely to be removed. To fully understand the dynamics of witchcraft, it's useful to look at some real examples of those who were executed for their diabolical activities. As we will see, even in case studies, these women are broadly congruous with the stereotypes outlined above.

Chapter 5

Marks of the Devil

Case Studies of Early Modern Witches

Witch crazes were not uniform throughout the countries in which they took place. They tended to center on specific areas, which had suffered through periods of economic hardship, which were fervently religious to begin with, or were marked by a combination of these and other factors. In this chapter, we will explore the dynamics of a number of witch crazes in order to see how they operated, based on the historical sources, as well as how and why people accused each other of witchcraft.

The Pendle Witches

One of the most famous witch crazes, which we already briefly alluded to, took place in Pendle in Lancashire in 1612. This was, essentially, the culmination of a long-running feud between two poor families, who competed with each other to be local healers, both of whom were reputed to practice witchcraft. Such practices were tolerated to a greater extent in the Catholic north, which developed a certain Pagan-Christian syncretization, than in the Puritan south.

It all began when a young girl, Alison Device, who was from one of these families of healers, cursed a Yorkshire pedlar, John Law, who proceeded to have a stroke. Alison, who was genuinely convinced she was a witch, confessed to what she'd done, leading to Law making an official complaint. Alison, her mother Elizabeth, and brother, James, were brought before a magistrate who had been tasked with investigating the affair. James testified that his sister had bewitched a local child, while Elizabeth admitted that her own mother, Elizabeth Demdike (also known as Elizabeth Southerns), had a mark on her body. These were known as "Devil's Marks" or "Witch's Marks." According to lore, the Devil would mark his witches in this way, after she had made a pact to serve him. Unusual marks on witches' bodies were used as part of a cumulative case against them.[1] Witches would then be "pricked" to discover if the marks were, in fact, the sign of the devil. It was believed that if you pricked one of these marks, the witch would not feel pain, nor would the mark bleed.

There was bad feeling between the Devices and a rival local family of reputed witches known as the Chattoxes. Perhaps motivated by revenge, Alison accused Anne Whittle (alias Chattox) of murdering four men by witchcraft and also of killing her father, John Device, who had died in 1601. On 2nd April 1612, Demdike, Chattox, and Chattox's daughter, Anne Redferne, were brought before the same magistrate. Both Demdike and Chattox, who were blind and in their 80s, confessed to witchcraft. Demdike also accused Redferne of witchcraft, and a witness was produced to substantiate the claim. Based on this evidence, all three were sent to Lancaster Gaol to be tried for witchcraft at the next assizes (a system whereby judges moved around a circuit of courts to try accused criminals), as was Alison Device.

On Good Friday, 1612, Elizabeth Device organized some kind of meeting at Malkin Tower, which was the home of the Demdikes. In order to feed those present, James Device stole a neighbor's sheep. Word of this meeting reached the investigating magistrate and he was naturally concerned that some sort of

1: T. Flotte and D.A. Bell, "Role of Skin Lesions in the Salem Witchcraft Trials," *American Journal of Dermotopathology*, 11 (1989): 582-587.

witch's coven had taken place. As a result, Elizabeth Device, James Device, Alice Nutter, Katherine Hewitt, John Bulcock, Jane Bulcock, Alice Grey, and Jennet Preston were all arrested for witchcraft. Preston lived just across the county border in Yorkshire, so she was to be tried at the York Assizes. The others were sent to Lancaster Gaol.

The York Assizes took place on July 27th, 1612. Preston was found guilty and hanged two days later. The Lancaster Assizes sat on the 18th and 19th of August. Alice Grey was found not guilty, and Elizabeth Demdike had died in prison awaiting trial. All of the rest were found guilty and hanged. At the trial, it was reported that Elizabeth Device had a deformed face, meaning that one eye was much higher than the other. The main witness called against her was her own 9-year-old daughter, Jennet. Elizabeth Device screamed at her daughter and cursed her, forcing the judges to have Elizabeth forcibly removed from the court.[2]

The Second Pendle Witch Craze

Witchcraft hit Pendle again in 1634, when a ten-year-old boy, Edmund Robinson, accused around 20 people of witchcraft, including of murder via witchcraft. One of these was Jennet Device, very possibly the same person who had testified against her mother in 1612. The accused were brought before the Lancaster Assizes and found guilty. However, the judges were seemingly unhappy about this verdict. They refused to pass the death sentence and, instead, sent the convicts to Lancaster Gaol. They then referred the case to the King, Charles I. This meant that Edmund Robinson had to testify in London.

Under cross-examination, he admitted to having fabricated allegations against four of the convicts, seemingly to

2: See Philip Almond, *The Lancashire Witches: A Chronicle of Sorcery and Death on Pendle Hill* (London: I. B. Tauris, 2017).

avoid a whipping for a minor offense. The four were pardoned. Precisely what happened to the convicts is unclear from the surviving records.[3] However, later in 1634, the events did result in a popular play by Thomas Heywood (c.1575-1641) and Richard Brome (c.1590-1652), entitled *The Late Lancashire Witches*. This was performed at London's famous Globe Theatre by a well-known theatre company, The King's Men. The popularity of the play kept what had happened in Lancashire in the public consciousness. Literary historian Frances Dolan writes, "In the early seventeenth century, the drama influenced and reflected the widespread interest in witchcraft," and *The Late Lancashire Witches* was the culmination of a series of plays on this subject, including *Macbeth* (1606).[4] One of the people who read about the Lancashire witches was the young son of a vicar. This vicar's son was named Matthew Hopkins.[5]

Matthew Hopkins: The Witch-finder General

Between 1644 and 1646, Matthew Hopkins (c.1620-1647), who claimed the title of Witch-finder General, was responsible for the execution of somewhere around 230 people, almost all of them in East Anglia in the east of England, where there was another localized witch craze.[6] Hopkins was born in Suffolk, the son of James Hopkins, the Puritan vicar of Great Wenham in that county. In the early 1640s, Hopkins moved to Manningtree

---

3: Alison Findlay, "Sexual and Spiritual Politics in the Events of 1633–1634 and the Late Lancashire Witches," in *The Lancashire Witches: Histories and Stories*, ed. Robert Poole (Manchester: Manchester University Press, 2002).

4: Frances Dolan, *Dangerous Familiars: Representations of Domestic Crime in England, 1550 – 1700* (Ithaca: Cornell University Press, 1994), 210.

5: Richard Deacon, *Matthew Hopkins: Witch Finder General* (London: Frederick Muller, 1976), 41.

6: Craig Cabell, *Witchfinder General: The Biography of Matthew Hopkins* (Stroud, Glos: The History Press, 2006).

in Essex, about 10 miles from Wenham. In this area, he met John Stearn (c.1610-1670), who had managed to persuade local lay magistrates—so-called "Justices of the Peace"—that he was skilled in persuading witches to confess to their crimes. This was in a society where there was, of course, no police force. Stearn appointed Hopkins as his assistant.

Their campaign focused on his own county, as well as nearby Suffolk, Norfolk, Cambridgeshire, and Huntingdonshire and, to a lesser extent, Bedfordshire and Northamptonshire, which were further afield. These were the most strongly Puritan areas of the country.[7] Hopkins claimed, however, in his pamphlet, *The Discovery of Witches*, that he had personal experiences of witchcraft in Manningtree and that it was this that inspired his activities:

> *The Discoverer never travelled far for it, but in March 1644 he had some seven or eight of that horrible sect of Witches living in the Town where he lived, a Town in Essex called Manningtree, with divers other adjacent Witches of other towns, who every six weeks in the night (being always on the Friday night) had their meeting close by his house and had their several solemn sacrifices there offered to the Devil, one of which this discoverer heard speaking to her Imps one night, and bid them go to another Witch, who was thereupon apprehended, and searched, by women who had for many years known the Devil's marks, and found to have three teats about her, which honest women have not: so upon command from the Justice they were to keep her from sleep two or three nights, expecting in that time to see her familiars, which the fourth night she called in by their several names, and told them what shapes, a quarter of an hour before they came in, there being ten of us in the room . . .*[8]

7: *Ibid.*

8: Matthew Hopkins, *The Discovery of Witches: In Answer to Severall Queries, Lately Delivered to the Judges of Assize for the County of Norfolk* (self-published, 1647), Query 4.

Hopkins's zeal soon made him more prominent than Stearn. And in the two-year period in which he investigated claims of witchcraft in these counties and brought them before the courts, more people in England were hanged for this crime than had been in the preceding 100 years. Hopkins and Stearn claimed, falsely, to have been appointed by parliament to find witches and charged locals fees for their work, billing them for every witch they made to confess.

When their methods of extracting confessions, which involved ducking and other tortures, began to be questioned by magistrates, especially in Norfolk, the duo retired from their work, with Hopkins dying the following year. In discovering whether women were witches, they often stripped them naked and had female assistants examine their bodies in order to find evidence of Witch's Marks or deformities, such as a third nipple or some other teat-like protuberance. It was believed that they would suckle devils using these deformities.[9]

The Witches of Cheshire and Libel

The events in East Anglia and in Lancashire have been widely discussed in the historical literature. Accordingly, to gain a greater understanding of the kind of people who were found guilty of witchcraft, it would be useful to conduct some primary research. Bordering Lancashire to the south is the county of Cheshire. Only one investigation of the history of witchcraft in this county has ever previously been presented,[10] meaning it would be an important contribution to understanding the history of witchcraft in England to expand on what has already been published on the matter.

Cheshire, historically, was something of an anomaly in England. At the beginning of Henry VIII's reign, England

9: See Cabell, *Witchfinder General*, *op cit.*

10: Deborah Lea, "Harlots, Whores and Witches," *Herstory*, 3 (2009): 32-37.

included three so-called "Palatinates" or "Palatines": Lancashire, Durham, and Cheshire. In the Medieval period, these counties had sat on the borders of crown power. Accordingly, they were given the status of "palatines," whereby a nobleman—the Bishop of Durham, the Duke of Lancaster, or the Earl of Chester—rather than the king, was their head-of-state. By the 16th century, the individual palatines had different relationships with the English state. By 1399, the Duchy of Lancaster, which had always had Members of Parliament, had reverted to the crown. It was effectively subsumed into the English state, though administered separately as it still is today by its Chancellor. The Bishop of Durham appointed his own sheriffs and maintained the absolute right to pardon offenses within the palatinate. Durham had no MPs until 1673.

Cheshire was also ardently independent. Although the Earldom of Chester had also reverted to the crown (in 1301), Cheshire's independence was strongly maintained. The original Earl of Chester had appointed hereditary deputies—eight of his feudal barons, known as the "Cheshire barons"—to rule parts of Cheshire in his place. These barons—they were gentry, only recognized as "barons" within Cheshire—could authorize executions without recourse to the crown. Cheshire had its own chief justice, who administered justice in the name of the Earl of Chester, its own Chamberlain (financial chief), who administered the county, and its own parliament ("mise"), composed of the Cheshire barons and the county's officers, such as the Sheriff, who decided on occasional grants to the crown. The king—as Earl of Chester—appointed Cheshire's officers, but Cheshire was still substantially beyond the reach of English Law and, to a degree, maintained a distinct culture. This distinct culture included being strongly Catholic even by the late 16th century, and Cheshire was dominated by its Catholic gentry.[11] This tended to mean that witchcraft was tolerated, meaning that only the most obvious "witches" were likely to

11: Tim Thornton, *Cheshire and the Tudor State, 1480-1560* (Woodbridge, Suffolk: The Boydell Press, 2000).

be found guilty. This makes Cheshire, by virtue of its relative independence, a particularly useful case study in understanding the essence of the Early Modern witch.

According to historians C.B. Phillips and J.H. Smith, only 11 people were hanged for witchcraft in Cheshire in the county's entire history.[12] I am unsure of the providence of this number, because I cannot find evidence even for that many. There were a number of cases of people suing others for libel after having been accused of witchcraft. In 1662, in Nantwich, Anna Wright accused Maria Briscoe of killing her daughter, Anna, by witchcraft, claiming that the little girl's "eyes hanged over her cheeks and sometimes would play on her forehead and sometimes up and down on her face like two bladders."[13] Anna Wright, however, is described as a "troublesome, contentious and ill-tempered woman."[14] According to English historian Deborah Lea, who has researched this case:

> *In an unfortunate coincidence after a number of, 'evil and bitter words and expressions', between the two, Anna's son Hugh was suddenly taken sick with strange distemper and died. Naturally, Maria was suspected to be the cause of his ailment.*

A year later, Anna's daughter, also called Anna, saw Maria look at her in a strange way. Soon after, the younger Anna became seriously ill and died. Anna Wright, who already had many earlier grievances with Maria, started spreading rumors that Maria was a witch. So Maria sued her and won, with Anna being compelled to apologize.[15]

In 1595, Jane Dickinson of Tarvin sued Margaret Dickinson for calling her "a whore and a witch."[16] In 1613, in

---

12: C.B. Phillips and J.H. Smith, *Lancashire and Cheshire from 1540 AD* (London: Routledge, 1994), 61.

13: Cheshire Records Office, Nantwich, 1662, EDC 5/1662/63.

14: Lea, "Harlots, Whores and Witches," *op cit.*

15: *Ibid.*

16: Cheshire Records Office, Tarvin, 1595, EDC 5/1595/44.

Warrington, Jane Bell sued Jacob Eaton for libel for calling her "a whore and a charming witch."[17] There were a number of other similar libel cases, such as one from 1601 in which an accused woman was found not guilty by virtue of being an "ignoramus."[18] Most of the few cases I have found where women were actually executed for witchcraft took place at the height of Puritan influence over the county, during Cromwell's Interregnum.

Ellen Stubbs of Warford, wife of farm laborer William Stubbs, her daughter, Elizabeth Stubbs, and Anne Stanley of Withington, wife of farm laborer John Stanley, were all hanged for witchcraft in 1654. All three were found to have bewitched a woman called Anne Lowe back in 1646. Ellen and Elizabeth Stubbs had bewitched a black cow owned by Warford gentleman Thomas Grastie's in 1652. Ellen Stubbs and Anne Stanley had entertained evil spirits and bewitched a gentlewoman called Elizabeth Furnivall, in June 1653, at Nether Alderley. Furnivall had died as a consequence.[19]

Consistent with broader research, all three of these women were poor, part of the "lower sort." They also appear to have been relatively old as well. The survival rate for parish records prior to the Interregnum is patchy. Consulting the baptism records of St Michael's, Macclesfield, which was close to Warford, I cannot find a christening for "Elizabeth Stubbs." However, Ellen, daughter of "William Stubbes," was baptized on November 1st, 1604, with babies usually being christened approximately a week after their birth.[20] Assuming this is the correct William Stubbes, we can estimate—based on the average age that laborers married at the time—that he was born no later than about 1582, nor would have been his wife, Ellen. The

---

17: Cheshire Records Office, Warrington, EDC, 5/1613/30.

18: Cheshire Records Office, John Ratcliffe, Mayor, Thomas Lawton, Recorder, QSF/50.

19: Richard Bradshaw, *God's Battle Axe: The Life of Lord President John Bradshawe* (Bloomington: Xlibris, 2010), 333-334.

20: See, Graeme Davis, *Solving Genealogy Problems: How to Break Down "Brick Walls" and Build Your Family Tree* (Begbroke, Oxon: How-to-Books, 2011).

average age of marriage for women at the time was about 26, though it was lower among the lower sort.[21] This would have made Ellen Stubbs 72 years old in 1654 and thus an elderly lady, of the kind who would have been targeted by witch-hunters. Elizabeth Stubbs herself would have, therefore, been a middle-aged spinster, also conforming to the broader analyses of who was convicted of witchcraft. Boys called "John Stanley" were christened at St. Michael's, Macclesfield, in 1584 and at Nether Alderley in 1615. Anne Stanley could have been the wife of either, but if it was the former, then she was also an elderly woman.

Three more convicted witches were hanged in Cheshire in 1656. In September 1651, Ellen Beach, wife of John Beach, a collier, was accused of conjuring up evil spirits by which she managed to a kill a spinster by the name of Elizabeth Cowper. These women both lived in the village of Rainow. John Beach was christened at St. Michael's, Macclesfield, in 1589, potentially implying that Ellen was an old lady by the standards of the time. Also in 1656, Ellen's neighbor, Ellen Osboston, wife of James Osboston, a husbandman, was accused of witchcraft. This is a very rare surname. Mary Osboston, daughter of James, was christened at St. Michael's, Macclesfield, on January 1st, 1633. Based on the average age at which the "middling sort" married, we can thus estimate that Ellen Osboston was no younger than 46 when she was accused of witchcraft. This James, however, was probably her son, because in 1595, "Ellen Osbaldeston" sued "Thomas Walmisley" and "Robert Tailor" for libel, after they claimed she had been practicing witchcraft for 20 years.[22] If this is the same Ellen, something which appears very probable, then she could have been well into her 80s by 1656.

Ellen Ostboston was also accused of having killed John Steenson of Rainow, also a husbandman, using witchcraft. In November that year she supposedly killed Anthony Booth of Macclesfield, Gentleman, with witchcraft. In 1653, she putatively

21: See Lawrence Stone, *The Family, Sex and Marriage in England, 1500-1800* (New York: Harper & Row, 1977).

22: Cheshire Records Office, Blackburn, EDC 5/1595/30.

murdered Barbara Pott of Rainow, a widow. And finally, in August 1655, she was said to have killed John Pott of Rainow, Yeoman, with her sorcery. The two accused witches were sent to Chester to stand trial along with a third accused, whom we will meet below. Husbandmen were part of the "middling sort," though they were the bottom rank of that class. There was no clear definition of these different social ranks. They were defined by a combination of lifestyle, wealth, and social culture. A husbandman could be extremely wealthy, wealthier than a yeoman or even a gentleman. If he took to the plough himself, however, then most people would regard him as a husbandman.[23] James Osboston may have been a very poor husbandman.

In February 1656, Anne Thornton of Eaton, a widow, was accused of having murdered Daniel Finchett, the baby son of a yeoman farmer called Ralph Finchett:

> *That Anne Thornton, late of Eaton in Cheshire, widow, on the 9th day of February 1655 [1656], and on divers other days and times as well before and since, at Eccleston, not having God before her eyes, but with instigation of the Devil, being moved and seduced [did] with force and arms wickedly, devilishly and feloniously exercise and practice certain devilish and wicked acts, enchantments, charms and sorceries in and upon one Daniel Finchett, son of Ralph Finchett, of Eccleston, yeoman, being an infant of the age of three days . . . he, the aforesaid Daniel by the said wicked and devilish acts so by her the aforesaid Anne Thornton used, exercised and practised, as aforesaid, upon him, the said Daniel, died.*

A widow is precisely the kind of person we would expect to be accused of witchcraft. The nearest church to Eaton at the time was at Eccleston. Elizabeth Thornton, daughter of James, was christened there on 1st October 1617. This would mean, if she were lower sort, that her mother was born no later than

23: See Edward Dutton, *The Ruler of Cheshire: Sir Piers Dutton, Tudor Gangland and the Violent Politics of the Palatine* (Northwich, Cheshire: Léonie Press, 2015), Chapter 2.

about 1605, making her a relatively old widow when she was accused of witchcraft. All three women were found guilty and hanged on October 15th, 1656.[24]

In 1670, a woman called Elizabeth Powell died in Northgate Gaol in Chester of "various ailments," having been held there for six years charged with witchcraft.[25] Powell had been convicted of witchcraft, according to another source, in 1669, so she may have died awaiting the execution of her sentence.[26] In April 1675, Mary Baguley of Wildboarclough, in the parish of Prestbury, was indicted for killing a married schoolmaster called Robert Hall of Wincle with her evil magic. He had lain in bed sick for many days before she used sorcery to "crush his heart to pieces." She was found guilty of witchcraft and hanged.[27] I have been unable to discover how old she was from the surviving records. In general, however, an examination of the Cheshire records adds to the broader finding that "witches" tended to be middle-aged or elderly women. In addition, there was a tendency for them to be close to the bottom of the Early Modern socioeconomic ladder. They were not, generally, part of the "middle class." Modern day "witches," by contrast, are most certainly part of the middle class. In the next chapter we will explore why this is the case.

24: Roger Stephens, *The Little Book of Cheshire* (Stroud, Glos: The History Press, 2018); John Earwalker, *The History of the Church and Parish of St Mary on the Hill, Chester* (London, 1898), 28-29.

25: Cheshire Records Office, March 7th, 1670, QCI/12/12.

26: Cheshire Records Office, Sheriff's Indentures Gaol, ZS/IG.

27: Gregory Durston, *Crimen Exceptum: The English Witch Prosecution in Context* (Sherfield on Lodden, Hants: Waterside Press, 2019), 196.

Chapter 6

The Middling Sort

Spiteful Mutants and the Middle Class

We have established the defining characteristics of the Early Modern witch. They tended to be physically unattractive females who acted in such a way as to undermine patriarchy, and by extension group selection. They also tended to be childless and unmarried. Being physically unattractive, they had poor genetic health, and this was reflected in their also being mentally maladapted, as we would expect most females to be evolved to accept patriarchy.[1] Under Industrial conditions, we would expect to find more and more females who, in pre-Modern times, would have been regarded as witches. This is because there would be more and more females, who wouldn't have survived childhood under Darwinian conditions, reaching adulthood. They would, therefore, likely be physically and mentally unhealthy and prone to advocating fitness-damaging ideas. As we will see, these "modern witches" tend to come from the middle class. Why is this? To understand what is happening, we first need to be clear on the nature of social class.

Social Class

Some people question the utility of dividing societies into social classes when analyzing them. But it can be countered that a

1: Rachael Grant and V. Tamara Montrose, "It's a Man's World: Mate Guarding and the Evolution of Patriarchy," *Mankind Quarterly*, 58 (2018): 384-418.

system of categories is useful if it permits correct predictions to be made. Psychologists of class in the UK, such as Michael Argyle (1925-2002), define the upper class as the traditional aristocracy and leaders in commerce and other areas. They are people who are very wealthy and influential in the running of society, including senior members of the various higher professions, such as the Law. In England, we would expect such people to be part of the approximately seven percent of the population who attend private schools, and, more so, part of the four percent who attend the most prestigious and expensive private schools. In England, these are known as "public schools," famous examples include Eton and Harrow.[2] Just as younger children of Early Modern "Gentlemen" might begin as "yeomen," the children of the upper class might begin their careers as socioeconomically "middle class," though they would have a different social culture from those who had been born into the middle class.

Argyle also distinguishes between a middle class of "higher professionals" and "lower professionals." Higher professionals would include lawyers, doctors, academics, architects, and members of other such professions, many, though not necessarily all of whom, would be relatively well-paid and highly educated. The wealthier members of this group would likely send their children to public schools. Lower professionals would be people such as school teachers, accountants, and nurses. Then there is a lower-middle class of "white collar workers," policemen, and other non-graduates, although with the rapid expansion of university education,

2: "Public schools" are so named because they are attractive to members of the wider public who can afford the costly residential fees; this is in distinction to "local schools" or "state schools." The term "public school" is specifically used with regard to particularly prestigious examples of these private boarding schools. In the United States, similarly prestigious institutions are known as "private schools," "boarding schools," or "prep schools," in distinction from the "public schools" that are government-funded and open to all in a locality. Hereafter, when I use the term "public school," I am referring to the British variety.

even they may now increasingly be university graduates. All of these people may regard themselves simply as "middle-class," but there remains, Argyle suggests, significant social differences between them. Beneath these classes are a "working-class," engaging in physical labor (such as car mechanics and builders) and an "under-class," comprised of the long-term unemployed, criminals, and marginalized immigrant groups.[3]

One problem with Argyle's model is that it does not take into account the importance of social background or social culture. Many British people would regard an "upper class" person who becomes a school teacher as "an upper-class teacher." This means that many people might be on the borders of different social classes, but this does not undermine the utility of making class divisions. Indeed, these divisions—based on income, education level, and occupational status—crossover with numerous other differences of culture and even language usage. For example, in England, when someone mishears what someone has just said, an upper-class person would typically say "What?"; higher professionals say "Sorry?"; lower professionals and lower middle-class people say "Pardon?"; and working class people say "What?"[4] Social-class differences also correlate with differences in average IQ, and people tend to assort, in friendships and relationships, along social class, and thus partly genetic lines.[5] Indeed, it has been shown that there are differences in average blood type between different social classes in the UK. As J. Philippe Rushton explains: "In Britain, blood type A is found to occur more frequently in SES 1, the highest group (57 percent of the time), than in SES 5, the lowest group (41 percent of the time)."[6] This genetic dimension to social class makes sense. It

3: Michael Argyle, *The Psychology of Social Class* (London: Routledge, 1994), 15-16.

4: Kate Fox, *Watching the English: The Hidden Rules of English Behaviour* (London: Hodder and Stoughton, 2004), 76.

5: Richard Herrnstein and Charles Murray, *The Bell Curve: Intelligence and Class Structure in American Life* (New York: Free Press, 1994).

6: J. Philippe Rushton, "Genetic Similarity, Human Altruism, and Group Selection," *Behavioral and Brain Sciences*, 12 (1989): 503-559.

is predicted by the high heritability of intelligence—which is central to socioeconomic status—and also by Genetic Similarity Theory, which we discussed earlier. This genetic dimension to class is also in line with the finding, previously noted, that across generations, social class is about 0.7 heritable.[7]

Industrialization and the Mind of Western Societies

Next, we have to understand what has been wrought by the Industrial Revolution. In 1800, the child mortality rate was about 50 percent, a rate that has now fallen to 1 percent. Industrialization heralded better medicine, inoculations against formerly devastating childhood diseases, cheaper food, and eventually, much healthier living conditions. As a consequence, the intensity of Darwinian selection was dramatically weakened, including the intensity of group selection. Until around 1800, the high child mortality meant that mutations that caused, for example, a poor immune system, were purged from the population every generation, meaning that the population was strongly adapted to the ecology and had a very low mutational load. With the Industrial Revolution, more and more people with more and more mutations, which would have previously caused them to die in childhood, began to survive and pass on their genes. This led to an increasingly genetically sick population, a process known as "dysgenics."[8] This has two key manifestations.

The first is declining intelligence, which had previously been positively selected for, as discussed above. Geoffrey Miller has argued that intelligence is extremely sensitive to mutation by virtue of the fact that the brain—as approximately 84

7: Gregory Clark, *The Son Also Rises: Surnames and the History of Social Mobility* (Princeton: Princeton University Press, 2014).

8: See Richard Lynn, *Dysgenics: Genetic Deterioration in Modern Populations* (London: Ulster Institute for Social Research, 2011).

percent of the genome[9]—is a massive mutational target.[10] Thus, increased mutational load will cause intelligence to decline, because genetic health and intelligence have been selected for together, as both are adaptive. Congruous with this, intelligence is weakly positively associated with having a symmetrical face, implying low mutational load. Low intelligence also correlates with other markers of high mutational load.[11]

In addition, declining mortality salience makes people less stressed and thus less religious. This helps to further contribute to the -0.2 correlation between intelligence and fertility in modern populations in a number of ways. These include the reality that many people seem to stop wanting to have children, especially those who are more intelligent. It is unclear why this happens but one possibility is that intelligent people—being low in instinct, as discussed above—are more reliant than less intelligent people on being directed along an optimally adaptive road map of life. Thus, if this is subverted, they will be more sensitive to it and feel a greater sense of dysphoria accordingly. In addition, if an individualistic, fitness-damaging ideology does become dominant, they will be more likely to absorb it and persuade themselves of its veracity. This may also be because, lacking traditional religiousness, they perceive everything, including having children, in more rational and thus less instinctive terms. They desire social status and, in their new "evolutionary mismatch," having children does not assist substantially in that regard, so they end up delaying having them until it is too late. When low in mortality salience, they also lose their religiousness. "*Life has no meaning*," many of them reason, "*So what is the point of having children? Wouldn't they*

9: Michael A. Woodley of Menie, Matthew Sarraf, Radomir Pestow, and Heitor Fernandes, "Social Epistasis Amplifies the Fitness Costs of Deleterious Mutations, Engendering Rapid Fitness Decline Among Modernized Populations," *Evolutionary Psychological Science*, 3 (2017): 181-191.

10: Geoffrey Miller, *The Mating Mind: How Sexual Choice Shaped the Evolution of Human Nature* (New York: Anchor Books, 2000).

11: *Ibid.*

just contribute to the destruction of the rain forests and oceans?"[12] In addition, more intelligent people also have the foresight and ability to successfully use contraception, developed due to the Industrial Revolution.

Feminism is another consequence of the decline of traditional religiousness, and, in particular, of the decline in patriarchal norms. Intelligent females tend to delay and limit having children in order to pursue higher education and careers.[13] Again, this reflects a strong evolutionary mismatch. Women ultimately desire status and to "fit in" with the group, as they have since time immemorial. But they are no longer directed towards forms of status that result in having children, such as a prestigious marriage, and the in-group has persuaded them to do something that damages their genetic interests in a way that it would not have done under harsher, and thus more religious, conditions.

It is quite clear that we are now becoming less intelligent for *genetic* reasons—and not just due to "dumbing down" through television, social media, and pop culture. This is evidenced by a decline across generations in the percentage of native European populations carrying alleles associated with very high educational attainment, as well as by many other markers including lengthening reaction times, worsening high-level vocabulary, and worsening color discrimination, all of which correlate negatively with intelligence.[14] The cleverer you are, the faster you are mentally and the better you are at

---

12: Edward Dutton and Dimitri van der Linden, "Why is Intelligence Negatively Associated with Religiousness?" *Evolutionary Psychological Science*, 3 (2017): 392-403.

13: See Lynn, *Dysgenics*, *op cit*.

14: Augustine Kong, Michael Frigge, Gudmar Thorleifsson, *et al.*, "Selection Against Variants in the Genome Associated with Educational Attainment," *Proceedings of the National Academy of Sciences, USA*, 114 (2017): E727-E732.

making subtle distinctions.[15] The so-called "Flynn Effect," the apparent rise in IQ scores across the 20th century, has been comprehensively demonstrated to be an illusion caused by the imperfect nature of the IQ test, something accepted by James Flynn (1934-2020), after whom the effect is named.[16]

The second result is simply a rise in congenital illness—a rise across time in the prevalence of numerous partly heritable physical conditions and similar ailments. These include: autism, schizophrenia, psychopathology, Narcissistic Personality Disorder, paranoia, hysteria, manic depression, suicide, obesity, diabetes, and many more serious conditions, such as haemophilia and cystic fibrosis.[17] Consistent with a rise in mutation, it has been shown, from analyses of skulls, that the average British face has become less symmetrical across time, which would also be congruous with declining intelligence and rising mutational load.[18]

What are these new mutated people going to be like? This growing body of people, who were high in mutational

---

15: See Edward Dutton and Michael A. Woodley of Menie, *At Our Wits' End: Why We're Becoming Less Intelligent and What It Means for the Future* (Exeter, Imprint Academic, 2018); Michael A. Woodley of Menie and Heitor Fernandes, "Showing Their True Colors: Secular Declines and a Jensen Effect on Color Acuity—More Evidence for the Weaker Variant of Spearman's Other Hypothesis," *Personality and Individual Differences*, 88 (2015): 280-284; Michael A. Woodley, Jan te Nijenhuis, and Regan Murphy, "Were the Victorians Cleverer Than Us? The Decline in General Intelligence Estimated From a Meta-analysis of the Slowing of Simple Reaction Time," *Intelligence*, 41 (2013): 843-850.

16: See Edward Dutton, Dimitri van der Linden, and Richard Lynn, "The Negative Flynn Effect: A Systematic Literature Review," *Intelligence,* 59 (2016): 163-169; James R. Flynn and Michael Shayer, "IQ Decline and Piaget: Does the Rot Start at the Top?" *Intelligence,* 66 (2018): 112-121.

17: Matthew Sarraf, Michael A. Woodley of Menie and Colin Feltham, *Modernity and Cultural Decline: A Biobehavioral Perspective,* (Basingstoke, Hants: Palgrave Macmillan, 2019), 141; Lynn, *Dysgenics, op cit.,* 83.

18: Michael A. Woodley, "The Cognitive Differentiation-Integration Effort Hypothesis: A Synthesis Between the Fitness Indicator and Life History Models of Human Intelligence," *Review of General Psychology,* 15 (2011): 228-245.

load, would be increasingly different from the pre-industrial norm of being strongly group-selected. In other words, they would have been, genetically, less group-selected and higher in "individualism," just as witches were. To the extent that they manifested in the higher social classes, these extreme individualists would have been influential in attacking and undermining tradition and undermining patriarchal standards, subtly influencing other people to be more like themselves. They are "geniuses," of a kind. As Bruce Charlton and I have explored in *The Genius Famine*, a genius is, to a great extent, group-selected.[19] His ideas and inventions make society more adaptive in the battle of group selection, whether it be a weapon that allows the group to better win wars; a medical innovation that boosts its population; a work of art that inspires it; or a form of spirituality that makes it more adaptive. Geniuses are characterized by outlier high IQ combined with a moderately anti-social personality, specifically they are moderately low in Agreeableness and low Conscientiousness. This means that they don't care about offending people (which new ideas always do), and they can "think outside the box" in a highly original (rule-free) way. Charlton and I term their opposite the "*evil genius.*" This would be a spiteful mutant who is *anti-group-selected* and who pushes the group in a *maladaptive* direction. Others have termed them "*anti-geniuses*," which also fits.[20]

An example of an anti-genius would be Oscar Wilde (1854-1900), who preached a philosophy of Aestheticism—"Art for Art's Sake"—and has been interpreted as critiquing, and even mocking, the traditional religious society, promoting instead one of individualism, sensation-seeking, and decadence.[21]

19: Edward Dutton and Bruce Charlton, *The Genius Famine: Why We Needs Geniuses, Why They're Dying Out, Why We Must Rescue Them* (Buckingham: University of Buckingham Press, 2015).

20: Sarraf, Woodley of Menie, and Feltham, *Modernity and Cultural Decline*, *op cit.*, 254.

21: Annette Magid, "Preface," in *Quintessential Wilde: His Worldly Place, His Penetrating Philosophy and His Influential Aestheticism*, ed. Annette Magid (Newcastle-Upon-Tyne: Cambridge Scholars Publishing, 2017).

Another would be the illustrator Aubrey Beardsley (1872-1898), another Aesthetic. Beardsley mainly drew grotesque and sexually licentious images, seemingly to outrage and undermine the traditional society.[22] Dimitri van der Linden and myself have shown that "evil geniuses" are very similar, in psychological terms, to geniuses.[23] However, evil geniuses in science and social science tend to be very low in mental stability, which does not generally appear to be the case with scientific geniuses of the past. In this sense, we argue, scientists who espouse fitness-damaging, ideologically-biased, and illogical ideas—such as cultural determinism and multiculturalism—are, psychologically, more similar to artistic geniuses than to scientific geniuses. But the key point is that, under industrial conditions, maladaptive ideas emanate from the top of society, due to increasing levels of individualism, combined with such people having considerable societal influence. A low-IQ underclass now comprises a large portion of the bottom of society. A century ago, an underclass of this size simply didn't exist. It's worth noting, as well, that late Victorians had an average IQ about 15 points higher than ours, 15 points being the difference between the average science teacher and the average research scientist.[24] Due to people like Wilde, the traditional structures that forced the growing body of individualists to behave in a group selected—such as traditional religiousness—were slowly being chipped away, until they could no longer hold back the tsunami.

How was this state of affairs reached? As pack animals, we have two sets of "moral foundations." On the one hand, we have to survive as a pack. Thus, we develop the *binding moral foundations* of in-group loyalty, obedience to authority

22: Chris Snodgrass, *Aubrey Beardsley: Dandy of the Grotesque* (Oxford: Oxford University Press, 1995).

23: Edward Dutton and Dimitri van der Linden, "Who Are the 'Clever Sillies'? The Intelligence, Personality, and Motives of Clever Silly Originators and Those who Follow Them," *Intelligence*, 49 (2015): 57-65.

24: Woodley, te Nijenhuis, and Murphy, "Were the Victorians Cleverer Than Us?" *Intelligence*, *op cit.*

and a sense that the group is "sacred," with things that might endanger it evoking "disgust." But each individual must also ascend the group hierarchy, which, at least in pre-industrial times, gave one the best chance of finding a mate and breeding. Thus, we also have *individualizing moral foundations*. These put the good of individual above that of the group. The values of this system are "harm avoidance" and "equality," such that all "individuals" have a fair share. These moral foundations broadly map on to "liberalism" and "conservatism," though with some nuances. Conservatives, for instance, are higher in generalized "disgust" but liberals are higher specifically in "moral disgust." Conservatives score about the same in all five moral foundations. Liberals score very high in individualizing moral foundations but very low in binding foundations. The result is that conservatives often sympathize with liberals in a way that is not reciprocated.[25] This allows liberals to hijack the culture and push it in an ever-more individualizing direction, until an extreme "evolutionary mismatch" (too many people feel a sense of chaos, for example) is reached, resulting in a "right-wing backlash" or a more catastrophic loss in the battle of group-selection, as the society is conquered or dissolves.

With the collapse of harsh Darwinian selection, including intense group selection, it is possible to have runaway individualism, at least once a critical mass of individualists is accumulated and people start to defected *en mass* to the up-and-coming way of seeing the world, which probably began in the 1960s. Having previously been selected to be group-oriented, rising mutational load will mean that people are increasing genetically individualistic. This will influence the culture, which will then start to gradually inculcate people into acting in more individualistic ways. With weakened group selection, there will be nothing to stand in the way of this process. Thus, more and more people will be more and more individualistic, until a tipping point is reached in which the whole society flips to being fundamentally concerned with

25: Jonathan Haidt, *The Righteous Mind: Why Good People Are Divided By Politics and Religion* (London: Penguin, 2012).

"equality" and "harm avoidance." Just as people once competed for status by signaling their binding moral foundations, people will now do so by signaling their commitment to "equality" and "harm avoidance." Doing so is not inherently fitness-damaging, as we will see below. But two processes ensure that it is maladaptive: first, the presence of spiteful mutants, who conceive of toxic ideas and promote them; second, the arms-race of outdoing the neighbors is signaling your individualism. We have an evolved desire for status, and an evolved ability to be inculcated by the group. Such instincts find themselves in an evolutionary mismatch when no longer under harsh Darwinian conditions, in which it is necessary to clamp down on individualism to ensure group cohesion against the enemy at the gates. So, eventually, people start signaling things that are against their group's genetic interests—and even against their individual genetic interests, such as that it is selfish and wrong to have children because doing so damages the environment, or because White people are inherently evil, or whatever it may be.

In addition, our ability to be inculcated—which, again, was previously adaptive—means that we can be inculcated with fitness-damaging ideas, of the kind espoused by spiteful mutants. Put another way, we are extremely environmentally plastic and evolved to live in a group that pushes towards individual and group-level adaptive behavior. If this breaks down, with spiteful mutants and extreme individualists pushing us towards maladaptive behavior, our adaptive instincts to conform to the group and play for status within it suddenly become our own worst enemy. And only those who are specifically resistant to maladaptive indoctrination—due to strong group-selected and natalist instincts—will survive.

The Middle Class and Maladaptive Ideas

One problem with this model of the spiteful mutant is the apparent prevalence of maladaptive ideas specifically among members of the "middle," rather than of the "upper" class, as we would expect the upper class to have greater societal influence. In British newspapers, the term "middle class" is generally used to mean "higher professional" or "upper-middle class." British newspapers report that radical left-wing movements tend to be dominated by these "middle class" people. For example, in Autumn 2019, a group called "Extinction Rebellion" led a series of protests in central London to draw attention to climate change. They occupied Smithfield Market, blockaded vital roads, and even glued themselves to government buildings.[26] Extinction Rebellion's demands include "climate justice."[27] This effectively means that Western nations curb their emissions, and thus massively reduce their living standards; non-Western nations, however, should not do this and should continue developing until Western and non-Western living standards are equalized. In effect, they demand that European people put the genetic interests of others above their own—a policy that is inherently fitness-damaging. The group, according to reports, was conspicuously "middle class."[28] Indeed, one researcher summarized such groups, based on data he collected on then, as "a white middle class ghetto."[29]

Why would the "middle class" —rather than the "upper class," who have been subject to harsh selection for the least time—dominate such movements?

26: Sarah Marsh, "Extinction Rebellion Activists Glue Themselves to DfT and Home Office," *The Guardian*, October 8, 2019), https://www.theguardian.com/environment/2019/oct/08/extinction-rebellion-activists-glue-themselves-to-home-office-and-dft.

27: Andre Spicer, "The Extinction Rebels Have Got Their Tactics Badly Wrong. Here's Why," *The Guardian*, April 19, 2019), https://www.theguardian.com/commentisfree/2019/apr/19/extinction-rebellion-climate-change-protests-london.

28: Charlotte Gill, "Extinction Rebellion Have Turned Climate Change into a Class War," *Telegraph*, October 17, 2019, https://www.telegraph.co.uk/news/2019/10/17/extinction-rebellion-have-turned-climate-change-class-war/.

29: Damien Gayle, "Does Extinction Rebellion Have a Race Problem?" *The Guardian*, October 4, 2019, https://www.theguardian.com/environment/2019/oct/04/extinction-rebellion-race-climate-crisis-inequality.

Middle-class dominance in Extinction Rebellion is in line with broader data that are extremely consistent over time in the UK. According to British sociologists Geoffrey Evans and James Tilley:

> *The professional classes are centrist economically and socially liberal; the managerial and bourgeois classes are right wing economically and socially authoritarian; the working class is left wing economically and socially authoritarian.*[30]

The British upper class is characterized by a combination of general conservatism and *noblesse oblige*—the belief that they have a duty to serve society, such as in the armed forces.[31] Indeed, it is these conservative and militaristic values that the public schools have traditionally instilled in the upper classes.[32] Thus, it is the "professional classes" who are the most likely to advocate socially liberal—and thus maladaptive—ideas. Why would this be the case, based on our understanding of the high heritability of social class? A possible answer lies in the very nature of the "middle class," something we touched upon earlier. They hold a position in society that makes questioning the *status quo*—either to make it more conservative or liberal—attractive as a means of gaining status. Members of the middle class distinguish themselves from those who are members of the two surrounding classes via their virtue and their intellect, something that has been observed even in analyses of the 16th century "middling sort."[33] They are distinct from the working class because they are, so they believe, wealthier, more educated,

---

30: Geoff Evans and James Tilley, *The New Politics of Class: The Political Exclusion of the British Working Class* (Oxford: Oxford University Press, 2017), 60.

31: Richard Carr, *One Nation Britain: History, the Progressive Tradition, and Practical Ideas for Today's Politician* (London: Routledge, 2016), Chapter 5.

32: See Donald Leinster-Mackay, "The Nineteenth-Century English Preparatory School: Cradle and Crèche of Empire?" in *Benefits Bestowed? Education and British Imperialism*, ed. J.A. Mangan (London: Routledge, 2012).

33: Tony McEnery, *Swearing in English: Bad Language, Purity and Power from 1586 to the Present* (London: Routledge, 2006).

more diligent, and more refined.[34] Valuing "education" as an inherent good is a particularly middle-class idea. Upper-class people are more inclined to regard university attendance as a means of networking, so that they can "meet the right people who can help influence their future." For this reason, it is only worth attending "the right schools."[35] Thus, the middle class is also distinct from the upper class. They admire the upper class and, to a certain extent, imitate their culture. This sociological process is known as "Trickle Effect": fashions tend to emanate from the upper classes and "trickle down" through society.[36] However, throughout English history it has been noted that the middle class is the engine of intellectual change. A mutant born into the upper class would, therefore, have less incentive to become "spiteful"—less incentive to play for status by espousing fitness-damaging ideas.

The middle class has long played for status by emphasizing that, although they are not as wealthy and powerful as the upper class, they are morally and intellectually superior and even more godly.[37] This is consistent with evidence that feelings of social exclusion elevate religiousness,[38] and that social insecurity is often dealt with via compensatory zeal with regard to "opinions, values, goals, groups, and self-worth."[39] The intellectual superiority, and status-playing, of the middle class can be seen in the way in which they question the current dispensation by pushing it in a more extreme direction. In this sense, they are "liberal," as they tend to promote individualizing values as a means of social signaling. They are prone to signing

---

34: See Fox, *Watching the English*, *op cit*.

35: Donna Tileston, *What Every Teacher Should Know About Diverse Learners* (Thousand Oaks: Corwin Press, 2004), 40.

36: Georg Simmel, "Fashion," *American Journal of Sociology*, 62 (1957): 541-558.

37: McEnery, *Swearing in English*, *op cit*.

38: Ara Norenzayan and Azim Shariff, "The Origin and Evolution of Religious Pro-sociality," *Science*, 322 (2008): 58-62.

39: Ian McGregor, "Zeal Appeal: The Allure of Moral Extremes," *Basic and Applied Social Psychology*, 4 (2006): 343-348.

petitions, going on marches, voting, generally acting to hold those in power to account and in voting for non-mainstream political parties, something predicted by education level.[40] As we have already discussed, it was the 16th century "middling sort" who questioned the current intellectual dispensation by adopting Protestantism, a form of extreme religiosity in an already highly religious society. However, this also promoted individualizing, pro-equality ideas, such as the "priesthood of all believers."[41]

Once spiteful, individualist ideas become accepted, they are particularly attractive to the middle class as a means of leveraging status. As noted earlier, intelligence is also associated with the ability to correctly perceive the social norm and force oneself to essentially accept it.[42] Thus, their intelligence would render the middle class easier to indoctrinate than the working class. Openness to new ideas correlates with IQ at 0.3, and those who are high in Openness are easier to inculcate.[43] And as we have seen, the position of the middle class, their modal personality and their intelligence, makes them attracted to supposedly virtuous and anti-traditional ideas. It would follow that the middle class would be attracted to anti-patriarchal ideas and would be good at convincing themselves of their validity, if doing so seemed to be the new "norm" and to their social benefit. By contrast, general conservatism and ethnocentrism are negatively

---

40: Heiner Rindermann, C. Flores-Mendoza, and Michael A. Woodley, "Political Orientations, Intelligence and Education," *Intelligence*, 40 (2012): 217-225; Ian Deary, G. David Batty, and Catherine Gales, "Childhood Intelligence Predicts Voter Turnout, Voter Preferences and Political Involvement in Adulthood; the 1970 cohort," *Intelligence*, 36 (2008): 548-555.

41: For an examination see, Cyril Eastwood, *The Priesthood of All Believers: An Examination of the Doctrine from the Reformation to the Present Day* (Minneapolis, MN, Augsburg Publishing, 1962).

42: Michael A. Woodley of Menie and Curtis Dunkel, "Beyond the Cultural Mediation Hypothesis: A Reply to Dutton (2013)," *Intelligence*, 49 (2015): 186-191.

43: Daniel Nettle, *Personality: What Makes You Who You Are* (Oxford, Oxford University Press, 2007).

associated with IQ.[44] So we can expect the working class to be socially conservative, as has been found, especially in a context in which the dominant way of thinking is "liberal."[45]

British linguist Tony McEnery has observed that the middle class adoption of new ideas involving moral superiority has been noted throughout English history in the form of "moral panics" about working-class behavior, panics that have been dominated by middle-class people.[46] Thus, in the 16th and 17th centuries, the middle class were dominated by the Puritans, who stressed their religiosity and moral constancy. Their ideological descendants in the 19th century also stressed these factors, leading to a strong sexual taboo and related moral panics. By this stage, however, the middle class had become more flamboyantly "virtuous," displaying their morality by assisting the working classes and being especially concerned about alcoholism among this group. Their virtue displays can even be seen in their use of language: the working class use strong swear words the most, then the upper class, and then the middle.[47] The result is an arms race of norm-questioning and moral virtue-signaling, which explains why it is among the middle class that spiteful ideologies are the most prominent in the modern day.

This would be expected to push society in an ever more anti-traditionalist direction, though this could still make it more religious. For example, Puritan Protestantism was appealing because it questioned the status quo, stressed moral virtue, and emphasized equality before God. In a sense, it involved identifying with the poor, but it also stressed moral purity. Additionally, once everyone was Protestant,

---

44: Gordon Hodson and Michael Busseri, "Bright Minds and Dark Attitudes: Lower Cognitive Ability Predicts Greater Prejudice Through Right-wing Ideology and Low Intergroup Contact," *Psychological Science*, 23 (2012): 187-195. See also Arthur Jensen, *The g Factor: The Science of Mental Ability* (Westport: Praeger, 1998).

45: Evans and Tilley, *The New Politics of Class*, *op cit.*, 60.

46: McEnery, *Swearing in English*, *op cit.*

47: *Ibid.*, 48.

Romantic Nationalism was appealing to the middle class in many countries, because it questioned the new "tradition" and it idolized peasant culture. This ideology was strongly related to religiousness and class status, in some respects, pushed in a more religious direction within a broadly religious society. Thus, it can be argued that middle class anti-traditionalism was previously adaptive for them, because it combined a play for status with adaptive desires, fertility, and nationalism.

This gradually changed, however, as anti-traditionalism started to push in an extreme liberal direction, after society flipped over to being high in individualizing. Runaway individualism eventually led to nihilism, as religiousness started to breakdown as a critical mass of individualists (inspired by spiteful mutants) was reached and people started to migrate, very quickly, over to leftist, maladaptive ideas. Middle-class identity then became a matter of competing to be more "Woke" than the next person. Marxism, which idolized working-class culture *internationally*, became appealing. This meant you were potentially placing another ethnic group above your own. This could be regarded as the first spiteful ideology, as it questioned religion and nationalism, but it appealed to the middle class desire to seem more virtuous and educated than the next man. This was, therefore, the turning point, where the combination of elevated mutation (leading to atheism), high intelligence (leading to high openness, low instinctiveness, and low traditionalism), the weakening of religious controls, and social-status insecurity resulted in the middle class beginning to push in a fitness-damaging direction by adopting a spiteful ideology. Once Marxism became highly influential, the next marginalized group had to be employed for virtue-signaling purposes: females, ethnic minorities, homosexuals, transsexuals, animals, plants . . . Under Darwinian conditions, especially of strong group selection, this arms race would be held in check by selection for religious, patriarchal, and ethnocentric groups. This selection for traditional religiousness, combined with high mortality salience, making people more religious and ethnocentric, was also holding this process in check, as was the vanishingly small number of spiteful mutants advocating maladaptive ideas. But with the breakdown of Darwinian Selection, these various protection mechanisms would collapse as well. The result, eventually, would be the explosion of a middle class-based anti-traditionalism nuclear bomb, as can be seen in highly spiteful but predominantly "middle class" movements such as Extinction Rebellion, where one signals group loyalty and virtue by espousing childlessness and the destruction of advanced society.

And this, of course, has serious implications for who has children. The strong advocates of these fitness-reducing ideas will tend not to breed. In addition, those who are particularly environmentally sensitive, even if they are not inculcated with these ideas, will increasingly feel despondent, experience a sense of dysphoria, and give up on life as a result.[48] Women will be unhappy due to their evolutionary mismatch and will increasingly find that there are not enough potential mates of higher status, leading them to forgo motherhood, as we will see below. Men, too, will suffer from greater depression. Those who can be inculcated with these ideas to any significant extent are, at the very least, likely to limit their fertility. Previously, such people had lived in a religious ecology, in which procreating and childrearing was deemed God's will; today, they are left adrift. So, all that is left is those who are, for genetic reasons, extremely religious and conservative and, thus, strongly desirous of children;[49] those who are simply strongly desirous of children either because they have

48: See, for example, Katherine Williams, Wendy Marsh, and Natalie Ragson, "Mood Disorders and Fertility in Women: A Critical Review of the Literature and Implications for Future Research," *Human Reproduction Update*, 13 (2007): 607-616; William Yates, William Mellor, Brian Lund, *et al.*, "Early-onset Major Depressive Disorder in Men is Associated with Childlessness," *Journal of Affective Disorders*, 124 (2010): 187-190.

49: Martin Fieder and Susanne Huber, "Political Attitude and Fertility: Is There a Selection for the Political Extreme?" *Frontiers in Psychology* (2018), https://doi.org/10.3389/fpsyg.2018.02343.

a strong desire to nurture (being altruistic)[50] or because, being Machiavellian, they perceive having children as useful to status or the ability to attain welfare;[51] those who have a low IQ (and thus cannot be inculcated properly with the dominant ideology); those who have low impulse control, which correlates with low IQ; and those with high Extraversion, meaning they accidentally have children due to sexual risk taking.[52]

In this sense, Wokesim has displaced child mortality and warfare as the new "Crucible of Evolution." Indeed, feminism is itself a "crucible of evolution." It creates an extreme evolutionary mismatch that makes males, and females, despondent and maladaptive, meaning only those who, for genetic reasons, are able to survive this new "harsh environment," which defeats most, are able to pass on their genes. And these people, in part, will be those that would have survived under pre-industrial conditions. Thus, ironically, feminism permits a return, in part, to a society dominated by religious, patriarchal anti-feminists. These feminists, however, are "spiteful mutants," because they push society in a maladaptive direction, just as witches did from the bottom-up. Let us look in more detail at how they do this and at their other points of crossover with witches.

50: Markus Jokela, "Birth-cohort effects in the association between personality and fertility," *Psychological Science,* 23 (2012): 835-841.

51: Fernando Gutiérrez, Miguel Gárriz, Josep M. Peri, *et al.*, "Fitness Costs and Benefits of Personality Disorder Traits," *Evolution and Human Behavior,* 34 (2013): 41-48; Adam Perkins, *The Welfare Trait: How State Benefits Affect Personality* (London: Palgrave Macmillan, 2015).

52: Markus Jokela, "Birth-cohort effects in the association between personality and fertility," *Psychological Science,* 23 (2012): 835-841.

Chapter 7

Without Remorse

Feminism, Postmodernism, and Neo-Matriarchy

Ardent feminists would appear to be precisely the kind of women that would have been accused of witchcraft in Early Modern England. In this chapter, we will show in detail that feminists can be understood as modern day witches, as feminism undermines group fitness by undermining the patriarchy. We will see that feminists, like stereotypical Early Modern witches, tend to be physically unattractive and masculinized, as well as single and childless. Like witches, they damage group selection by feminizing politics (reducing ethnocentrism) and academia; they push out geniuses (who benefit the group), who are obsessed with truth, in favor of "Head Girls," who are more interested in social accord and empathy. As with witches, feminists promote abortion and damage the fertility of other women. Witches supposedly used spells to make others barren or otherwise childless. Feminists, on the other hand, promote "lies as truth," as part of the general leftist trend, to the extent of normalizing transgenderism. Indeed, we will note the points of commonality between some transsexuals and stereotypical witches. Most importantly, this agenda can harm children, another stereotypically witch-like trait. The world which they create also undermines masculinity in boys, further damaging group selection by creating weak males.

Fertility and Conservatism

We would expect that those who strongly espouse feminism—having higher mutational load—would be physically unattractive and less feminine than "normal" women, who, under harsh conditions, would be adapted to the patriarchal system.[1] As runaway individualism has taken hold, many relatively genetically fit people have been inculcated into believing that they are "feminists." Thus, when we employ the word "feminist" in this discussion, we refer to those at the vanguard of the feminist movement.

Like witches, feminists tend to be childless spinsters, as maladapted organisms tend to be less fertile. Feminism is an example of a left-wing ideology, and we have already observed that fertility, mental and physical health, and assorted markers of low mutational load are associated with traditional religiousness, which is a strong proxy for being conservative. We can, however, go much further than that. Due to the current association between conservatism and such adaptive traits as traditional religiousness and ethnocentrism, we would expect conservatism itself to be associated with health and fertility. In this regard, it has been found, based on large samples, that being left-wing is associated with mental illness. This may be because both are an expression of underlying mutation—deviation from the mental health and focus on group over individual interests to which we were selected under harsh conditions—and it may also be because depression is associated with Neuroticism. Neurotics feel negative feelings strongly—including a sense of futility, resentment, guilt, and so on—and this pushes you towards left-wing ideas.[2] Neuroticism, with the exception of subcomponents such as social anxiety, is an adaptation to an unstable environment, in which you must simply survive, so you become focused on yourself. Therefore you

1: Rachael Grant and V. Tamara Montrose, "It's a Man's World: Mate Guarding and the Evolution of Patriarchy," *Mankind Quarterly*, 58 (2018): 384-418.

2: Emil Kirkegaard, "Mental Illness and the Left" *Mankind Quarterly*, 60 (2020): 487-510.

push for the individualizing values: harm avoidance and attaining personal power, including through pushing for "equality." You do this because you perceive yourself as not having power. People who are neurotic are likely to have aspects of low self-esteem and thus see themselves as lacking power, no matter how much they have in reality, and identify with others who lack power, feeling resentment and fear towards those whom they perceive as powerful. In the West, people who are "conservative" are more physically healthy, when controlling for key variables such as age, than people who are liberal.[3] In addition, there is evidence that being extremely politically conservative, independent of religiousness, is itself associated with fertility worldwide. Within Europe, there is a clear association between fertility and extreme conservatism: the strongly politically conservative have the most children, as noted in the previous chapter.[4]

Feminism and Physical Unattractiveness

There is also direct evidence that feminism is a manifestation of dysgenics, providing a clear parallel with witches. Women who are active feminists have more masculinized hands—a lower 2D:4D ratio, essentially stubbier fingers—than controls, a sign that they are biologically less feminine.[5] Another study found that even in relatively gender-equal Norway, "feminist women are visually represented as more masculine whereas the

3: Eugene Chan, "Political Orientation and Physical Health: The Role of Personal Responsibility," *Personality and Individual Differences*, 141 (2019): 117–122.

4: Martin Fieder and Susan Huber, "Political Attitude and Fertility: Is There a Selection for the Political Extreme?" *Frontiers in Psychology,* (2018), https://doi.org/10.3389/fpsyg.2018.02343.

5: Guy Madison, Ulrika Aasa, John Wallert, and Michael A. Woodley, "Feminist Activist Women are Masculinized in Terms of Digit-ratio and Social Dominance: A Possible Explanation for the Feminist Paradox," *Frontiers in Psychology*, 5 (2014): 1011.

opposite is true for feminist men."[6] This perception of feminists as facially masculine is likely true, as stereotypes have been shown to have a high level of empirical accuracy.[7] Congruous with this finding, 45 percent of self-identified feminists in a U.S. sample claimed to be non-heterosexual and predominantly homosexual.[8] This is despite the fact that only about 0.7 percent of Western females identify as "lesbian."[9] Lesbians are generally (and not surprisingly) more physically and psychologically masculinized than are heterosexual females.[10]

Similarly, females regard males who are feminists—who are "woke" with regard to gender equality—as less sexually attractive than they do benevolent "sexist" males.[11] The benevolent sexist male, in essence, considers females to be different from males in exactly the ways in which they are actually objectively different.[12] One manifestation of this is the traditional chivalrous male who holds doors open for ladies and offers them his coat when they're cold, but who is also prepared to fight to protect women against those who attempt

6: Aleksander Gunderson and Jonas Kunst, "Feminist ≠ Feminine? Feminist Women Are Visually Masculinized Whereas feminist Men Are Feminized," *Sex Roles*, 80 (2019): 291-309.

7: Lee Jussim, *Social Perception and Social Reality: Why Accuracy Dominates Bias and Self-Fulfilling Prophecy* (Oxford: Oxford University Press, 2012).

8: Miriam Liss and Mindy Erchull, "Everyone Feels Empowered: Understanding Feminist Self-labeling," *Psychology of Women Quarterly*, 34 (2010): 85–96.

9: Office of National Statistics, *Sexual Orientation, UK, 2012-2017*, 2017, https://www.ons.gov.uk/peoplepopulationandcommunity/culturalidentity/sexuality/datasets/sexualidentityuk.

10: Ray Blanchard, "Review and Theory of Handedness, Birth Order, and Homosexuality in Men," *Laterality*, 13 (2008): 51-70.

11: Pelin Gul and Tom Kupfer, "Benevolent Sexism and Mate Preferences: Why Do Women Prefer Benevolent Men Despite Recognizing That They Can Be Undermining?" *Personality and Social Psychology Bulletin*, 2018, https://doi.org/10.1177/0146167218781000.

12: R.A. Lippa, "Gender Differences in Personality and Interests: When, Where, and Why?" *Social and Personality Psychology Compass*, 4 (2010): 1098-1110.

to take advantage of their lesser physical strength.[13] It has been found that women's strength of feminist attitudes correlates with the extent to which they are dissatisfied with their own bodies, which may imply that the more feminist a woman is the more objectively unattractive her body is, or that the more feminist she is, the more mentally unstable she is.[14] Either way, it implies elevated mutational load among feminists. Another study found a weak positive relationship between identifying as a feminist and feeling unattractive.[15] This summary of the research implies that feminists tend to be masculinized females, and thus unattractive females, because males are attracted to more feminine females. This is because females are evolved to have "feminine" features.[16] In addition, features that are perceived as "feminine"—such as large eyes and full lips—signal fertility, hence their also being associated with youth.[17] Obviously, it would make sense in evolutionary terms for males to be attracted to fertile females.

This research raises another point of commonality between witches and feminists: many ordinary people shun them. Men regard females who are feminists as physically unattractive, and they are usually correct to do so. Females, despite the fact that they might sometimes claim to be feminists who favor sexual equality, find men who espouse these views to be sexually unattractive and prefer benevolently sexist men with traditional views on sex roles. There is some evidence that those with a

13: Gul and Kupfer, "Benevolent Sexism and Mate Preferences," *op cit.*

14: Michelle Dionne, Caroline Davis, John Fox, and Maria Gurevich, "Feminist Ideology as a Predictor of Body Dissatisfaction in Women," *Sex Roles*, 34 (1995): 277-287.

15: Thomas Cash, Julie Ancis, and Melissa Strachan, "Gender Attitudes, Feminist Identity, and Body Images Among College Women," *Sex Roles*, 36 (1997): 433-447.

16: Anthony Little, Benedict Jones, and Lisa DeBruine, "Facial Attractiveness: Evolutionary Based Research," *Philosophical Transactions*, 366 (2011): 1638–1659.

17: Urszula Marcinkowska, Mikhail Kozlov, Huajian Cai, *et al.* "Cross-cultural Variation in Men's Preference for Sexual Dimorphism in Women's Faces," *Biology Letters* (2014), https://doi.org/10.1098/rsbl.2013.0850.

feminist viewpoint, in the more traditional sense of the term, are happier and have higher self-esteem than traditionalist women, at least in countries where the influence of female equality is relatively low, such as Poland.[18] But as modern feminism is strongly linked to leftism or liberalism, "Second Wave Feminists" are more likely to suffer from mental illnesses, such as depression. Ideological feminists, like witches, are unhappy malcontents who are rejected by more content members of society. There is a degree to which they should be pitied.

The Spinster Problem

Based on this, we would expect that what we might call "proto-feminists," like witches, would have been regarded as physically unattractive in their lifetimes, and we would expect comment to have been passed on this. There is some evidence for this if we look at the campaign for female suffrage in the UK, which began in 1851 with the founding of the Sheffield Female Political Association and culminated in women being given the vote on the same basis as men in 1928.[19] This is particularly true if we look at the more extreme manifestations of this movement. In 1851, a mere 14 percent of men could vote. Even by 1910, only 60 percent of men could vote. As British independent researcher Steve Moxon observed, "The female suffragist cause was an extremely well-to-do affair generally: not middle- but upper-class

18: Justyna Kucharska, "Feminist Identity Styles, Sexual and Non-Sexual Traumatic Events, and Psychological Well-Being in a Sample of Polish Women," *Journal of Interpersonal Violence*, 33 (2018): 117-136.

19: See Diane Atkinson, *Rise Up Women! The Remarkable Lives of the Suffragettes* (London: Bloomsbury, 2018). It should be noted, however, that female rate-payers (wealthy spinsters and widows) had enjoyed the right to vote in local elections but gradually lost this as small towns and villages were incorporated into larger municipal corporations after 1835, with women lacking the right to vote in corporation elections. Female rate-payers gained the right to vote in corporation elections in 1869. In some instances, wives of ratepayers were able to vote as well.

. . . Very well politically-connected, wealthy, and titled women made up the Women's Social & Political Union." Indeed, many female suffrage campaigners specifically argued that "the vote initially should be extended to women through an education qualification. The converse of this was also argued, and quite openly—*that uneducated men should be denied the vote*."[20] In the year 1913, 63 percent of members of the Women's Social and Political Union—the organization led by Emmeline Pankhurst (1858-1928), which violently campaigned for female suffrage—were confirmed spinsters.[21] Indeed, they were specifically "middle class" spinsters: "well educated, wealthy middle class women."[22] This is unsurprising. The WSPU specifically *opposed* the vote for all females. They campaigned only for middle class females—university graduates, rate-payers, or the wives of rate-payers—to have the vote.[23]

Historian Claudia Nelson has explored the dynamics of 19th century spinsterhood in depth.[24] By 1801, "spinsters" (meaning unmarried women over 30) were an acutely noticeable presence among the educated classes, which provoked increasing social comment and spinsters were regarded as a significant social problem. The spinster was perceived as unnatural, a failure as a woman, and a burden on her family, as there were few jobs available for middle-class women. By the time of the 1851 census, just five years after the unmarried 31-year-old Charlotte Brontë (1816-1855) published *Jane Eyre*, there were 355,159 more women than men in England and Wales. Of this

---

20: Steve Moxon, *The Woman Racket: The New Science Explaining How the Sexes Relate at Work, at Play and in Society* (Exeter: Imprint Academic, 2008).

21: Celia Kitzinger, *The Social Construction of Lesbianism* (London: Sage, 1987), 41; Claudia Nelson, *Family Ties in Victorian England* (Westport: Praeger, 2007), 112.

22: June Hannam, "'I Had Not Been to London': Women's Suffrage: A View from the Regions," in *Votes for Women*, eds. Sandra Holton and June Purvis (London: Routledge, 2000), 231.

23: Simon Webb, *The Suffragette Bombers: Britain's Forgotten Terrorists* (Barnsley: Pen & Sword, 2014).

24: Nelson, *Family Ties in Victorian England, op cit.*, Chapter 4.

number, 204,650 were unmarried women over the age of 45. Spinsters grew as a percentage of the population. By 1901, there were not 700,000 surplus women—as 1851 population trends would predict—but a million (1,068 women to 1,000 men); 421,549 of these were spinsters over the age of 45.

Working-class spinsters, to the extent that they existed, could simply remain servants, working their way up the service hierarchy. This was not possible for middle-class spinsters, however, whose work prospects were severely limited. If they were lucky, they might, like Jane Eyre, find a position as a governess or even, with the expansion of female education, a school teacher. Nursing, rendered more respectable by (spinster) Florence Nightingale (1820-1910), was another option, but there were few others, until the professions began to open up to women at the end of the 19th century, though even then women had to struggle against forces keeping them out. Accordingly, many of these genteel spinsters ended-up as life-long dependents on their parents and, thereafter, their nieces and nephews, often living in genteel poverty, especially in old age. Ridiculed by Victorian writers, novelist Eliza Lynn Linton's (1822-1898) savage attack is fairly representative: "Such an old maid stands as a warning to men and women alike of what and whom to avoid."[25]

A series of factors had converged to create this middle-class "spinster problem." In general, boys were more likely to die young than girls, due to accidents caused by boisterous behavior. From the Industrial Revolution onwards, fatal or crippling work-place injuries became ever more common, and these mostly affected men. The 19th century witnessed the rise of the British Empire, and it was men, especially of the higher echelons, who were the most likely to emigrate to South Africa, India, or some other distant land. In fact, in the early years of the 20th century, half a million men were leaving Britain (which had a population of 29 million) for the Empire every year. By contrast, only confirmed spinsters were inclined to emigrate,

25: Quoted in Nelson, *Family Ties in Victorian England*, *op cit.*, 133.

to be governesses for colonial families. In addition, during this era, middle-class men tended to delay marriage and marry a younger woman when they eventually did. And finally, there was strong social pressure on young girls not to disgrace their families by "marrying down." The percentage of middle-class spinsters grew and grew.[26]

It should be noted that, in general, females and males operate different sexual strategies. Males have little to lose from the sexual encounter, so it pays for them to be promiscuous and, to the extent that they are picky, to select youth, as a sign of fertility, and beauty, as a sign of fertility and health. Females also sexually select for physical traits in males, including facial qualities. But, as the female *does* have something to lose from the sexual encounter, it pays for her to select a male who can and will look after her and invest in her and the offspring. As such, females tend to sexually select for high-status males. In other words, they tend to marry upwards—*hypergamously*. This desire is so strong that many would rather not marry at all than marry downwards—*hypogamously*. This female instinct appears to be as strong in highly gender-equal societies as it is in patriarchal ones.[27]

With no families to raise, spinsters tended to involve themselves in social campaigns and church activities, and it seems to be more than a coincidence that feminist ideas began to develop during this period. Many of the leading thinkers were spinsters themselves, often insisting that spinsterhood was their "choice." Sisters Maria Grey (1816-1906) and Emily Shirreff (1814-1897) wrote in 1871, "in marrying, a woman gives up many advantages. Her independence is, of course, renounced

---

26: *Ibid.*

27: See Edward Dutton and Guy Madison, "Why do Finnish Men Marry Thai women but Finnish Women Marry British Men? Cross-National Marriages in a Modern Industrialized Society Exhibit Sex-dimorphic Sexual Selection According to Primordial Selection Pressures," *Evolutionary Psychological Science*, 3 (2017): 1-9.

by the very act that makes her another's."[28] Florence Nightingale proclaimed that a woman must "annihilate herself" in order to marry.[29] The suffragette Christabel Pankhurst (1880-1958) went even further, advocating the shunning of men: "There can be no mating between the spiritually developed woman of this new day and the men who in thought and conduct with regard to sex matters are their inferior," she proclaimed.[30] A body of suffragettes, centered around the magazine *Freewoman*, were scathing of the influence of what they regarded as man-hating, embittered spinsters on the movement, with an editorial referring to the "violated spirit" of the spinster that "haunts every library." Free women wanted equality with men, rather than their utter rejection.[31]

Simply from what we know about the sexual strategy that males adopt, it seems extremely likely that the excess of unmarried middle-class females in 19th- and early 20th-century England would be in this situation for a very obvious reason: they were physically unattractive. There were far fewer males than females, especially among the middle class. The campaign for female suffrage was an overwhelmingly middle-class activity. Thus, we would expect the unattractive females to be left over, though there may also have been attractive females who chose not to marry for political reasons. These would be the females who were high in mutational load and, as discussed, we would expect this to extend to their adopting ways of thinking that would have been previously maladaptive. It should thus be no surprise that spinsters tended to be stereotyped as unattractive. It has been noted that Charlotte Brontë was: "a spinster (she married in her late thirties, in the last year of her life). She was physically unattractive, socially obscure, and financially

28: Quoted Nelson, *Family Ties in Victorian England*, *op cit.*, 112.

29: *Ibid.*

30: *Ibid.*

31: Sheila Jeffreys, *The Spinster and Her Enemies: Feminism and Sexuality, 1880-1930* (North Melbourne: Spinifex, 1997), 95.

insecure. Unlike [Jane] Austen, she had little sense of humor."[32] This is how spinsters tended to be portrayed in Victorian fiction, because they were associated with these characteristics by people in general.[33] Spinsters were regarded as having "proved too physically unattractive or too psychologically strong-willed to capture a man."[34] The Victorian governess, always a spinster, was perceived as: "sour, ugly and aging—characteristics which were supposed to be the result of her disappointment in love but which were invoked to explain why she had been left on the shelf."[35] A letter penned in the 1870s refers to a widow who has "3 oldish spinster daughters, all ugly but very worthy."[36]

This perception of being physically unattractive was also associated with members of the Women's Social and Political Union. The popular press portrayed suffragettes as "unattractive, unfeminine and mannish," precisely because this was the common "stereotype" about them.[37] This should be unsurprising considering the evidence for the veracity of physiognomy that we have already explored. Members of the WSPU specifically wanted power for people such as themselves, implying they were high in Dark Triad traits such as Machiavellianism and Narcissism, which relates to a sense of entitlement. The latter has been shown to be associated

32: Joseph Carroll, *Literary Darwinism: Evolution, Human Nature, and Literature* (London: Routledge, 2004).

33: *Ibid.*

34: Laurel Yourke, *From Tradition Beyond Androgyny: Character Models in Kesey, Barth, and Lessing* (Madison: University of Wisconsin Press, 1979), 27.

35: Kathryn Hughes, *The Victorian Governess* (London: A&C Black, 2001), 118.

36: Louise Creighton, *A Victorian Family: As Seen Through the Letters of Louise Creighton to Her Mother, 1872-1880* (Lampeter: Edwin Mellon Press, 1998), 87.

37: Krista Cowman, "Suffragette Attacks on Art, 1913-1914," in *Suffrage and the Arts: Visual Culture, Politics and Enterprise*, eds. Garrett and Zoë Thomas (London: Bloomsbury Publishing, 2018), 197. Sarah Pederson, *The Scottish Suffragettes and the Press* (Basingstoke, Hants: Palgrave Macmillan, 2017), 121.

with testosterone and thus with masculinization.[38] The WSPU were wantonly violent, bombing theaters, banks, museums, and public buildings, sending letter bombs, sometimes causing serious injury, and risk to life.[39] This kind of aggression is associated with testosterone.

Many prominent members of the WSPU displayed evidence of serious mental instability, which we would expect to reflect mutational load and potentially be reflected in an unattractive face. For example, spinster Emily Davison (1872-1913) assaulted a pastor with a whip at Aberdeen railway station because he resembled a senior cabinet minister and tried to kill herself a number of times, ultimately succeeding. A number of WSPU activists were involved in assorted extreme, violent, and oppositional political groups, such as the WSPU, as well as Communism and even Fascism. For example, suffragette and convicted arsonist Mary Richardson (1882-1962) went on to be a Labour Parliamentary candidate and then Chief Organiser of the Women's Section of the British Union of Fascists, a prominent inter-war group in the UK. Adela Pankhurst (1885-1961), Emmeline's daughter, went into Communist activism and then the extreme nationalistic Australia First Movement.[40] This would be congruous with very high Neuroticism and even with Borderline Personality Disorder, which predicts an intense desire for order and pronounced black-and-white thinking, frequent changes in identity (and thus political perspective) due to neurotic self-doubt, and violent outbursts.[41] It has been found that people can correctly infer from facial

---

38: Stefan Pfattheicher, "Testosterone, Cortisol and the Dark Triad: Narcissism (But Not Machiavellianism or Psychopathy) is Positively Related to Basal Testosterone and Cortisol," *Personality and Individual Differences*, 97 (2016): 115-119.

39: See Webb, *The Suffragette Bombers, op cit.*

40: Verna Coleman, *Adela Pankhurst: The Wayward Suffragette 1885-1961* (Melbourne: Melbourne University Press, 1996).

41: Daniel Fox, *Antisocial, Narcissistic, and Borderline Personality Disorders: A New Conceptualization of Development, Reinforcement, Expression, and Treatment* (London: Routledge, 2020).

photographs that a person has Borderline Personality Disorder more accurately than could be the case by chance, consistent with sufferers being more likely to be physically unattractive, if only subtly so, due to elevated mutational load.[42] In some cases, the contradictions might be explained by being attracted to that which males stereotypically desire: political power and thence militarism and ethnocentrism, including, in a number of cases, the militarism of the British Union of Fascists.[43] Such identification is associated with high levels of pre-natal testosterone and thus with physical masculinization.[44]

The Rise of the Head Girls

With the nature of feminists established, we can now turn to how they damage group fitness. Providing females with political power, which female suffrage does, manifestly challenges the patriarchal society, and this has vital implications for ethnocentrism and group selection. Most obviously, females are higher in Agreeableness and empathy than are males, perhaps because these traits are so important in successfully raising children.[45] Females score considerably lower, on average, on measures of negative ethnocentrism than do males, likely because of their high levels of generalized empathy. These differences are found even between young boys and girls,

---

42: Alexander Daros, Anthony Ruocco, and Nicholas Rule, "Identifying Mental Disorder from the Faces of Women with Borderline Personality Disorder," *Journal of Nonverbal Behavior*, 40 (2016): 255-281.

43: See Simon Webb, *Suffragette Fascists: Emmeline Pankhurst and Her Right-Wing Followers* (Barnsley: Pen & Sword, 2020).

44: Beth Atkinson, Tom Smulders, and Joel Wallenberg, "An Endocrine Basis for Tomboy Identity: The Second-to-fourth Digit Ratio (2D:4D) in 'tomboys,'" *Psychoneuroendocrinology*, 79 (2017): 9–12.

45: Christopher Soto, Oliver John, Samuel Gosling, and Jeff Potter, "Age Differences in Personality Traits From 10 to 65: Big Five Domains and Facets in a Large Cross-sectional Sample," *Journal of Personality and Social Psychology*, 100 (2011): 330-348.

indicating that the difference has biological causes.[46] It would follow that the empowerment of females, such as permitting them to vote or work in high-status and influential professions, would push society in a less negatively ethnocentric direction (that is, make it less hostile to outsiders). This would be a particular problem in a society with many childless women, because there is evidence that females display elevated positive ethnocentrism when they are pregnant, possibly as a means of avoiding foreign parasites or simply due to stress making them more instinctive.[47] It would follow that any society that subjugated females would be at an evolutionary advantage in terms of ethnocentrism.

It should be noted that, in relatively religious societies, females tend to be *more* politically conservative than males, seemingly because females are more religious. However, when the influence of religiousness breaks down, the female propensity towards higher empathy and lower ethnocentrism—and thus generalized Leftism—begins to manifest. By the 1990s, older women—who tended to be more religious than older men—were *more* conservative than older men. Younger women, however, were *less* conservative than males of the same age.[48] These younger women (no longer as influenced by traditional religious ideas) tend to promote leftist ideas—including pathological altruism towards competing ethnic

46: James Neuliep, Michelle Chaudoir and James McCroskey, "A Cross-cultural Comparison of Ethnocentrism Among Japanese and United States College Students," *Communication Research Reports*, 18 (2001): 137-146; Markus Kemmelmeier, "Gender Moderates the Impact of Need for Structure on Social Beliefs: Implications for Ethnocentrism and Authoritarianism," *International Journal of Psychology*, 45 (2010): 202-211; Yang Lin and Andrew Rancer, "Sex Differences in Intercultural Communication Apprehension, Ethnocentrism, and Intercultural Willingness to Communicate," *Psychological Reports*, 92 (2003): 195-200.

47: Carlos Navarette, Daniel Fessler, and Serena Eng, "Elevated Ethnocentrism in the First Trimester of Pregnancy," *Evolution and Human Behavior*, 28 (2007): 60-65.

48: Pippa Norris, "Mobilising the 'Women's Vote': The Gender Generation Gap in Voting Behaviour," *Parliamentary Affairs*, 49 (1996): 333-342.

groups—with a kind of religious zeal, to the extent that they have been termed "The New Church Ladies."[49] Accordingly, in the short term, female suffrage may have slowed down the rise in fitness-damaging ideas. But, in the longer term, it helped to undermine confidence in the traditional society, undermine confidence in religion, and, eventually, it ushered in a female-influenced and less ethnocentric kind of society, a society that would be expected to lose in the battle of group selection.

Another problem, in terms of female-influence damaging group selection, is that females are, on average, less focused on systematizing than are men. Psychologist Simon Baron-Cohen has shown that the "extreme male brain" is intensely focused on systematizing, but deficient when it comes to empathizing.[50] In the "extreme female brain," this is reversed: it is strongly focused on empathizing but it is "system blind." Males are more focused on the overall consequences of complex systems, such as a company or a society, whereas females are focused on local consequences of social interactions, such as the feelings of specific individuals. There is general agreement among psychologists who have explored this area that those acknowledged as scientific geniuses, who are brilliant and original, allowing them to solve very difficult problems, tend to combine outlier high IQ with moderately low empathy and moderately low Agreeableness. They also have moderately low Conscientiousness, as already noted.[51] In fact, it has been

---

49: Jim Goad, *The New Church Ladies: The Extremely Uptight World of Social Justice* (Stone Mountain: Obnoxious Books, 2017).

50: Simon Baron-Cohen, "The Extreme Male Brain Theory of Autism," *Trends in Cognitive Sciences*, 6 (2002): 248-254.

51: Edward Dutton and Bruce Charlton, *The Genius Famine: Why We Needs Geniuses, Why They're Dying Out, Why We Must Rescue Them* (Buckingham: University of Buckingham Press, 2015). See also, Gregory Feist, "A Meta-analysis of Personality in Scientific and Artistic Creativity," *Personality and Social Psychology Review*, 2 (1998): 290-309; Hans Eysenck, *Genius: The Natural History of Creativity* (Cambridge: Cambridge University Press, 1995); Dean Simonton, *Genius, Creativity and Leadership* (Cambridge, MA: Harvard University Press, 1988).

found that Agreeableness is weakly negatively correlated with valuing "academic rigor" (-0.24) and with a desire to "advance knowledge" (-0.17), in line with Baron-Cohen's model.[52]

Geniuses are overwhelmingly male, because the male IQ distribution is wider, meaning that a larger proportion of males have both outlier high and low IQs, whereas females are more bunched close to the mean.[53] In terms of personality, more males are geniuses because they are overall lower in Agreeableness and Conscientiousness. A society with more female influence will be one in which people *do* care more about feelings. Indeed, liberals are lower in systematizing and higher in overtly valuing empathy than are conservatives, so we can see how "liberal" ideas, which are less systematic, would become increasingly dominant in female-influenced societies, placing "empathy" over the search for truth.[54] Indeed, it has been found that conservatism (in contrast to liberalism) predicts "academic rigor" and a desire to "advance knowledge."[55] As discussed above, it is has been argued that there are five "Moral Foundations" on which people vary. Liberals have been found to value the moral foundations of equality and harm avoidance (which are also more typically female concerns), whereas conservatives value hierarchy and structure (an element of which is "truth"), group-loyalty, and sanctity. In this sense, objective truth—which could

52: Glenn Gehrer, Olivia Jewell, Rich Holler, *et al.*, "Politics and Academic Values in Higher Education: Just How Much Does Political Orientation Drive the Values of the Ivory Tower?" (2020). Unpublished Manuscript.

53: Paul Irwing, "Sex Differences on *g*: An Analysis of the US Standardization Sample of the WAIS III," in *Race and Sex Differences in Intelligence and Personality: A Tribute to Richard Lynn at 80*, ed. Helmuth Nyborg (London: Ulster Institute for Social Research, 2013); Edward Dutton, "The Male Brain, Testosterone and Sex Differences in Professional Achievement," *Mankind Quarterly*, 58 (2017): 93-100.

54: Ravi Iyer, Spassena Koleva, Jesse Graham, *et al.*, "Understanding Libertarian Morality: The Psychological Dispositions of Self-Identified Libertarians," *PLOS ONE*, 2012, https://doi.org/10.1371/journal.pone.0042366.

55: Gehrer, Jewell, Holler, *et al*, "Politics and Academic Values in Higher Education," *op cit.*

be regarded as a component of hierarchy and order—is less important than the feelings of the individual.[56] For this reason, we should not be surprised that there are contradictions in liberal ideologies, such as "race" being a "social construct" one day and there being a desperate need for more Black organ donors the next. These contradictions are unproblematic for people who are unconcerned with truth, or consistent, systematic truth. This would all have the effect of suppressing geniuses, meaning that such societies would not benefit from as many genius inventions, including superior weapons and military technology, for example. Thus, all else being equal, in the battle of group selection, the more patriarchal society is likely to out-compete the more female-influenced one as it will produce more geniuses. And this would be made even worse by the female propensity to feel empathy for suffering members of competing groups.

Bruce Charlton and I have discussed the impact of females on academia—which, at its best, provided geniuses with a space in which to solve problems—in our book *The Genius Famine*.[57] Indeed, it could be argued that female influence in academia inherently helps to undermine the search for truth because, as we discussed earlier, on average, males are higher in systematizing (and thus desiring truth, even if it offends) and females are higher in empathizing, potentially suppressing truth in favor of social harmony.

With sexual equality, females will be appointed over males as they will tend to be easier to work with, having higher Conscientiousness and higher Agreeableness. They will be what Bruce Charlton has called the "Head Girl" types, the kinds of popular and academically high-achieving, though conformist, females who are appointed head prefects at British

56: Jonathan Haidt, *The Righteous Mind: Why Good People Are Divided By Politics and Religion* (London: Penguin, 2012).

57: Dutton and Charlton, *The Genius Famine, op cit.*

girls' secondary schools.[58] These kinds of women may well not be spiteful mutants themselves, but they will be influenced, maladaptively, by them, such as with regard to their fertility. Indeed, the higher conformism of females means that they are even more subject to peer-pressure, and if there is a movement towards the ideas of "evil geniuses," then they are more likely to adopt them. Interestingly, feeling "White guilt" has been shown, in females, to be associated with bulimia. According to the researchers who discovered this relationship: "Body image and White guilt both involve internalizing how others see one's self." This is something that females are more prone to do.[59] This finding would also be consistent with evidence that left-wing people have poorer mental health, possibly for genetic reasons, than do conservatives, as bulimia sufferers are highly neurotic.[60]

There is, in fact, a body of evidence indicating that females are likely to become more maladaptive than males once the traditional, adaptive society breaks down. In this sense, feminists, like witches, damage the fertility of other women. This is something that those who might vociferously condemn females who have engaged in what they regard as problematic behavior might wish to keep in mind. Greek psychologist Menelaos Apostolou has argued that, being adapted to patriarchy, females are adapted, to a greater extent than males, to a situation in which choices are made for them, usually by their parents, particularly by their fathers.[61] In other words, they are acutely reliant on being lead along an evolutionarily

---

58: Bruce Charlton, "The Head Girl Syndrome—The Opposite of Creative Genius," *Intelligence, Personality and Genius*, July 25, 2013, http://iqpersonalitygenius.blogspot.com/2013/07/the-head-girl-syndrome-opposite-of.html.

59: Janet Lydecker, Rebecca Hubbard, Carrie Tulley, *et al.*, "White Public Regard: Associations Among Eating Disorder Symptomatology, Guilt, and White Guilt in Young Adult Women," *Intelligence*, 15 (2014): 76-82.

60: Carol Peterson, Paul Thuras, Diann Ackard, *et al.*, "Personality Dimensions in Bulimia Nervosa, Binge Eating Disorder, and Obesity," *Comprehensive Psychiatry*, 51 (2010): 31-36.

61: Apostolou, *Sexual Selection Under Parental Choice*, *op cit.*

adaptive life road map. Left to their own devices, they are, accordingly, more likely to make maladaptive choices. These choices would be rendered even more maladaptive by the influence of spiteful mutants. This is in line with evidence that being wealthy is far more damaging to the fertility of females than to the fertility of males. Equivalently wealthy women in Britain are far less likely than men to have children. Indeed, wealth—though not IQ—weakly positively predicts fertility among British men.[62] Moreover, it has been found that more intelligent people express a preference to remain childless when they are young, but only more intelligent women actually do so. This is the case even controlling for factors that might limit female fertility, such as education and earnings (and the consequent trading of fertility for a career).[63] This implies that females are more maladapted than males in a non-patriarchal environment. Females, being higher in empathy and rule-following than males, are much more concerned with social harmony and keeping everyone happy. Accordingly, they are less concerned with systematizing and less obsessed with the truth.[64] As a result, they are much more socially conformist than males, as experiments have shown.[65]

In addition, females pursue a slower Life History Strategy than males,[66] obvious in the way in which they invest proportionately less energy in sex and more in nurture than do males. Slow Life History Strategists are more environmentally plastic than fast Life History Strategists, meaning that they

---

62: Daniel Nettle and Thomas Pollett, "Natural Selection on Male Wealth in Humans," *American Naturalist*, 172 (2008): 658-666.

63: Satoshi Kanazawa, "Intelligence and Childlessness," *Social Science Research*, 48 (2014): 157-170.

64: Soto, John, Gosling, and Potter, "Age Differences in Personality Traits From 10 to 65," *op cit.*; Baron-Cohen, "The Extreme Male Brain Theory of Autism," *op cit.*

65: Alice Eagly and Carole Chrvala, "Sex Differences in Conformity: Status and Gender Role Interpretations," *Psychology of Women Quarterly*, 10 (1986): 203-220.

66: Margo Daly and Martin Wilson, *Homicide* (New Brunswick: Transaction Publishers, 1988), 140.

are more sensitive to their environment. This environmental sensitivity allows the organism to be optimally adapted to its environment at any given time, giving it a competitive edge in the highly competitive ecology that produces a slow Life History Strategy.[67] As such, the adaptive development of females is far more reliant on a precisely optimum environment than is the adaptive development of males. If this environment deviates from the one in which female development is evolved to take place, we would thus expect females to become far more psychologically maladapted than males, as evidenced in the fertility patterns outlined above.

Often these Head Girls, also being intelligent though never of outlier high IQ, will dedicate all of their twenties and even the first half of their thirties to their careers and end up having very few children or even none at all. This, it might be argued, is an interesting means by which feminism ultimately unravels itself. A society becomes increasingly intelligent until it industrializes, allowing it to reduce environmental harshness. This leads to the rise spiteful mutants, who advocate fitness-damaging ideas such as atheism and feminism. This ideology tells women that they are "losers" if they are merely wives and mothers and encourages them to enter higher education and the professions. More intelligent females are better able to do this, so they delay having children and limit the number of offspring. For this reason, the intelligence-fertility correlation among Western females is -0.2, stronger than it is among males.[68]

In addition, as American researcher F. Roger Devlin has observed, once females become equal to males, at least in terms

67: Christopher Kuzawa and Jared Bragg, "Plasticity in Human Life History Strategy: Implications for Contemporary Human Variation and the Evolution of Genus *Homo*," *Current Anthropology*, 53 (2012): 369-383.

68: Edward Dutton and Michael A. Woodley of Menie, *At Our Wits' End: Why We're Becoming Less Intelligent and What It Means for the Future* (Exeter: Imprint Academic, 2018).

of education levels, a very serious problem arises.[69] Females are evolved to sexually select upwards, socioeconomically. However, among highly educated females—such as those with PhDs—there simply won't be enough suitable males to go round. They will have to marry hypogamously or downwards, at least in educational terms, which they may find very unappealing. Consequently, among females, the more intelligent a female is, the more likely she is to be childless. The consequence of all this, we can predict, is that the intelligence of society declines and eventually, therefore, society starts to regress: mortality salience increases, stress levels increase, and religiousness increases. This is because, as we discussed earlier, the genetically religious will always reject feminism, even if it is the group norm, because religiousness is associated with rejecting anything that would have been fitness-damaging under Darwinian conditions. Rejecting feminism, the religious will outbreed the non-religious and anti-feminists (or half-hearted feminists) will outbreed feminists. Instinctiveness increases, conservatism increases, and feminism goes into reverse, as discussed above. feminism creates a new "Crucible of Evolution" by spreading dysphoria and brainwashing people to behave maladaptively. Only the carriers of genes that are resistant to this, which is, in part, extreme conservatives and the extremely religious, survive: the anti-feminists will inherit the Earth . . . eventually.

Head Girls in Power

We should return to the growing female influence on academia, as it impacts what kinds of ideas are accepted by the elites and thus whether or not society is pushed in an adaptive direction at the group level. The growth in the presence of these kinds of women at universities has fundamentally changed the culture of academia, rendering it less focused on the unbridled

69: F. Roger Devlin, *Sexual Utopia in Power: The Feminist Revolt Against Civilization* (San Francisco: Counter Currents Publishing, 2015).

pursuit of truth. Indeed, since the 1960s, universities have become more bureaucratic and business-like. Academics must get funding, publish frequently, and attend conferences. All of this is repellent to the genius, who wants to be left alone to solve his chosen problem. These trends will push out the male genius types, who will combine very high intelligence with a moderately anti-social personality. Indeed, feminism—as spearheaded by anti-geniuses, as we will see below—makes this even worse. They refuse to accept that there are genetic sex differences in intelligence and personality, and so demand "equality of outcome" in university appointments, ensuring that more competent male candidates are not appointed.[70] Naturally, this feminizes higher education—including publication venues such as journals, which senior academics often run, pulling it even further away from the unbridled pursuit of truth.

A number of studies have charted the decline of freedom in academia, as it has become increasingly concerned with female traits, such as empathy over and above systematizing, "safe spaces," not offending people's feelings, avoiding subjects that are "controversial," and enforcing unquestioning acceptance of environmentalist and equalitarian dogmas.[71] This gradual change has resulted in more and more "controversial" academics being persecuted, subject to biased misconduct investigations, condemned by their universities, and even fired from their jobs simply for presenting empirically accurate research findings, which the political Left—who now dominate universities in Western countries—dislike for ideological reasons. This is a particular problem with regard to research on the subject of intelligence.[72] Thus, with greater female influence, society will become less

---

70: See Joanna Williams, *Women vs Feminism: Why We All Need Liberating from the Gender Wars* (Bingley, West Yorks: Emerald Publishing, 2017).

71: Joanna Williams, *Academic Freedom in an Age of Conformity* (Basingstoke, Hants: Palgrave Macmillan, 2016).

72: Noah Carl and Michael A. Woodley of Menie, "A Scientometric Analysis of Controversies in the Field of Intelligence Research," *Intelligence*, 77 (2019): 101397.

efficient at nurturing genius, less inventive, and so less likely to win the battle of group selection.[73]

In many ways, universities in England—under pressure from left-wing, equality-focused and, in that sense, feminine ideologies—have reverted to what they were like before the year 1877, when the system was reformed. At that time, if you wanted to work at an English university, you had to profess England's state religion, Anglicanism, and if you desired a permanent position as a fellow, you had to be ordained and unmarried.[74] Even once this qualification was met, many Oxford and Cambridge college statutes restricted certain numbers of fellowships to graduates from areas where the college owned land, to members of certain families, or to pupils from specific schools.[75] Only after the candidate had cleared these hurdles was his potential for academic excellence taken into consideration.

Today, the state religion is multiculturalism and equality. To realistically attain an academic position, you must not dissent from, and sometimes you must assent to, this New Church. In other words, universities once more uphold the religious order.[76] After that, it is helpful if you tick a few identity boxes, such as being non-White or female. Only then is intellectual ability of interest. This drives geniuses out of the universities, leaving them with no clear, nurturing environment. It may also help to undermine public confidence in universities, but it means universities are, as in the title of Charlton's book on this issue, *not even trying* to be genuinely focused on the pursuit of truth.[77] Feminists have taken a leading role in this transformation.

73: Dutton and Charlton, *The Genius Famine*, *op cit.*

74: Julie Melnyk, *Victorian Religion: Faith and Life in Britain* (New York: Praeger, 2008), 19.

75: Alan Haig, *The Victorian Clergy* (London: Routledge, 1984).

76: Joel Kotkin, *The Coming of Neo-Feudalism: A Global Warning to the Middle Class* (New York: Encounter Books, 2020).

77: Bruce Charlton, *Not Even Trying: The Corruption of Real Science* (Buckingham: University of Buckingham Press, 2012).

To make matters worse, it can be argued that female dominance has pushed the university, and society as a whole, towards obsession with female concerns. The problems caused by this can be seen in terms of the issue of power. Males are evolved to want to ascend the hierarchy and attain power, meaning they are concerned with who holds actual power in society. Thus, when males bully each other, they do so in a struggle for social dominance, implying that the victim is weak. Females are evolved to want to attain the highest status male, which they do through beauty, social skill, and a reputation for being submissive to the patriarchy. The height of power is thus recognition, unconditional acceptance, and being adored. Female bullies often spread rumors about another women, subtly exclude her, and imply she is ugly.[78] We see that for females, power struggles are about "soft power"—or influence—and under female influence, we are, therefore, more concerned about these forms of power. Those with power are those who do not feel excluded, who do not feel offended, who feel validated, and who feel accepted. All the while, as we focus on these issues—of people not feeling left out and attacking those who appear to make others feel left out—academia has ignored the growth of real power structures, whether it be Silicon Valley or even its own bureaucratic apparatus.

Just as females have come to dominate academia in the wake of increasing sexual equality, the same process of the dominance of the "Head Girl" can be predicted to occur in society more broadly. Although genius-types and charismatic politicians are always likely to be males, "Head Girls" are likely to out-compete males at many other influential levels of society. Genius types are not needed in these contexts because *outlier* high intelligence is not important. So we can expect females to attain ever more influence. And this will be exaggerated by a feminist ideology that insists that females are

78: See Anthony Volk, Joseph Camilleri, Andrew Dane, *et al.*, "If, When, and Why Adolescent Bullying is Adaptive," in *The Oxford Handbook of Evolutionary Perspectives on Violence, Homicide, and War*, eds. Todd Shackelford and Vivian Weekes-Shackelford (Oxford, Oxford University Press, 2012).

disadvantaged and discriminated against, despite this being palpably untrue, as detailed research by educationalist Joanna Williams has demonstrated. Williams shows that females are under-represented at the extremes of power because they make conscious decisions to achieve a family-life balance. The more equality you give females, the less inclined they are to want to pursue science degrees, with qualifications in science predicting higher earnings.[79] The result is "positive discrimination" in favor of women, which further, and unfairly, disempowers more competent males.

Guy Madison has shown that arguments for sex quotas in Sweden have nothing to do with raising quality and everything to do with simply empowering women, even if they are less competent.[80] Interestingly, Madison has also found that research on gender issues conducted in departments of "Gender Studies"—which is centered around ideologically promoting feminism—is of an objectively worse standard, based on various markers of academic quality assessment, than research that explores gender differences from a scientific perspective.[81] One of the ways in which females are able to attain the status of a university professor is through academic standards being lowered, such that something that was previously not considered "academic" is now considered to be so. From this base, females can then become increasingly influential in the overall culture and administration of universities, including in the operation of more science-influenced departments.

79: Williams, *Women vs Feminism*, *op cit.*

80: Guy Madison, "Explicating Politicians' Arguments for Sex Quotas in Sweden: Increasing Power and Influence Rather than Increasing Quality and Productivity," *Frontiers in Communication*, 2019.

81: Guy Madison and Therese Söderlund, "Comparisons of Content and Scientific Quality Indicators Across Peer-reviewed Journal Articles With More or Less Gender Perspective: Gender Studies Can Do Better," *Scientometrics*, 115 (2018): 1161-1183.

Abortion and Selection

Another example of female control is the issue of what has become known as "reproductive rights." As we discussed, legal abortion can be seen as empowering females and undermining the system of patriarchy. Consequently, some Early Modern women who were accused of witchcraft were so accused because they carried out abortions. This being the case, if feminists are best understood as latter-day witches, we would expect them to be stridently in favor of abortion, and this is, of course, the case. Many feminists argue that it is *their* body at issue, and they have absolute dominion over it, to the extent of aborting any fetus they don't desire to carry. Indeed, feminist philosopher Judith Jarvis Thomson has stated that "even if the fetus has the right to life, it need not also have the right to use the mother's body to stay alive."[82] American sociologist Kelsy Kretschmer has charted how, since the 1960s, abortion has increasingly become a defining issue both for feminists and the "New Right."[83] This has meant that, increasingly, to be accepted as a feminist, at least by prominent feminist organizations, you must be in favor of abortion, and to be accepted by many conservative organizations in the United States, you must be "pro-life."

The evidence that something may be on some level "problematic" about abortion can be seen in the way that, despite it becoming legal in England at about the same time as homosexuality became legal, homosexuality is now relatively socially acceptable. There remains, however, a degree of shame around having undergone an abortion, perhaps because it involves terminating a baby or, at least, a life form that would have become a baby. And this is simply not something that, until quite recently, people in Western countries would

82: Sally Markowitz, "Abortion and feminism," *Social Theory and Practice*, 16 (1990): 1-17, 1.

83: Kelsy Kretschmer, "Shifting Boundaries and Splintering Movements: Abortion Rights in the feminist and New Right Movements," *Sociological Forum*, 29 (2014): 4.

expect a mother to do, no matter how painful or difficult her circumstances. It could be argued that doing so betokens a woman who is, in essence, not a very nice person.

I've only ever met one woman who admitted to me that she'd had an abortion. In 2010, I was at a cultural anthropology conference. This was shortly before I made my move into evolutionary psychology, so I was still doing research on the anthropology of Finnish culture at the time. While at this conference, the attendees at which were overwhelmingly young females, I got talking to a pretty, slightly underweight female doctoral researcher who was 34-years-old. She was introverted with a dry sense of humor, and we kind of got along. In 2012, in my last year working for an English-language newspaper aimed at foreigners living in northern Finland, I decided to do an article on abortion, as Finland has by far the lowest abortion rates of the Nordic countries. This fact had recently been reported in the national news, providing me with what journalists term a "hook." I sent out a message on Facebook inviting any female Finnish friends who had undergone the procedure and were prepared to be interviewed about it—without being named, of course—to get in touch. To my surprise, one woman promptly did, writing, "I volunteer." It was the woman from the conference.

The fake name she used in the article was "Susanna Urpi." I interviewed her over the phone. In 2001, she had been studying at Helsinki University:

> *I wasn't on the pill. I just wasn't paying attention to anything. I had a boyfriend who was seven years younger than me, he was a junkie. . . . It was a wild time in my life. . . . I kind of thought, I wouldn't get pregnant! I was kind of in denial.*

But she *did* get pregnant. Crying on the phone to her mother, Susanna ruminated on how it would interfere with her studies and mean that she'd have to keep in touch, for a very long time, with a heroin-abusing father.

> *It was such a big shock! I thought to myself, "What should I do? Is it right to have an abortion?" I thought, "What does God want me to do?" even though I'm just an ordinary Lutheran who only goes to church at Christmas!*

Susanna got an appointment at her university's Health Center, where she had to explain to a doctor and a nurse why she wanted an abortion. She was then given a week to mull over her decision. These are legal requirements in Finland if you want an abortion, whereas in Sweden abortion is simply on-demand. The termination deadline, in Finland, is 12 weeks, unless the female is under 17 (20 weeks) or a serious defect is found in the fetus (24 weeks). Eventually, Susanna went for her hospital appointment. The night before the operation occurred, Susanna took a pill to help dilate her vagina.

> *Once you take the pill, that's it! There's no going back or if you do the baby may be harmed.' She recalled that she could not put out of her head the thought that, 'I'm killing my baby.*

Susanna was placed under general anesthetic, and the fetus was removed. When she came round, Susanna continued to be haunted by the feeling that she'd "done an awful, terrible, terrible thing." One summer morning, she burst out crying to her family that, "My baby will never see this sunrise!" A year or so after her abortion, while taking the pill "not so regularly," Susanna got pregnant again. This was actually pleasing, in a way, because "one of my fears after having an abortion was that I wouldn't be able to get pregnant again." Susanna was adamant that she would keep this baby, especially as she was in "a stable relationship" with the baby's father at the time.

But four years later "the relationship went to Hell. I had an affair with an ex-boyfriend and became pregnant again." Susanna took the morning-after pill "well within the time it says" but, for some reason, it didn't work. "This time, I knew how much a baby gives but also how much it takes . . . I felt I had done the right thing (by taking the morning-after pill) . . . I was being responsible," she told me. So she felt less guilty about having this pregnancy terminated, which would have aborted anyway if the morning-after pill had worked. Susanna was very happy to be interviewed about all this, regarding it almost as a kind of therapy.

> *I don't often get to talk about it . . . But this is me. And sometimes I think, "I could have three kids now. Oh my God! I have killed two babies! Is it for me to decide?!" I guess I've decided that it is for me to decide.*

It was August 2012 when I interviewed Susanna.[84] In November that year, I ran into her in a café and we decided to have a coffee. This was a mistake. The entire experience was very tense. We suddenly had nothing to say to each other. When we'd done the interview, we implicitly assumed we'd never meet again, but now we had. I felt uncomfortable. I knew far too much about her. I knew her far too intimately, and I suspect she felt the same way.

In many ways, Susanna fit a certain personality type of women who have abortions. She had clearly experienced some degree of Post-Traumatic Stress after her first abortion, and this syndrome is more likely to manifest in people who are neurotic.[85] Unplanned pregnancies, not surprisingly, are common in women who are extroverted and risk-takers, and not particularly conscientious.[86] Susanna, though, wasn't particularly extroverted and seemed very high in self-control, but there did seem to be something beneath the surface. Mental instability

84: Edward Dutton, "The Lowest Abortion Rate in Scandinavia," *65 Degrees North*, August 2012.

85: Inger Lundell, Inger Poromaa, Lisa Ekselius, *et al.*, "Neuroticism-related Personality Traits Are Associated With Post-Traumatic Stress After Abortion: Findings From a Swedish Multi-center Cohort Study," *BMC Women's Health*, 17 (2017): 96.

86: Venla Berg, Anna Rotkirch, Heini Väisänen, *et al.*, "Personality is Differentially Associated With Planned and Non-planned Pregnancies," *Journal of Research in Personality*, 47 (2013): 4: 296-305.

is a key predictor of seeking an abortion.[87] This factor showed up in her responses to the survey, as well as in her description of her sex life. A study in the Netherlands found that women who had undergone an abortion were three times more likely than controls to have presented with a psychiatric disorder prior to their pregnancy. The highest odds related to "conduct disorder," a term which is effectively the same as "psychopathic personality disorder."[88] So, put simply, females who have had abortions, compared to those who have not, are more likely to be mentally unstable and psychopathic. They are the kind of people who will be temperamental, spiteful, and who will sow social discord. They can come across as selfish people and act in contrast to group selection. They are the kind of women one would be best advised to keep away from.

If extreme feminists can be understood as modern day witches, then we would expect them not only to be in favor of abortion but to be perversely proud of it. There is anecdotal evidence that many of them are. In May 2018, the Republic of Ireland voted to legalize abortion in a referendum. Pro-Abortion placards said a great deal about the attitudes of the females that wanted abortion legalized in Ireland. Consistent with the research already discussed, they were highly individualist and selfish, epitomized in such placards as: "MY BODY. MY CHOICE."[89] The rights of the fetus, the father, the family, and the extended national family were irrelevant. It was just "me,

87: Sana Mhamdi, Arwa Ben Salah, Ines Bouanene, *et al.*, "Obstetric and psychological characteristics of women seeking multiple abortions in the region of Monastir (Tunisia): results of a cross-sectional design," *BMC Women's Health*, 15 (2014): 40.

88: Jenneke van Ditzhuijzen, Margreet ten Have, Ron de Graaf, *et al.*, "Psychiatric History of Women Who Have Had an Abortion," *Journal of Psychiatric Research*, 47 (2013): 1737-1743.

89: May Bulman, "Northern Ireland's Abortion Law Violates Human Rights Supreme Court Rules – But Challenge rejected On Technical Grounds," *Independent*, June 7, 2018, https://www.independent.co.uk/news/uk/home-news/northern-ireland-abortion-law-supreme-court-human-rights-violation-ruling-dup-latest-a8387206.html.

me, me." Another placard was "IRISH WOMEN DESERVE CHOICE," expressing the sense of entitlement that is a trait of forms of psychopathic personality.[90] Yet another placard manifested the callousness that is associated with psychopathic personality. It demanded that, unlike with Susanna, females who undergo abortion shouldn't feel *any* guilt about their termination. A woman with short, partly shaven, dyed-red hair and a Yasser Arafat head scarf around her neck held a placard stating: "ABORTION ON DEMAND WITHOUT APOLOGY."[91] At a "pro-life" rally in Texas in September 2019, hecklers wielded placards which said "I Love Abortion."[92]

Returning to Ireland, this callousness was also expressed in the use of humor in placards demanding that women have the absolute right to abort their fetuses. "THAT WOULD NOT BE AN ECUMENICAL MATTER" read one.[93] This is a reference to the 1990s sitcom *Father Ted*, about three Irish priests living together on a small island. In one episode, three bishops come to the island to upgrade "the Holy Stone of Clonrichert"—which has moved from Fermanagh, in the far north, to Craggy Island, off the West coast, because "it wasn't doing great business" in Clonrichert—to a "Class II Relic." Father Ted is concerned about how the bishops will react to Father Jack, a foul-mouthed, violent, alcoholic, elderly priest

---

90: Suzie Kerrigan, "I Killed Savita Halappanvar by Choosing to Stay Silent About My Abortion—and I'm So Sorry," *Independent*, May 22, 2018, https://www.independent.co.uk/voices/savita-halappanavar-ireland-abortion-referendum-vote-latest-eighth-amendment-a8363166.html.

91: Pat Leahy, "Ireland's Abortion Laws Are Set to Rage Again," *Irish Times*, September 24, 2016, https://www.irishtimes.com/news/social-affairs/ireland-s-abortion-wars-are-set-to-rage-again-1.2803570.

92: Shawn Carney and Steven Karlen, "The 'Most Anti-Choice Place in the Country' is Not a Bad Place to Live," *Life Site*, September 30, 2019,https://www.lifesitenews.com/pulse/the-most-anti-choice-place-in-the-country-is-not-a-bad-place-to-live.

93: *The Irish Times*, "Abortion: A Green Light From the Cabinet," January 30, 2018, https://www.irishtimes.com/opinion/editorial/abortion-a-green-light-from-cabinet-1.3372948.

with whom he lives. Father Dougal, a young simpleton who is Father Ted's curate, suggests that they try to teach Father Jack some words "apart from drink, or feck, or girls," so Father Ted decides to teach him the phrase, "That would be an ecumenical matter," because, Ted reasons, almost any theological question can be answered with it. So it was to this famous Irish sitcom that the placard was alluding. At another protest, a humorous placard piquantly expressed the relationship between "reproductive rights" and group selection. It read "Patriarchy is for Dicks"; it was accompanied by a cartoon picture of a man's (comically undersized) genitals.[94] After Ireland voted to legalize abortion, another woman posed with a shirt upon which was a heart, stretched across her breasts, which she'd made artificially enormous for the photo. Within the heart was written "Repeal the 8th"—the 8th amendment to the Irish constitution, which outlawed abortion—and on top of this was a sticker asserting "WE MADE HISTORY."[95]

The most extreme example of this callousness was recorded in a group of Irish feminists who filmed themselves on a bus on the way to Belfast to protest against an anti-abortion march. In the video, they sang the famous song "I Love You Baby" with the lyrics changed to "We Need Abortion," as they clapped along and smiled. A group of feminists sung the same song during a speech at an anti-abortion rally in London in May 2019, as a woman who had undergone an abortion, and regretted it, discussed this in front of a crowd of 5,000 anti-abortion campaigners:

> *A few dozen pro-choice activists had gathered at the side of Parliament Square, and during Obden's testimony they parodied*

94: Lizzy Buchan, "Government 'Using Devolution as an Excuse' to Avoid Abortion Reform in Northern Ireland, Campaigners Warn," *Independent*, March 17, 2018), https://www.independent.co.uk/news/uk/politics/government-devolution-northern-ireland-abortion-reform-theresa-may-dup-a8258841.html.

95: Henry MacDonald, "Pro-choice Group Plans to Offer Abortion Pills in Northern Ireland Tour," *The Guardian*, May 28, 2018, https://www.theguardian.com/uk-news/2018/may/28/pro-choice-group-plans-to-offer-abortion-pills-in-northern-ireland-tour.

> *Engelbert Humperdinck's song 'I love you baby, and if it's quite all right,' as 'we need abortion and if it's quite all right.'*[96]

Of course, it could be argued that abortion on demand is, in fact, adaptive—in terms of group selection. The desire for abortion is partly predicted by psychopathic personality, and this is approximately 0.7 heritable.[97] Abortion has surely had a significant impact on Western gene pools. In Finland, for example, in the 2000s, approximately 20 percent of pregnancies were aborted every year.[98] Accordingly, legal abortion permits individualist and selfish females to remove themselves from the gene pool, which might be argued to be a good thing. It can be countered, however, that this is an over-simplification. Abortion has become legalized on-demand due to the breakdown of a patriarchal society. Thus, the fact of abortion being legal should be understood as a symptom of a more profound underlying condition. Finally, in that the pro-Abortion movement is likely led by spiteful mutants, it will influence even women who are relatively low in mutation to remove themselves from the gene pool, just as witches were accused of causing barrenness. These would be women who would return to adaptive behavior if the spiteful mutants, instead of their fetuses, were removed.

SJWs, Transsexuals, and Postmodernism

A key way in which many people leverage social status is via virtue-signaling: flamboyant displays of personal virtue, through

---

96: *Catholic Herald*, "5,000 March for Life in Westminster," May 14, 2019, https://catholicherald.co.uk/news/2019/05/14/5000-march-for-life-in-westminster/.

97: Catherine Tuvblad, Serena Bezdjian, Adam Raine and Laura Baker, "The Heritability of Psychopathic Personality in 14- to 15-Year-Old Twins: A Multirater, Multimeasure Approach," *Psychological Assessment*, 2014, https://doi.org/10.1037/a0036711.

98: Mika Gissler, "Registration of Births and Induced Abortions in the Nordic Countries," *Finnish Yearbook of Population Research*, XLV (2010): 171-178.

extreme affirmation and denunciation. Stereotypically, so-called "Social Justice Warriors" will wax lyrical about how "Diversity is our strength," along with condemning broader society for its irrepressible "racism." They will even openly attack "The Patriarchy," or whatever vestiges there is of it left. While it is easy to dismiss such people as unhinged and so unusual as to be irrelevant, the problem is that "vocal minorities" can have tremendous power in shifting debate and forcing a new consensus upon the "silent majority." Moreover, once some of the basic tenets of the SJW creed are accepted—for example, that "racism" is wrong or that homosexuals should have equal rights to heterosexuals in marriage and adoption—it then becomes much more difficult for anyone to attain status by arguing for these things. What results is an ongoing "ratcheting effect" of causes, outrages, taboos, and sensitivities—in a word, "micro-aggressions."

Dutch psychologist Dimitri van der Linden and I have argued in the journal *Intelligence* that in a secular society, Social Justice Warriors—we call them "Clever Sillies," a term coined by Charlton[99]—must constantly push things in an ever more anti-traditional and anti-group-selected direction in order to showcase their altruism and dogmatic progressivism, as well as their virtuous and intelligent nature.[100] They essentially conform to a left-wing worldview, but, as mentioned above, to display status, they must endlessly critique other leftists as, in effect, not left enough. The more extreme and influential of these "clever sillies" can be regarded as "evil geniuses." They advocate very radical change, and take a considerable risk in doing so, though potentially gaining a very considerable reward of fame and eminence. Advocating for homosexuality, homosexual marriage, or gender reassignment were considered

---

99: Bruce Charlton, "Clever Sillies: Why High IQ People Tend to be Deficient in Common Sense," *Medical Hypotheses*, 73 (2009): 867-870.

100: Edward Dutton and Dimitri van der Linden, "Who are the 'Clever Sillies'? The Intelligence, Personality, and Motives of Clever Silly Originators and Those who Follow Them," *Intelligence*, 49 (2015): 57-65.

to be unspeakable, outrageous positions by wider society when they were first broached. The "clever silly" followers of these evil geniuses will offer tepid, self-defeating critiques of the patently maladaptive, bizarre pronouncements, which mostly succeed in pushing things further leftward still.

Currently, the "woke" thing to do is to campaign for the rights of transgender people. There are some self-identified feminists, however, who don't exactly "go with the flow" and oppose the idea that a male can become a female. Indeed, they say, transsexuals bring into question or even demean female identity. Such feminists, who count J.K. Rowling, the author of the *Harry Potter* series, among their number, have been labeled "Trans Exclusionary Radical Feminists" (TERFs) by their detractors.[101] Perhaps we can hear echoes of the many suffragettes who were attracted to the Right a century earlier. Regardless, there is now a clear intersection between feminism and transsexuality, which will reveal both conflicts and common cause.

It could be argued that some transsexuals have some of the traits that would cause one to be accused of witchcraft. Most obviously, they question the very fact of biological sex, a stance that implicitly undermines patriarchy. There is also evidence that transsexuals are high in mutational load. Male-to-female transsexuality correlates with hearing problems, arthritis, and Fibromyalgia (characterized by chronic pain, insomnia, and memory problems), among numerous other physical complaints.[102] Female-to-male transsexuality is associated, for example, with asthma, menstrual irregularities, and delayed menarche.[103] As we

101: See Sophie Lewis, "How British Feminism Became Anti-Trans," *New York Times,* February 7, 2019, https://www.nytimes.com/2019/02/07/opinion/terf-trans-women-britain.html.

102: Saria Reisner, Tonia Poteat, JoAnne Keatley *et al.*, "Global Health Burden and Needs of Transgender Populations: A Review," *Lancet*, 388 (2016): 412-436.

103: Dana Levit, Jakob Ablin, Valerie Aloush, and Iris Yash, "Evaluating Fibromyalgia Symptoms in Transgender Patients," *Arthritis and Rheumatology*, 71 (2019): (suppl 10).

will see below, they also implicitly undermine central adaptive religious ideas, such as the importance of truth, they (on average) tend to be anti-social, and they (indirectly) harm children, to the extent that they create an environment where it is acceptable to encourage children to regard themselves a transgender and to have their puberty blocked.

When I was an undergraduate at Durham University in the year 2000, I had to "live out" of my college in my second year, in a house in the city. A female friend, a History undergraduate, who was a practicing witch (Wiccan) and had a particular interest in the history of witchcraft, had a spare room in a house that she shared with two other witches. I took up her offer and briefly lived with three practicing witches, the other two of whom were a lesbian couple. My evangelical Christian friends, also female, insisted that I not sleep the night in my new house on Halloween, and they suggested that I move in with them, which, after three weeks, I sensibly did. Though my friends thought it was hilarious—"What are you going to do next, Ed? Move in with a group of midget wrestlers?!"—it was very interesting living with two lesbian witches, in a Victorian house decorated with pagan symbols. Oddly, the following year, the *femme* of this couple—a public school girl who was studying philosophy—shaved off her attractive, ginger locks and became increasingly androgynous. Approximately a decade later, we were put back in touch on Facebook, by a mutual friend, also a Wiccan. My former housemate—once a pretty, lively young girl—looked like a transman (female-to-male transsexual) and was using a man's name. We corresponded on her Facebook "wall," and she seemed to imply that, though she was a transsexual, she also had a vagina. I was genuinely baffled by this and innocently asked how she was defining "transsexual." Her Facebook friends were outraged, though would not explain why. She later told me that my question was "like asking someone who has been raped 'How are you defining rape?'" I was amazed. She appeared to believe that if she thought something was the case, then it was—an utterly self-centered and delusional view of the world. According to psychologist Ray Blanchard, most female-to-male transsexuals make themselves look as much like men as possible, but retain their vaginas, being, in essence, extremely masculinized lesbians.[104]

A number of studies have shown that transsexuals score very high on measures of Narcissistic Personality Disorder (and other personality disorders).[105] The violent and intense reaction of transmen to academics who objectively explore the causes of transsexuality can been argued to be a clear manifestation of "Narcissistic Rage." This is when the Narcissist must destroy that which questions his exalted understanding of himself.[106] Narcissists have a weak and unclear sense of self. They, in a sense, have low self-esteem and suffer an intense fear of rejection, causing them to be plagued by self-doubt and a sense of emptiness. They deal with this by descending into grandiose fantasies about themselves. However, this fundamental sense of emptiness, which is also found in other personality disorders such as Borderline Personality Disorder, means that a Narcissist's sense of self can be unstable. A period of intense emptiness may result in a sudden identity change, with the new, clear identity providing a sense of structure and certainty, and so relieving the emptiness. Narcissists are also extremely self-entitled, selfish, anti-social, manipulative, and highly sensitive to criticism, as this punctures their grandiose self-image—this being their defense-mechanism against the void that haunts them.[107] This makes sense when we consider that some transwomen (male-to-female transsexuals), for example, demand that they be accepted as "real women" to the extent of being able to use women's changing rooms (sometimes simply because they "identify" as a woman, despite still having a penis) and being

104: Ray Blanchard, personal discussion, February 25, 2021.

105: Azadeh Meybodi, Ahmad Hajebi and Atefeh Jolfaei, "The Frequency of Personality Disorders in Patients with Gender Identity Disorder," *Medical Journal of the Islamic Republic of Iran*, 28 (2014): 90.

106: Anne Lawrence, "Shame and Narcissistic Rage in Autogynephilic Transsexualism," *Archives of Sexual Behavior*, 37 (2008): 457-461.

107: See Fox, *Antisocial, Narcissistic, and Borderline Personality Disorders*, *op cit.*

able to participate in female sport. They can be understood to be, in this sense, extreme individualists who simply do not care about the feelings of other people. All that matters is that the society absolutely accepts that who they say they are is, indeed, who they are, even though this is manifestly not the case.

In 2019, a British "gay trans man" called Freddy McConnell, of Deal in Kent, hit the headlines due to a legal case over the registration of the birth of the baby to which *he*—his preferred pronoun—had given birth.[108] This person, a journalist for British newspaper *The Guardian*, was born in 1986 as the child of Esme Chilton.[109] Consulting public records of births and marriages, it would seem that this person, born in Camberwell in London, was originally named Jessica Mimi McConnell. Freddy studied Arabic at Edinburgh University,[110] as did "Jess McConnell," who wrote for the *Edinburgh Middle East Report* while she was there.[111] McConnell decided to "transition" when he was 23 and came out as a "transman" while working for an NGO in Kabul in

108: Lily Wakefield, "Seahorse Review: Trans Dad's Birth Story is a Moving Account of Love and Family," *Pink News*, July 22, 2019, https://www.pinknews.co.uk/2019/07/22/seahorse-review-documentary-dad-giving-birth-trans-family/.

109: Lily Waddell, "Transgender Dad Documents Pregnancy and Giving Birth in Emotional BBC Documentary," *Mirror*, September 11, 2019, https://www.mirror.co.uk/3am/celebrity-news/transgender-dad-documents-pregnancy-giving-20008060.

110: Simon Hattenstone, "The Dad Who Gave Birth: 'Being Pregnant Doesn't Change Me Being a Trans Man,'" *The Guardian*, April 20, 2019, https://www.theguardian.com/society/2019/apr/20/the-dad-who-gave-birth-pregnant-trans-freddy-mcconnell.

111: Jess McConnell, "Veil Debate: Here and There," *Edinburgh Middle East Report*, January 2007, http://emeronline.blogspot.com/2007/01/veil-debate-here-and-there.html.

2011.[112] McConnell is biologically female and was undergoing hormone treatment, as part of his "transition" to living as a man, when he decided that he wanted to have a child. According to *The Guardian* newspaper:

> *McConnell has long lived as a male, starting testosterone treatment in April 2013 and undergoing chest reshaping surgery in Florida. In 2016, he sought advice from a fertility clinic about becoming pregnant. His hormone treatment was suspended, which had the effect of reversing some of the gender-reassignment process, leaving him destabilised, which he described as a "loss of myself." His menstrual cycle restarted and he became pregnant in 2017 using sperm from a donor. He gave birth in 2018.*[113]

He then returned to his hormone treatment.

When he gave birth—which he did as part of a documentary about himself, with the birth thus being filmed—he demanded to be registered as the "father" on the child's birth certificate.[114] The registrar refused, McConnell went to court, and the judge ruled against him, arguing that in English Common Law, the "mother" is the person whose egg is inseminated. McConnell, who went on to lose an appeal against the judgment in April 2020, responded to the original ruling:

112: Freddy McConnell, "The Gift of a Lifetime: How Trans 'Top Surgery' Changed My Life," *The Guardian*, June 30, 2014, https://www.theguardian.com/society/2014/jun/30/trans-top-surgery-changed-my-life; McConnell, "Trans Life: Fond Memories of Coming Out in Afghanistan," *The Guardian*, March 12, 2015, https://www.theguardian.com/lifeandstyle/2015/mar/12/trans-life-fond-memories-of-coming-out-in-afghanistan.

113: Robert Booth, "Transgender Man Loses Court Battle to be Registered as Father," *The Guardian*, September 25, 2019, https://www.theguardian.com/society/2019/sep/25/transgender-man-loses-court-battle-to-be-registered-as-father-freddy-mcconnell.

114: Sara Hughes, "Seahorse: The Dad Who Gave Birth, Review: An Unflinchingly Honest Film That Doesn't Sugarcoat its Subject," *The Telegraph*, September 10, 2019,https://www.telegraph.co.uk/tv/2019/09/10/seahorse-dad-gave-birth-review-unflinchingly-honest-film-doesnt/.

> *It has serious implications for non-traditional family structures. It upholds the view that only the most traditional forms of family are properly recognized or treated equally. It's just not fair.*[115]

Thus, McConnell not only demanded that people accept that he is a man, and just as much of a man as a biological male, but concomitantly accept that he pause his transition and use a sperm donor in order to get pregnant. He also demanded that people accept him as a man to the extent of falsifying public records, such that future genealogists will wrongly believe that he was a biological male. All that matters, it seems, is how he feels.

In essence, some transgender activists demand that society ignores what it sees with its own eyes and accepts lies as truth. Bruce Charlton has argued that this should be regarded as an extreme manifestation of postmodernism.[116] Put simply, postmodernism is the idea that there is no such thing as objective "truth" and that all "truth" is ultimately reducible to power dynamics. What we are told is the "truth" is, in fact, a means of maintaining the powerful in their position of power. Surely, therefore, it is our moral duty to "deconstruct" their "truth"—to highlight the subjective and inconsistent nature of their systems of categories—and create a more equal world in which there are competing and equally valid "truths" that vary according to your cultural background.[117]

115: Amie Gordon, "Transgender Man, 34, Loses Battle to be Named as Father on his Child's Birth Certificate After Telling Appeal Court Judges That Decision to Call Him Mother 'Has Caused Psychological Scarring,'" *Mail Online*, April 29, 2020, https://www.dailymail.co.uk/news/article-8268729/Transgender-man-loses-battle-named-father-childs-birth-certificate.html; Booth, "Transgender Man Loses Court Battle to be Registered as Father," *The Guardian*, *op cit.*

116: Bruce Charlton, "Spiritual War, Transhumanism and the Transgender Agenda," *Bruce Charlton's Notions*, November 6, 2018, http://charltonteaching.blogspot.com/2018/11/spiritual-war-transhumanism-and.html.

117: See Roger Scruton, *Modern Culture* (London, Continuum, 2000).

The inconsistencies in this position should be obvious. If there is no objective truth, and logic and reason are merely "Western constructs," created to empower White people, then how can postmodernists logically convince anyone that they are correct? It might be countered, of course, that they don't. They tend to simply present verbose, deep-sounding prose to beguile the naïve reader into believing that he is in the presence of a "profound mind," a point made by the American philosopher Denis Dutton (1944-2010; no relation).[118] If there is no objective truth, then why do postmodernists use Western medicine when they become ill instead of going to see a witch doctor? Why do wealthy Africans come to Europe for heart operations? The answer, as Australian anthropologist Roger Sandall (1933-2012) notes, is that Western science gets results, because it is grounded in reality—in the objective truth.[119] Moreover, postmodern "deconstruction" of categories fails the test of pragmatism. If we cannot divide the world up into sets of (admittedly imperfect) categories, into which some phenomena will not quite fit, then we cannot make predictions. We thus would find it all but impossible to function and survive.

Postmodernism is a maladaptive ideology. It asks us to overturn traditions for the sake of doing so, and even if there is no scientific reason to do so. These traditions were adopted for a reason, otherwise they wouldn't have become traditions. Worse, postmodernism ultimately strips us of truth itself. Indeed, it strips us of reason. It takes us into a fantasy world in which everything is "subjective," meaning that anyone can assert anything, and it is "true" for them, and you are being willfully imperialistic (and thus evil) if you question or do not accept their "truth." And it is no good appealing to objective reality or logic, because there is no objective reality or logic.

118: Denis Dutton, "Language Crimes: A Lesson in How Not to Write Courtesy of the Professoriate," *The Wall Street Journal*, February 5, 1999. http://denisdutton.com/language_crimes.htm.

119: Roger Sandall, *The Culture Cult: On Designer Tribalism and Other Essays* (Boulder: Westview Press, 2001).

These are just constructs of the powerful, and if you attempt to appeal to them then perhaps it is because you are "privileged" and require some humility. In such a world, stripped of truth or reason, everything is reduced down to "power" and, perhaps by extension, violence.

Postmodernism, argues Charlton, demands that you accept that things you know to be lies are, in fact, truth. Witches were always understood to be in league with the Devil, who is described as the "father of lies": "When he lies, he speaks his native language, for he is a liar and the father of lies" (John, 8:44). By contrast, God is understood to be the truth and to value truth: "The one whose walk is blameless, who does what is righteous, who speaks the truth from his heart" (Psalm, 15: 2); "I, the Lord, speak the truth; I declare what is right" (Isaiah, 45: 19). According to Isaiah, in a world that has forsaken God, "truth has stumbled in the streets, honesty cannot enter. Truth is nowhere to be found, and whoever shuns evil becomes prey" (Isaiah, 59: 14-15). Charlton avers that, in a sense, accepting postmodernism, and especially transgender ideology, can be seen as a rejection of God's Creation—or of objective reality, to put it another way—in favor of an alternative reality in which Man is God. If she decides he's a man that morning, then he's a man. And if he's the Empress of China the next morning, then who are you to question her? As Charlton puts it:

> *The trans-agenda should be seen as a perfectly rational step towards the kind of Alternative Reality (AR) that the demonic powers need to be successful in the context of God's creation. It is part of a world picture that has been building-up over several generations; which has denied God, Creation and Reality—and asserted that this world is humanly constructed ("socially" constructed). The "Reality" in the phrase itself assumes that reality is man-made, at will. The appeal of the Alternative Reality is the promise of freedom and pleasure—since, if the AR really were equivalent to created-reality, then in principle we might make reality any way we pleased, without constraint. For instance; people*

> *could choose to be men or women, and swap back and forth at whim! Differences between sexes, classes, races, nations, and individual people could be made or abolished!*[120]

This situation gets worse almost by the day. In December 2019, there was an employment tribunal in London. A 45-year-old woman called Maya Forstater had been fired from the "Center for Global Development" for supposedly an "offensive" post on Twitter, in which she questioned government plans to allow people to self-identify their gender according to how they felt. Forstater argued that her sacking was against her human rights, because she was fired for expressing her beliefs. Reporting this, the *Mail Online* noted, "The case was viewed as a test of whether gender critical views—that there are only two biological sexes and it is not possible to change between them—could be protected philosophical beliefs under the 2010 Equality Act." Judge James Taylor, presiding over the tribunal, made the following ruling:[121]

> *If a person has transitioned from male to female and has a Gender Recognition Certificate (GRC), that person is legally a woman. That is not something [Miss Forstater] is entitled to ignore. [Miss Forstater's] position is that even if a transwoman has a GRC, she cannot honestly describe herself as a woman. That belief is not worthy of respect in a democratic society. Even paying due regard to the qualified right to freedom of expression, people cannot expect to be protected if their core belief involves violating others' dignity and creating an intimidating, hostile, degrading, humiliating, or offensive environment for them.*[122]

120: Charlton, "Spiritual War, Transhumanism and the Transgender Agenda," *Bruce Charlton's Notions*, *op cit.*

121: Forstater v. CGD Europe & Anor (Religious or Belief Discrimination), United Kingdom Employment Tribunal, December 18, 2019.

122: See also Jake Hurfurt, "Britons Have No Right to Ask Whether a Transgender Person is Male or Female," *Mail Online*, December 19, 2019 https://www.dailymail.co.uk/news/article-7808685/Britons-ask-transgender-person-male-female-judge-says.html. In June 2021, the decision against Maya Forstater was overturned on appeal. Doug Faulkner, "Maya Forstater: Woman wins tribunal appeal over transgender tweets," *BBC News*, June 10, 2021, https://www.bbc.com/news/uk-57426579.

In other words, believing in the empirical truth, and asserting that you believe in the empirical truth, is a stance that is not, in itself, "worthy of respect in a democratic society." There should be no legal protection for those who construct a worldview based on science, reason, and empirical evidence if aspects of this worldview lead to negative emotions in some people, specifically people who have mind-body dysphoria. In addition, if the government asserts that something that is empirically wrong is true, then it must be accepted, even if it is obviously preposterous.

One of the phenomena that the transgender movement has led to is, in effect, the serious abuse of children, something with which witchcraft was also associated. Children are being raised in an environment in which parents, social workers, and teachers are positively encouraged to accept at face value any confusion they may experience about their gender-identity. Accordingly, what once might have been a passing phase has now resulted in, for example, little boys being raised as girls and actually having their puberty medically stopped. It was reported in 2011, in California, that a lesbian couple had adopted a boy and that the boy, by then aged 11, wanted to be a girl. He had even threatened to mutilate his genitals when he was 7 years old. The boy was going to be given hormone blockers. "This is child abuse. It's like performing liposuction on an anorexic child," declared Paul McHugh, Professor of Psychiatry at Johns Hopkins University.[123]

McHugh's criticism effectively encapsulates a theory propounded by Ray Blanchard. Blanchard argues that some transwomen are "homosexual transsexuals" who are highly feminized and want to become, as far as possible, heterosexual

---

123: NewsCore, "We'll Stop Puberty so Tommy Can Become Tammy: Lesbian Couple Want to Help Boy to Become Girl," *The Courier Mail*, October 18, 2011, https://www.couriermail.com.au/news/well-stop-puberty-so-tommy-can-become-tammy-lesbian-couple-want-to-help-boy-to-become-girl/news-story/6cceb0151fcd59e89c4cc26489522996?sv=81059ba6d20d25de054e90828l682d6.

women (in the case of male sufferers).[124] They show signs of opposite-sex behavior at very young ages. The rest are what he calls "autogynephilic transsexuals." These are male fetishists, argues Blanchard, who are deeply emotionally satisfied by the idea of having a female body, something that correlates with wanting to take action to obtain one, and which becomes an interest for such people during or after adolescence. In other words, they are aroused by the idea of themselves as the opposite sex, something which sounds strikingly similar to mythological Narcissism, in which Narcissus falls in love with his own reflection.[125] More recently, Blanchard has averred that his model is also likely to apply to some transmen.[126] They are much like anorexics, in the sense that they have body dysphoria and are deluded about and alienated from who they really are. Anorexics regard themselves as overweight despite being dangerously underweight. Transsexuals, in turn, regard themselves as the opposite sex. Unsurprisingly, these different dysphoria correlate: transsexuals are prone to also being anorexic.[127] Anorexics, like transsexuals, have elevated levels of Narcissistic Personality Disorder.[128] This makes sense, because, as discussed above, Narcissism is characterized by a weak and confused sense of who you are, which you deal with by convincing yourself of your own perfection, resulting in

---

124: Ray Blanchard, "Varieties of Autogynephilia and Their Relationship to Gender Dysphoria," *Archives of Sexual Behavior*, 22 (1993): 241–251.

125: Kenneth Levy, William Ellison, and Joseph Reynoso, "A Historical Review of Narcissism and Narcissistic Personality," in *The Handbook of Narcissism and Narcissistic Personality Disorder: Theoretical Approaches, Empirical Findings, and Treatments*, eds. W. Keith Campbell and Joshua Millar (Hoboken, NJ: John Wiley & Sons, 2011).

126: J. Michael Bailey and Ray Blanchard, "Gender Dysphoria is Not One Thing," *4thWaveNow*, December 14, 2017, https://4thwavenow.com/tag/autohomoerotic-gender-dysphoria/.

127: Jiska Ristori, Alessandra Fisher, Giovanni Castellini, *et al.*, "Gender Dysphoria and Anorexia Nervosa Symptoms in Two Adolescents," *Archives of Sexual Behavior*, 48 (2019): 1625-1631.

128: Anthony Winston, "An Island Entire of Itself: Narcissism in Anorexia Nervosa," *Journal of Infant, Child and Adolescent Psychotherapy*, 15 (2016): 309-318.

a constant need for praise.[129] It has been observed that boys who later suffer from Gender Dysphoria tend to be raised in suboptimal environments, in which the parents frequently fight and in which the fathers have low self-esteem and are distant, while the mothers are high on psychopathology.[130] It has also been found that many children who present to doctors as suffering from gender dysphoria are, in fact, suffering from autism.[131] Autism, which is also associated with anorexia[132] and Borderline Personality Disorder[133] is itself characterized by a weak sense of self. Autistics lack the feeling that they are the same person across time and that they are in control of their thoughts and actions, possibly because, lacking empathy, they find that they cannot predict the consequences of their actions and, hypersensitive to stimuli, they easily become overwhelmed by the world.[134] The result is a chaotic and frightening void, which can result in Narcissism, Borderline Personality, and pronounced changes in identity, including in gender identity. In that autism, with its focus on objects, is also

---

129: Lawrence, "Shame and Narcissistic Rage in Autogynephilic Transsexualism," *Archives of Sexual Behavior*, *op cit.*

130: Kenneth Zucker, Susan Bradley, Dahlia Ben-Dat *et al.* "Pychopathology in the Parents of Boys With Gender Identity Disorder," *Journal of the American Academy of Child Adolescent Psychiatry*, 42 (2003): 2-4.

131: Elizabeth Hisle-Gorman, Colin Landis, Apryl Susi *et al.*, "Gender Dysphoria in Children with Autism Spectrum Disorder," *LGBT Health*, 6 (2019): 95-100.

132: Jess Kerr-Gaffney, Daniel Halls, Amy Harrison, and Kate Tchanturia, "Exploring Relationships Between Autism Spectrum Disorder Symptoms and Eating Disorder Symptoms in Adults With Anorexia Nervosa: A Network Approach," *Frontiers in Psychiatry*, 2020, https://doi.org/10.3389/fpsyt.2020.00401.

133: Robert Dudas, Chris Lovejoy, Sarah Cassidy, *et al.*, "The Overlap Between Autistic Spectrum Conditions and Borderline Personality Disorder," *PLoS One*, 12 (2017): e0184447.

134: Viktoria Lyons and Michael Fitzgerald, "Atypical Sense of Self in Autism Spectrum Disorders: A Neuro-Cognitive Perspective," *InTech Open*, 2013: doi: 10.5772/53680.

associated with sexual fetishes,[135] we can begin to understand why fetishism, Narcissism, and autism all come together in trans-sexuality.[136] Thus, the transgender movement—by pushing their ideology—are effectively abusing vulnerable children and creating an atmosphere in which it is difficult for them to obtain the psychiatric help they require. It may even be that some mothers encourage their sons to become female. Indeed, the commentator Steve Sailer has suggested that such mothers may have Munchausen's Syndrome By-Proxy.[137] This is when someone lives out their own delusion through somebody else, such as by being convinced that their child is ill and so making that child ill. In these cases, mothers are manipulating their children into mutilating their bodies.

The Annihilation of Masculinity

It is probable that the impact of feminism has been rendered all the more acute by changes in the male population, which have, in turn, made males more open to accepting the new dogma. This only further evidences the extent to which feminists, like witches, undermine the adaptive patriarchal system. The kind of "woke" males who are the most prone to accepting feminism are mockingly known as "soy boys." This is because left-wing

---

135: Daniel Schöttle, Peer Briken, Oliver Tüscher, and Daniel Turner, "Sexuality in Autism: Hypersexual and Paraphilic Behavior in Women and Men With High-functioning Autism Spectrum Disorder," *Dialogues in Clinical Neuroscience*, 19 (2017): 4.

136: It has been demonstrated that transwomen are actually highly mentally and physically masculinized, implying that transgenderism is a function of the (autistic) "extreme male brain," which would correlate with an extreme male body and be underpinned by high testosterone. See Edward Dutton and Guy Madison, "Gender Dysphoria and Transgender Identity Is Associated with Physiological and Psychological Masculinization: A Theoretical Integration of Findings, Supported by Systematic Reviews," *Sexuality Research and Social Policy*, 2020, https://doi.org/10.1007/s13178-020-00489-z.

137: Steve Sailer, "Munchausen's-Syndrome-By-Proxy?" *Unz Review*, January 15, 2018, http://www.unz.com/isteve/munchausens-syndrome-by-proxy/.

men are more likely to eschew meat and dairy in favour of soy, and soy (supposedly) reduces libido and makes males less masculine.[138] Whatever the case, it is demonstrably true that males in Western countries are becoming less masculine. Between 1989 and 2004, there was a substantial and age-independent decrease in average levels of serum testosterone in American males. The researchers found that there was no apparent environmental factor that would explain this.[139]

Many have blamed chemicals (endocrine disruptors) found in plastics, cosmetics, and food, as well as modern clothing and even the ubiquity of pornography, though these theories have not proved conclusive.[140] What might explain it, at least in part, is males becoming genetically less "masculine," due to the breakdown of harsh Darwinian selection. Similarly, we would expect females to become more masculine, making them more prone to adopting aspects of feminist ideology. I cannot find a study that has tested whether or not average testosterone levels in females have increased over time. It has, however, been reported that the prevalence of Polycystic Ovary Syndrome, which is a leading cause of infertility in women, in on the rise in the UK.[141] One of the causes of Polycystic Ovary Syndrome is the production of relatively high levels of

---

138: Rachel Hosie, "Soy Boy: What is this New Online Insult Used by the Far Right?" *Independent*, October 30, 2017, https://www.independent.co.uk/life-style/soy-boy-insult-what-is-definition-far-right-men-masculinity-women-a8027816.html.

139: Thomas Travison, Andre Araujo, Amy O'Donnell, *et al.*, "A Population-Level Decline in Serum Testosterone Levels in American Men," *Journal of Clinical Endocrinology and Metabolism*, 92 (2007): 196-202.

140: See Nicholas Kristof, "What Are Sperm Telling Us?" *New York Times*, February 20, 2021, https://www.nytimes.com/2021/02/20/opinion/sunday/endocrine-disruptors-sperm.html.

141: Tessa Copp, Jesse Jansen, Jenny Doust, *et al.*, "Are Expanding Disease Definitions Unnecessarily Labelling Women with Polycystic Ovary Syndrome?" *British Medical Journal*, 358 (2017): j3694.

testosterone.[142] The rise of "soy boys" is also likely to reflect not just increasing mutational load but also an increasing evolutionary mismatch. We are all evolved to be raised in an optimal environment—specifically the environment that is created by a group composed of people under harsh Darwinian selection. If this environment changes significantly—as it has done due to the influence of ideologies such as feminism—then we can expect males, as well as females, to become increasingly maladapted.

As stated, a number of environmental factors may have reduced drive among Western males. High levels of anxiety are associated with reduced testosterone levels.[143] Boys are increasingly educated in schools that are dominated by females, even at secondary schools. In Britain, as of 2019, 85 percent of primary school teachers were female, and, as of 2018, 75 percent of secondary school teachers were female.[144] Such schools naturally start to reflect female interests such as social harmony, emotional expression, and caring, inculcating young men away from more manly interests, such as competition, fighting for status, and suppressing emotion to signal dominance.

As Steve Moxon has noted, a "health and safety culture" at schools prevents boys from pursuing their natural propensity to take risks, meaning that it is little wonder

---

142: Leticia Morales-Ledesma, Juan Antonio Diaz Ramos, and Angelica Trujillo Hernandez, "Polycystic Ovary Syndrome Induced by Exposure to Testosterone propionate and Effects of Sympathectomy on the Persistence of the Syndrome," *Reproductive Biology and Endocrinology*, 15 (2017): 50.

143: Linnea Berglund, Hanne Prytz, Alexander Perski, *et al.*, "Testosterone Levels and Psychological Health Status in Men from a General Population: The Tromsø Study," *Aging Male*, 14 (2011): 37-41.

144: Laura FitzPatrick, "Male Teachers Ruling Out Primary School Jobs Because They Fear Being Viewed with Suspicion," *Telegraph*, January 13, 2019, https://www.telegraph.co.uk/news/2019/01/13/male-primary-teachers-speak-fears-perceived-suspicious-working/; GOV.UK, "School Teacher Workforce," *Ethnicity Facts and Figures*, September 24, 2018, https://www.ethnicity-facts-figures.service.gov.uk/workforce-and-business/workforce-diversity/school-teacher-workforce/latest.

that 75 percent of children diagnosed with Attention Deficit Hyper-Activity Disorder (ADHD) are male.[145] As females have become increasingly influential, masculinity is "pathologized," with terms such as "toxic masculinity," and mocked with such concepts as "man-splaining." This encourages boys to believe it is good to be non-aggressive and cooperative—to be, essentially, feminine. This is occurring despite the correlation between masculine traits, within certain boundaries at least, and socioeconomic success.[146] In effect, boys are taught that it is bad to be manly, and they are discouraged from acting in a natural fashion, and even prevented from doing so.

Pre-schools are attempting to be "gender-neutral" by teaching girls to shout and boys to dance, as was reported in Sweden.[147] There is, of course, a strong degree to which sex differences in psychology are products of evolution and are thus innate.[148] However, for boys to constantly witness masculinity being denigrated by powerful societal organs from a very young age may well have some negative effect on them in terms of drive, and it may create anxiety. Interestingly, it has been found that boys who regularly play computer games—which tend to involve competition and fighting—are low in anxiety, whereas girls, placed in the same situation, are high in it. These girls become even more anxious when these games are two-player and thus involve competing with other players.[149] This finding

---

145: Steve Moxon, *The Woman Racket: The New Science Explaining How the Sexes Relate at Work, at Play and in Society* (Exeter: Imprint Academic, 2008).

146: Nick Drydakis, Katerina Sidiropoulou, Vasiliki Bozani, *et al.*, "Masculine vs Feminine Personality Traits and Women's Employment Outcomes in Britain: A Field Experiment," *IZA Institute of Labor Economics*, 2017: 11179.

147: Ellen Barry, "In Sweden's Preschools, Boys Learn to Dance and Girls Learn to Yell," *New York Times*, March 24, 2018, https://www.nytimes.com/2018/03/24/world/europe/sweden-gender-neutral-preschools.html.

148: David Buss, *The Evolution of Desire: Strategies of Human Mating* (New York: Basic Books, 1989).

149: Christine Ohannessian, "Video Game Play and Anxiety During Late Adolescence: The Moderating Effects of Gender and Social Context," *Journal of Affective Disorders*, 226 (2018): 216-219.

would be congruous with the hypothesis that girls become anxious when forced to behave, to an extreme degree at least, like males (such as by being made to be highly competitive), so we would expect boys to become anxious when compelled to behave like females. In addition, as males grow older, they are less able to achieve their evolved role as head of a family, provider, and so on, and are more likely to be competing with females for status. They are also more likely to find themselves working in environments that are increasingly dominated by women—universities, schools, and healthcare practices are all examples—which force them to adapt to feminine rules.

As Canadian psychologist Jordan Peterson has pointed out, such environments become a "girls' game."[150] But, from a very young age, boys display a visceral loathing of having to play girls' games, which is not reciprocated as strongly by girls.[151] This makes it much easier for girls to continuously encroach on traditionally male spaces, constantly turning them into "girls' games." This, in evolutionary terms, "unnatural" situation for males—where they are constantly made to conform to a female-influenced environment—would be expected to lead to depression, anxiety and, thus, reduced testosterone. Thus, again, feminism creates a new hostile evolutionary environment in which those who are environmentally sensitive, because they lack the most adaptive genes, are selected out over time. We are thus experiencing, not simply lamentable social trends, but a profound change in environment—perhaps approaching that brought on by the Industrial Revolution—that is leading to genetic change in the population.

150: Jordan Peterson, "Decline in Men at Universities Bad for Both Sexes," *The Australian*, February 3, 2018, https://www.theaustralian.com.au/nation/inquirer/decline-in-men-at-universities-bad-for-both-sexes/news-story/eccc91aeb9d772c874feac873b7b4493.

151: Horatiu Catalano, "The Importance of Free Play in Early Childhood and Primary School Education: Critical Analysis for Romania," *Educational Research Applications*, ERCA-150 (2018), DOI: 10.29011/2575-7032/100050.

Having looked at the nature of feminism and its impact, let us now turn to the most important leading feminists whom, will we see, have much in common with traditional witches.

Chapter 8

Waking the Witch

The Case of Andrea Dworkin

Who are the modern modern-day witches? Considering the support for and even popularity of destructive and bizarre ideas in our time, the Western world seems to be dominated by coven of sorcerers. But who would exemplify a head witch, such as "The Grand High Witch" described by Roald Dahl? In this chapter, we will examine in detail just such a person. She appears as a manifestations of the psychological type associated with the "anti-genius" or "evil genius."

As far as I can see, Andrea Dworkin (1946-2005) was, in fact, a witch. Dworkin, the archetypal "radical feminist," was born in Camden, New Jersey, in 1946, to a Jewish family.[1] Her father was a school teacher and a socialist, and her mother, a campaigner for legalized abortion.[2] Aged 9, so she claimed, Dworkin was molested by a male stranger in a cinema.[3] So began her life of negative sexual experiences with men. According to her autobiography, when Dworkin was at "junior high school" (aged about 11 to her teens), she had a male "pedophilic" teacher who "liked little girls, especially little Jewish girls," and she

1: Andrea Dworkin, *Life and Death* (London: Virago Press, 1997), 3.

2: Andrea Dworkin, *Heartbreak: The Political Memoir of a Feminist Militant* (London: Continuum, 2006), 20.

3: Marissa Pagnattaro, "The Importance of Andrea Dworkin's "Mercy": Mitigating Circumstances and Narrative Jurisprudence," *Frontiers*, 19 (1998): 147-166.

had a "sexualized relationship" with him, as did a number of Dworkin's Jewish female friends.[4] According to Dworkin, this teacher "drew me pictures of all the sex acts, including oral and anal sex . . . He suggested I become a prostitute. . . ." Dworkin implies that this teacher persuaded her and her friends to do quasi-sexual things together for his titillation:

> *[H]e created configurations of sex and love that manipulated, sexualized, and intensified our friendships with each other—it was a menage a quatre; he knew what each of us wanted and there he was dangling it and if you were part of his sexual delight he'd give you a taste.*[5]

What these girls wanted was time with him, however:

> *He fucked one of us on graduation night and kept up an abusive relationship with her for years. I almost committed suicide at sixteen because I didn't think he loved me, though he later assured me that he did in a hot and heavy phone call."*[6]

Aged 10, Dworkin moved from Camden to the suburbs, specifically Cherry Hill, New Jersey, where she remembers refusing to sing the carol "Silent Night" at school, despite attempts to force her to do so, because, "I knew I wasn't a Christian and didn't worship Jesus. I even knew that Christians had made something of a habit of killing Jews."[7]

Dworkin went to a private Liberal Arts college in Vermont, Bennington College. While there, in 1965, she attended anti-Vietnam protests and was arrested in front of the United Nations in New York. Taken to prison at the New York Women's House of Detention, Dworkin claimed that prison medics performed a rough internal examination on her, which resulted in bleeding for days. She testified about this in front

---

4: Dworkin, *Heartbreak*, *op cit.*, 22.

5: *Ibid.*, 23-24.

6: *Ibid.*, 24-25.

7: Dworkin, *Life and Death*, *op cit.*, 8.

of a grand jury, making international news headlines; however, a grand jury declined to indict those whom she accused of medical malpractice.[8] Dworkin then took a year-long sabbatical in Crete to write a novel and some poetry before returning to college.[9] There she continued to campaign against the Vietnam War, as well as against the college's student code of conduct, against the lack of availability of contraception on campus, and for the legalization of abortion.[10]

Dworkin graduated from Bennington College in 1968 and moved to Amsterdam to live with a group of anarchists stationed in the Netherlands. She married one of them, later claiming that he raped and physically abused her, sometimes until she lost consciousness. According to Dworkin, her ex-husband stalked her throughout the country, and she eventually began living with another American activist who was also in Holland. This woman introduced Dworkin to the most extreme feminist ideas.[11]

Dworkin returned to America in 1972. Thereafter, she was effectively a full-time feminist writer and activist and became famous in this capacity, especially with her campaign against pornography. Dworkin began a relationship, of sorts, with John Stoltenberg in 1974, and the pair married in 1998, though she always insisted she was a lesbian and he insisted he was gay.[12] She created controversy in the year 2000, while regularly writing for *The Guardian*, when she claimed to have been drugged and raped in a hotel room in Paris the previous year, with it coming to light that she had likely fabricated the entire story.[13] Dworkin went

---

8: Dworkin, *Heartbreak*, *op cit.*, 74-79.

9: *Ibid.*, 79.

10: *Ibid.*, 61-63.

11: *Ibid.*, 102-113.

12: John Stoltenberg, "Living with Andrea Dworkin," *Lambda Book Report*, May-June 1994.

13: Andrea Dworkin, "They Took My Body From Me and Used It," *The Guardian*, June 2, 2000, https://www.theguardian.com/books/2000/jun/02/society.

into recluse for two years after this and eventually died of heart problems aged 58. She never had children.

A piece about Dworkin just after she died, in *The Guardian*, provides a reasonable summary of her views, through a series of quotations.[14] With regard to crime, she asserted that, "I really believe a woman has the right to execute a man who has raped her." Rape is clearly an appalling crime and most people would agree that those found guilty of it should be severely punished, but what Dworkin is calling for here is anarchy. If a man rapes a woman, then that woman should have the legal right to track him down and kill him, or pay others to assassinate him for her. In effect, Dworkin is espousing the breakdown of law and order, something which would produce a society marked by chaos.

With regard to romance, Dworkin claimed, "In seduction, the rapist often bothers to buy a bottle of wine." This implies, in effect, that all men who are interested in having sex, and thus procreating, or at least fornicating, should be viewed as "rapists." Moreover, according to Dworkin, it seems that *all* inter-gender sexual intercourse inherently involves the rape of a female. If she has been "seduced," through the male advertising his status and behaving in a chivalrous manner, it is as much rape as if the woman was grabbed off the street and assaulted in a dark alleyway. In effect, Dworkin is arguing that sex, for women, is *always* rape, and if they consent to it, they must have been manipulated. Dworkin stated this more directly in discussing the nature of sexual intercourse: "Intercourse remains a means, or the means, of physiologically making a woman inferior: communicating to her, cell by cell, her own inferior status . . . pushing and thrusting until she gives in."[15] Dworkin argued that sex is inherently degrading to women because their being penetrated inherently involves abject submission:

14: Katharine Viner, "'She Never Hated Men,'" *The Guardian*, April 12, 2005, https://www.theguardian.com/books/2005/apr/12/gender.highereducation.

15: Quoted in Viner, "She Never Hated Men," *op cit.*

> *She learns to eroticize powerlessness and self-annihilation. The very boundaries of her own body become meaningless to her, and even worse, useless to her. The transgression of those boundaries comes to signify a sexually charged degradation into which she throws herself, having been told, convinced, that identity, for a female, is there—somewhere beyond privacy and self-respect.*[16]

This being the case, Dworkin wants to stop men and women who love each other from expressing intimacy through sexual intercourse; she, indeed, wants to stop people from having sex at all. Dworkin's ideology, if taken seriously, would thus lead to nothing less than the end of humanity.

Dworkin is fairly clear about this extension of her logic.

> *Intercourse appears to be the expression of that contempt [held by men for women] in pure form, in the form of a sexed hierarchy; it requires no passion or heart because it is power without invention articulating the arrogance of those who do the fucking. Intercourse is the pure, sterile, formal expression of men's contempt for women; but that contempt can turn gothic and express itself in many sexual and sadistic practices that eschew intercourse per se. Any violation of a woman's body can become sex for men; this is the essential truth of pornography. So freedom from intercourse, or a social structure that reflects the low value of intercourse in women's sexual pleasure, or intercourse becoming one sex act among many entered into by (hypothetical) equals as part of other, deeper, longer, perhaps more sensual lovemaking, or an end to women's inferior status because we need not be forced to reproduce (forced flicking frequently justified by some implicit biological necessity to reproduce) . . .*[17]

Dworkin is arguing that heterosexual sex is inherently bad and proposing that one way round it is to not reproduce

16: Andrea Dworkin, *Intercourse* (New York: Free Press, 1987).

17: *Ibid.*

at all. Humanity should come to an end. Dworkin, though, had a tendency to make extreme statements—presumably for shock value—and then nuance them, in a verbose manner, when challenged. Thus, in response to the quite reasonable conclusion that she thought all sex was rape, Dworkin stated:

> *If you believe that what people call normal sex is an act of dominance, where a man desires a woman so much that he will use force against her to express his desire, if you believe that's romantic, that's the truth about sexual desire, then if someone denounces force in sex it sounds like they're denouncing sex. If conquest is your mode of understanding sexuality, and the man is supposed to be a predator, and then feminists come along and say, no, sorry, that's using force, that's rape—a lot of male writers have drawn the conclusion that I'm saying all sex is rape.*[18]

This is a clever tactic. It allows you to espouse your view and then claim, when critiqued, that you have been "taken out of context"; that your critics are engaging in a "straw man argument"; or that they have "oversimplified" your view. But Dworkin's views were not distorted by the critic. They were fairly represented, and Dworkin is simply engaging in deflection.

There are many other ways in which Dworkin appeared to contradict herself. For example, she claimed to be a rabid opponent of pedophilia, espousing anarchy in dealing with it:

> *Women have the right to avenge crimes on their children. A woman in California shot a paedophile who abused her son; she walked into the court and killed him there and then. I loved that woman. It is our duty as women to find ways of supporting her and others like her. I have no problem with killing paedophiles.*[19]

Yet she seemed to also advocate child abuse. In 1974, Dworkin wrote:

18: Quoted in Viner, "She Never Hated Men," *op cit.*

19: *Ibid.*

> *The parent–child relationship is primarily erotic because all human relationships are primarily erotic. . . . The incest taboo, because it denies us essential fulfilment with the parents whom we love with our primary energy, forces us to internalize those parents and constantly seek them. The incest taboo does the worst work of the culture. . . . The destruction of the incest taboo is essential to the development of cooperative human community based on the free-flow of natural androgynous eroticism.*[20]

Dworkin sued when, based on these statements, she was accused of defending incest, claiming the accusation was defamatory. As it was an obviously fair comment, she lost the case.[21]

Even those who supported Dworkin conceded that she was physically repellent. Katherine Viner wrote in *The Guardian*:

> *For many, Dworkin was famous for being fat. She was the stereotype of the Millie Tant feminist made flesh—overweight, hairy, un-made-up, wearing old denim dungarees and DMs or bad trainers—and thus a target for ridicule. The fact that she presented herself as she was—no hair dyes or conditioner, no time-consuming waxing or plucking or shaving or slimming or fashion—was rare and deeply threatening; in a culture where women's appearance has become ever more defining, Dworkin came to represent the opposite of what women want to be. "I'm not a feminist, but . . ." almost came to mean, "I don't look like Andrea Dworkin but . . ."*[22]

"Millie Tant" is a feminist cartoon character in the British satirical magazine *Viz*. Viner quotes British commentator Mimi Spencer as having written: "The only visibly hairy woman at the forefront of feminism today appears to be Andrea Dworkin,

20: Andrea Dworkin, *Woman Hating* (New York: Penguin Books, 1974), 189.

21: Laura Kipnis, *Men: Notes from an Ongoing Investigation* (New York: Metropolitan Books, 2014).

22: Viner, "She Never Hated Men," *op cit.*

and she looks as though she neither waxes nor washes, nor flushes nor flosses, and thus doesn't really count." She didn't count, it is implied, because of how she looked; she only cared about rape because no man could fancy her. Indeed, for many, Dworkin's hideousness made it difficult to believe her claims that she was raped in a Paris hotel in 1999, after allegedly being drugged by young bartender, who spiked her drinks. According to Dworkin, she blacked out, and, when she awoke, realized she'd been raped, even though she had no memory of the act.[23]

According to Viner, Dworkin's account was questioned by some journalists, who asked why Dworkin hadn't reported the incident to the police, and how she could be so certain she had been sexually assaulted if she was drugged at the time. She claimed, as evidence, that she suffered vaginal pain, bleeding, infection (despite not having had sex for a very long time), had a bruise on her breast, and "deep gashes" on her leg. But as she had not reported any of this, there was only her word to go on.[24] "But the undercurrent," writes Viner, "tapping into the myths that Dworkin herself had so carefully undermined in her work, was this: how could she be raped? She's old, she's fat, she's ugly. As if anyone still thought that rape was about sex and not about power."

In fact, Dworkin's critics, most of them female, raised serious questions about Dworkin's story that were never answered. Why did Dworkin never go to hospital if she was seriously injured? If this was because she couldn't bear reliving the ordeal of the rape—which she would presumably have had to explain to the doctors—then why did she publicly write about what happened in British magazines, *The New Statesman* and *The Guardian*, only a year later?[25] If Dworkin is so passionately against rape, then why did she not report this bartender at her hotel—whom she claimed raped her—to the police, so

23: Dworkin, "They Took My Body From Me and Used It," *The Guardian, op cit.*

24: *Ibid.*

25: *Ibid.*

he couldn't claim any more innocent victims? Another critic noted that, in her *New Statesman* piece, Dworkin recalled going through a mental checklist of points that get you raped, "no short skirt . . . I didn't drink a lot," concluding none applied to her and thus wondering why she had been raped. In a sense, she was conceding that rape is about sex, not just "power." Another female commentator concluded that Dworkin had simply lost her mind.[26] Interestingly, a prominent American Second Wave Feminist Kate Millett (1934-2017) also "lost her mind" to the extent of having to involuntarily spend time in a psychiatric institution.[27]

Regardless of whether Dworkin had gone mad or not, it's understandable why some journalists reached the conclusion that she was lying. The level of detail Dworkin provides is quite incredible; it is too much detail, of the kind that is provided by liars who are trying to persuade: "*I was in a garden in a hotel. I was reading a book.* French Literary Fascism. *I was drinking kir royale. This is a French cocktail: crème de cassis mixed with champagne*." More importantly, Dworkin claims to be, essentially, ashamed and traumatized by her experiences to the point of being suicidal:

> *Now I take on average 12 pills to sleep and they only work sometimes. How can I close my eyes and voluntarily become unconscious? For the first time in my life I go to shrinks, a lucid one who prescribes drugs and an empathetic one whose speciality is in dealing with people who have been tortured. I have been tortured and this drug-rape runs through it, a river of horror. I'm feeling perpetual terror, they both tell me. I stare blankly or I say some words. I'm ready to die.*[28]

26: Julia Gracen, "Andrea Dworkin in Agony," *Salon*, September 20, 2000, https://www.salon.com/2000/09/20/dworkin/.

27: Millett wrote a book about her incarceration, *The Loony-Bin Trip,* in which she attempted to argue that she was perfectly sane, such as by imagining what it would be like to have sex with a horse whom she also imagined to be her father. See Kate Millett, *The Loony-Bin Trip* (New York, Touchstone, 1990), 130.

28: Dworkin, "They Took My Body From Me and Used It," *The Guardian, op cit.*

Such feelings are hardly consistent with having the energy, presence of mind, and lucidity, to pitch an article to *The New Statesman* and write it to an acceptable standard.

The Evolutionary Psychology of Rape and of Female Rape Fantasies

A more plausible explanation, consistent with evidence from evolutionary psychology, would go entirely against the dogmas of Dworkin's radical feminism. Firstly, it is inaccurate to claim that rape is about nothing more than "power." It is, in evolutionary terms, about passing on your genes, and men are more likely, therefore, to rape females who are attractive and young (implying genetic health and fertility). It would be a waste of bio-energetic resources to rape an old, unattractive woman.

Psychologist Lee Ellis, in reviewing a large number of studies, concludes that as women are attracted to high-status males, low-status males will tend to adopt a strategy of passing on their genes through rape.[29] In particular, their situation will favor gang rape, as this affords the rapist the protection of a gang, diluting the risk of being prosecuted, and it means that the victim can be more easily overpowered. Moreover, according to biologist Randy Thornhill and anthropologist Craig Palmer's literature review, there is evidence that rape elevates the likelihood of a woman becoming pregnant, because the rapist produces more semen to compensate for the possibility that somebody else may have recently had sex with the victim.[30] This is because it was specifically those who gang-raped who tended to pass on their genes, and if you are part of

---

29: Lee Ellis, *Theories of Rape: Inquiries into the Causes of Sexual Aggression* (New York: Hemisphere Publishing, 1989), 53.

30: Randy Thornhill and Craig Palmer, *A Natural History of Rape: Biological Bases of Sexual Coercion* (Cambridge: The MIT Press, 2001), 174.

a rape-gang you are engaging in sperm competition, so it makes sense to produce more semen. Further, any woman you rape—unless you know her personally—may have had sex with other people recently, so it again makes sense for more ejaculate to be produced during rape than during consensual sex. Ellis has conducted a detailed literature review that shows that being a low-status, single male is a key predictor of being a rapist and that predatory rapists—opportunists who do not know their victims well or at all—tend to be of particularly low status.[31] It is simply incredible to suggest that the only motivation for males to rape females is to have "power" over them.

In light of this understanding, females would be evolved to have sex with desirable males; if males needed to resort to rape, they would likely be undesirable, so rape would stand as violation from a female perspective.[32] That said, it has been found that men are more aroused by violent or sadomasochistic sexual encounters than by normal sexual encounters. It has been proposed that this is because, in pre-history, males who raped passed on more of their genes; since rape is a fusion of sex and violence, it would make sense for men to be acutely aroused by sexual violence.[33] In line with this, some studies indicate that in sado-masochistic sexual relationships, males are more likely to be aroused by taking the sadistic or dominant role, while females are more aroused by taking the submissive or masochistic role.[34] The fact that there is some crossover—that males may have both sadistic and masochistic fantasies—also makes sense. A fast Life History Strategy male may fantasize about being dominated by a female, as the fact of her dominance would prove that she was genetically fit, though,

31: Ellis, *Theories of Rape*, *op cit.*, 53.

32: Thornhill and Palmer, *A Natural History of Rape, op cit.*, 148-149.

33: *Ibid.*, 76.

34: Nele de Neef, Violette Coppens, Wim Huys, and Manuel Morrens, "Bondage-Discipline, Dominance-Submission and Sadomasochism (BDSM) from an Integrative Biopsychosocial Perspective: A Systematic Review," *Sexual Medicine*, 7 (2019): 129-144.

as with a female rape fantasy, it would be a dominance that he ultimately controlled.[35] Females are also much more likely than males to be aroused by the idea of being sexually dominated than by the idea of sexually dominating others.[36] Indeed, there is evidence that a large majority (two thirds) of women report having had sexual fantasies in which they are raped. The specifically arousing dimension to this was being forced into sex by a highly powerful male against whom they must struggle, but ultimately relent. Part of the motivation for this fantasy, it was found, was that they, the females, were so alluring that dominant males simply couldn't keep their hands off them. The fantasy was to be ravished by a dangerous alpha male, who, in effect, the female eventually tames, as in classic romance novels. It is a self-esteem boosting fantasy, as the rapist is aroused by his victim's looks.[37]

35: In this regard, it is worth noting that sado-masochistic spanking fantasies can be comprehended as an intense focus on a particular sexual object, the buttocks, combined with an evolved propensity to find submission and violence arousing for reasons already discussed. It makes sense that this common fetish, as with fetishes in general, is associated with autism, due to the autistic focus on objects and the ritualistic and repetitive dimensions, combined with the fast Life History Strategy components of autism, such as low empathy, leading to a sexual focus on submission and violence. Consistent with this, hyper-sexuality (a fast LHS trait) is associated with sexual sadism. Such a model also explains why people can develop spanking fetishes despite few or no childhood spankings. See Daniel Schöttle, Peer Briken, Oliver Tüscher, *et al.*, "Sexuality in Autism: Hypersexual and Paraphilic Behavior in Women and Men with High-functioning Autism Spectrum Disorder," *Dialogues in Clinical Neuroscience*, 19 (2017): 4; Giovanni Castellini, Alessandra Rellini, Cristina Appignanesi, *et al.*, "Deviance or Normalcy? The Relationship Among Paraphilic Thoughts and Behaviors, Hypersexuality, and Psychopathology in a Sample of University Students," *Journal of Sexual Medicine*, 15 (2018): 1322-1335; and Jillian Keenan, *Sex with Shakespeare: Here's Much to Do With Pain, But More With Love* (New York: HarperCollins, 2016).

36: Jenny Bivona, Joseph Critelli, and Michael Clark, "Women's Rape Fantasies: An Empirical Evaluation of the Major Explanations," *Archives of Sexual Behavior*, 41 (2012): 1107-1119.

37: John Bancroft, *Human Sexuality and Its Problems* (New York: Elsevier, 2009), Chapter 9.

Both males and females have rape fantasies, though males are likely to fantasize about raping a desirable female, while females are more likely to fantasize about being raped by a dominant man.[38] This makes sense in evolutionary terms. In pre-history, the males who passed on their genes to the greatest extent would have defeated other tribes in war and would have forcefully dominated their women. In other words, males who violently took what they wanted dominated the gene pool, including impregnating women whether the women were willing or not. Males who raped women, as long as they got away with it, would pass on more of their genes. Counter-intuitive as it may seem, violent males of the kind who would engage in rape would be attractive, because they would reach the top of the hierarchy and would generally have constituted an attractive mate from an adaptive perspective. Let us assume that the rape, or at least subsequent intercourse with the rapist, would bear offspring. Let us also assume that this offspring would have at least the same probability of reaching adulthood as the offspring of the woman's consensual mate. This is likely, as men in the position to rape in prehistory were either stronger or, in some other sense, in a position of power, and that typically entails greater resources. Even though having children by her rapist does not necessarily increase the woman's number of offspring, it would still increase the woman's fitness, by means of her genes being propagated to more women in the next generation by her rapist's son, who would inherit his father's violent, dominant traits. Such males would tend to reach the top of the hierarchy in prehistory, as attested to in studies of hunter-gatherer tribes, and would have the highest genetic fitness.[39] (However, low-status males might want to rape but find it hard to get away with it in communities where everyone knows each other. Thus, they could only get away with it as part of a gang).

38: Patricia Hawley and William Hensley, "Social Dominance and Forceful Submission Fantasies: Feminine Pathology or Power?" *Journal of Sex Research*, 46 (2019): 568-585.

39: Napoleon Chagnon, *Yanomamö: The Fierce People* (New York: Holt, Rinehart and Winston, 1968).

In this context, women would want to fight off to the very last all sexual advances from all males, such that only the fittest male could attain them. They would have done this physically and also by creating female groups in which women who received little investment from their male partners protected each other and "alloparented" each other's offspring (that is, shared in partnering duties, even of non-kin). In a sense, this struggle—which could even take the form of an actual fight—would be a test of the male's fitness, which he would ultimately win, rendering any further female resistance futile. Once this rape would be completed, and assuming that her previous mate, if she had one, was eliminated, it would be adaptive to succumb to this oppression, unpleasant as it may be, to increase the fitness of her child. From an evolutionary perspective, females who were capable of putting up a fight, and who followed this strategy, would be impregnated by the fittest males, meaning that their genes would be more likely to propagate. It is this conflict between being subject to force and violence, and that of propagating one's genes, which might help explain by women's contradictory reactions to rape and sexual coercion. It could be argued that females who ultimately submitted to rape—and even eroticized it—would be more likely to survive the struggle. Thus, it would make sense for females to fantasize about rape—but only rape at the hands of an extremely fit male. To accept rape in general would mean impregnation by unfit males and the likely collapse of the female's genetic line. Perhaps this situation can be compared to sperm selection. The female immune system fights off half a billion spermatozoa such that only the fittest sperm fertilizes the egg. And even this sperm is fought off until the very final moment.

These findings have fascinating implications. The nature of the "rape fantasies" outlined is consistent with females who follow a fast Life History Strategy, a concept we discussed above. They want to be regarded as irresistible expressly due to their physical qualities, and they want to be dominated by a male who is attractive solely because of his own highly masculine traits, which are indicative of genetic quality and his ability to defend them in an unstable ecology. Consistent with this, it has been found that evidence of "sociosexuality" (that is, promiscuity) predicts having rape fantasies in females (again, where the victim is so alluring that the rapist cannot keep their hands of her).[40] Sociosexuality—investment of energy in promiscuous sex—is a central component of a fast LHS. And it has been shown that the more socially dominant a female is—and in that sense the more masculine she is—the more likely she is to fantasize about being raped. It has been suggested that this is adaptive because it allows dominant females to be attracted to dominant males, who would, it might be argued, be evolved to the same unstable ecology.[41] As we have seen, feminists are masculinized, and there is also evidence that they are more socially dominant than non-feminists.[42] So we would expect feminists to be particularly likely to reject male domination over their lives—but also particularly likely to have intense fantasies about being raped. In fact, as noted earlier, one study has found a weak but significant correlation between strength of "feminist" identification and having fantasies about being raped.[43] This would be consistent with the evidence, already discussed, that patriarchy selects for socially submissive women. Patriarchy, as we have seen, both reflects and elevates a more *K*-strategy ecology (a group-selected ecology), in which males invest in their off-spring and energy is directed away from copulation and towards nurture, and in which a more cooperative group develops, where certain alphas are less dominant. It would follow that non-feminists, who accepted patriarchy, would be less likely to fantasize about rape and more likely to fantasize about males being kind and loving. In line with this, "sex guilt" (which would be associated with religiousness and thus patriarchy) is

40: Bivona, Critelli, and Clark, "Women's Rape Fantasies," *op cit.*

41: Hawley and Hensley, "Social Dominance and Forceful Submission Fantasies," *op cit.*

42: Alyssa Zucker and Laina Bay-Cheng, "Minding the Gap Between Feminist Identity and Attitudes: The Behavioral and Ideological Divide Between Feminists and Non-Labelers," *Journal of Personality*, 78 (2010): 1895-1924.

43: Julie Schulman and Sharon Horne, "Guilty or Not? A Path Model of Women's Sexual Force Fantasies," *Journal of Sex Research*, 43 (2006): 368-377.

negatively correlated with rape fantasies, whereas being easily sexually aroused—"erotophilia"—is positively associated with them.[44] All of this implies that "feminism" is an evolutionary strategy, adopted, initially, by r-strategy females, who would have been high in mutational load because our pre-industrial norm was a pronounced *K*-strategy and developed patriarchy. Feminism acts to psychologically crush and repel the males, so that only the genetically strongest males might overcome it.

Thus, a likely interpretation of Dworkin's rape account is that she was a fantasist who—as a socially dominant female and a feminist—entertained potent fantasies of being raped. As an extreme outlier feminist, it would make sense that her rape fantasies were both frequent and particularly intense and violent. This would have created cognitive dissonance, which she might have coped with by convincing herself that she hadn't merely fantasied about being raped but that it had actually occurred. The fact that she regarded all sex as rape may have been an honest description of how she felt. When she fantasized about sex, she fantasized about rape, for only the idea of being raped aroused her.

It might be argued that, stereotypically, feminists are picky about whom they will have sex with, turning to lesbianism if they cannot find a desirable male, and that this pickiness evinces a slow LHS trait. It can be countered, however, that lesbians tend to be masculinized females, and that the inclination to turn to lesbianism is a sign of a fast LHS. Such a female is evolved to a polygamous ecology (meaning little investment in wife and offspring), in which the male will cast off the older females and they, and their offspring, will survive by co-parenting in a strongly bonded relationship.[45] Some feminists might supposedly desire a bonded relationship with a specific kind of male: high status and tough, dominant in an

44: *Ibid.*

45: Austin Jeffery, Todd Shackelford, Virgil Zeigler-Hill, *et al.*, "The Evolution of Human Female Sexual Orientation," *Evolutionary Psychological Science*, 5 (2019): 71–86.

unstable ecology. However, unable to obtain him, homosexual tendencies might emerge as a backup strategy, as predicted by a fast LHS context. A slow LHS female, on the other hand, would lack such tendencies and would, anyway, be attracted, not only to males of status and physical prowess, but also to males who would be caring husbands and fathers. Indeed, she might even further discount "status" for "caring." Unable to obtain a desirable male, we would expect her, beyond exercising patience to pursue kin selection, or even wider spheres of inclusive fitness. These are all group-selection strategies.

In terms of understanding Dworkin as a witch, her supposed suicide attempt indicates extreme levels of Neuroticism, which is negatively associated with religiousness. Her weight and general aggressiveness implies poor impulse control and her lack of concern for her appearance, combined with this aggressiveness, betokens low Agreeableness. In these ways, she is the kind of anti-social female who would have likely been accused of witchcraft under Darwinian conditions. And, like those who were accused of witchcraft, her way of life, and worldview, act to undermine group selection, both in terms of questioning patriarchy and, more generally, in undermining adaptive societal structures. It can be reasonably argued that Andrea Dworkin was a latter-day witch and an obvious example of a spiteful mutant. Her views on how women should see the world influenced the modern feminist movement and so influenced less mutated women to behave in a fitness-damaging way.

Chapter 9

Happily Ever After?

The Future of the Witches of the West

Let us return to where we started. *Once upon a time*, there were peoples known as the Europeans. We inhabited a world that was cold and harsh, and our various bands battled for survival and dominance. The groups that won out were the best suited to the struggle: bonded to one another and hostile towards outsiders. We were spirited, fertile, and hardy, as this was God's will. Soundness of body and soundness of mind went together. We lived lives of toil, even tragedy, but we reached the pinnacle of health, intelligence, and organization. We spun a connecting thread between ancestor and offspring.

Sometimes, though, the witches would come around. When they did, they were persecuted with a vengeance. The witches poisoned everything they touched. They formed communities apart. They disobeyed God with their spells, magic healing, and lives away from men. These women bore marks that announced them as unholy. A person's face can tell you quite a bit about her soul: *Monstrum in fronte, monstrum in animo*. Witches were at the bottom of society because that is where they belonged. Upright people rose to the top.

The Industrial Revolution, with all its marvels, changed everything. In 1800, half of all those born died as children; two centuries later, almost none did. More and more people who would not have survived in the old times walked among us. They were mistakes made flesh. They no longer uplifted the established rules; they endlessly criticized and undermined them, like the witches of yore. Unwell in body and mind, they were, at best, selfish and impulsive; at worst, they promoted depression and despair.

Some of these villains were born into society's highest ranks, or rose there due to their cleverness. The really spiteful ones advocated for ideas that were catastrophic. Worse still, people listened to them, since most are born to obey. The nature of our communities changed, including our outposts and colonies around the world. We all went mad, you could say—everyone, except those who were naturally resistant or too slow to conform. Deviancy became the norm; patriarchy was overturned. Those who were brightest were the first to accept the new religion, as they could talk themselves into anything. They even talked themselves into having small families or no children at all.

These new witches lived out in the open and were even celebrated. So many women were taken in by their spells: they behaved like men; they cared about careers more than children; they raised boys as girls. Even men listened to the witches. Our societies were feminized, though that didn't mean they became kinder and gentler. The persecuted became the persecutors, the judged became judges, the last came first. Everything was out of joint.

These are dizzying times . . . but nothing lasts forever. Those susceptible to the witches' spells are cursed with barrenness; those who are religious still multiply. We Europeans thus stand at a fork in the road. Some say that the children will bring about a revival of the old ways, though in a population that is much dimmer than in previous times. Some see a civil war or breakdown over the horizon. Others warn of a return to the harsh conditions of the past. Whichever way destiny takes us, the witches, and those under their spell, are not long for this world.

So how is this going to turn out?

Head Girls in Charge

Some events embody social trends to such an extent that they are difficult to look away from. One of these took place on December 10th, 2019, when a 34-year-old woman named Sanna Marin was elected leader of Finland's Social Democratic Party (SDP), becoming Finland's youngest ever Prime Minister. Antti Rinne, a portly, middle-aged trade-union lawyer, who had won Finland's parliamentary elections earlier that year and who had been leading a multi-party coalition, had been forced to stand down as PM. This was, apparently, because he'd been less than entirely honest with regard to a postal strike. Due to this dishonesty, his coalition partners, the Centre Party, threatened to withdraw from the arrangement, and likely force another General Election, if Rinne did not go. But the result was that a pretty, young mother became the leader of Finland, the youngest head-of-government in the world at the time.

This was all the more newsworthy, internationally, because every party leader in the five-party coalition was now female. The so-called "Spice Girls"[1] were: Sanna Marin (SDP, Prime Minister, b.1985), Katri Kulmuni (Centre Party, Finance Minister and Deputy Prime Minister, b.1987), Maria Ohisalo (Green League, Interior Minister, b.1985), Li Andersson (Marxist "Left Alliance," Education Minister, b.1987), and Anna-Maja Henriksson, Swedish People's Party, Minister of Justice, b.1964). It was even more newsworthy because four of these women were in their 30s. Indeed, there was very little interest in Henriksson, implicitly—and ironically considering the "feminist" stance of the reporting—because she was menopausal and thus less attractive. Britain's *Mail Online*, for example, published a lavishly illustrated article on the new Finnish government, including five close-up photographs of the four Millennial Ministers posing together. Henriksson was presented only in a photograph of all the ministers in the female-majority cabinet or blurred in the

1: This term for the Finnish government was coined by Mr. Tommy McCrossan.

background of a close up of Marin. She wasn't young and pretty, so she wasn't relevant.[2] Indeed, all four of the female Millennial Ministers were not unattractive, with three of them—Marin, Kulmuni, and Andersson—being quite good-looking for their age. The *Mail Online* ran a long article on Marin when she was elected, copiously illustrated with photographs of her looking pretty, including one of her breast feeding with a coquettish expression on her face.[3]

What kind of women were these? Sanna Marin is the daughter of problem parents. Her father was an alcoholic. Her parents' marriage broke down when she was a few years old, and her mother placed her in a children's home. Her mother eventually withdrew her from the care home. The mother entered into a lesbian relationship with another woman, and Marin was raised by these two women. Marin is extremely left-wing, focused on "equality" and other such mantras. Around 70 percent of Finns are members of the Lutheran Church—for which they pay a small church tax—at the time of writing, but Marin is not.[4] She had at the time a common-law husband (they have since married) and an illegitimate baby daughter, who has taken the mother's surname. Marin has a degree, from Tampere University,

2: Chris Dyer, "Finland's Sanna Marin Becomes the World's Youngest Serving Prime Minister and Prepares to Lead the Country With a New, Female-majority Cabinet," *Mail Online*, December 10, 2019), https://www.dailymail.co.uk/news/article-7776351/Finnish-parliament-picks-world-s-youngest-sitting-prime-minister.html.

3: Hayley Richardson, "A Politician for the Instagram Generation: World's Youngest Prime Minister Sanna Marin, 34, of Finland Shares VERY Candid Breastfeeding Snaps and Glamorous Nights Out on Social Media," *Mail Online*, December 9, 2019), https://www.dailymail.co.uk/femail/article-7771821/A-politician-Instagram-generation-Meet-worlds-youngest-prime-minister-Sanna-Marin-34.html.

4: *YLE*, "Half of Lutheran Parishes in Finland Report Financial Loss," July 9, 2019), https://yle.fi/uutiset/osasto/news/half_of_lutheran_parishes_in_finland_report_financial_loss/10868737.

in administration.[5] Kulmuni, who is from Tornio in southern Lapland, studied Social Science at the University of Lapland. She is the daughter of a father with an agricultural business and a mother who is a special-needs teacher. She has a male "partner" but no children. Kulmuni took the Centre Party in a left-wing and environmentalist direction.[6] In June 2020, Kulmuni resigned as Finance Minister and Deputy Prime Minister due to allegations that she had used public money for coaching sessions to improve her public-speaking and debating skills.[7]

Maria Ohisalo has a similar kind of background to Marin. As a child, she spent a year in a shelter due to her frequently unemployed parents losing their home, and her parents broke up because of her father's alcoholism.[8] She studied social sciences at Helsinki University, and has a doctorate in the subject from the University of Eastern Finland. She is married and childless. As leader of the Green League, she is left-wing and feminist in orientation. Li Andersson, who is from Finland's five percent Swedish-speaking minority, who constitute its traditional elite and are 50 percent of its nobility,[9] is the daughter of an artist and a journalist, both from Finland's former capital of Turku, known as Åbo in Swedish. There, Andersson studied political science at

5: Saara Tunturi and Lauri Nurmi, "Rinteen Sijainen on Napakka Nuori Konkari ja Kaksinkertainen Äänirohmu—Yksi Video Näyttää, Kuinka Sanna Marin Laittoi Tampereen Valtuuston Ruotuun," *Aamulehti*, January 23rd 2019, https://www.aamulehti.fi/a/201418683.

6: Katri Kulmuni, "Katri Esittäytyy," *Katri Kulmuni,* 2019, https://www.katrikulmuni.fi/katri-ja-media/.

7: *YLE*, "Kulmuni Resigns as Minister of Finance Over €50k Coaching bill," June 5, 2020, https://yle.fi/uutiset/osasto/news/kulmuni_resigns_as_minister_of_finance_over_50k_coaching_bill/11387871.

8: U.-M. Paavilainen, "Yksivuotispäivä Turvakodissa—Maria Ohisalo Nousi Syrjäytymisvaarasta Politiikan Huipulle," *Kotiliesi*, January 14, 2018: https://kotiliesi.fi/ihmiset-ja-ilmiot/ihmiset/nain-lukutaidoton-matonkutoja-intiasta-koki-suomen-jos-olisin-taman-kokenut-kolmekymppisena-huomio-olisi-voinut-nousta-paahan/.

9: See Edward Dutton, Dimitri van der Linden, Guy Madison, *et al.*, "The Intelligence and Personality of Finland's Swedish-speaking Minority," *Personality and Individual Differences*, 97 (2016): 45-49.

the city's Swedish-language university, Åbo Akademi. She began her career campaigning for "human rights" and for the "rights of refugees." Andersson co-wrote a book in 2012 entitled *The Extreme Right in Finland*, in which the authors discussed the civic-nationalist *Perussuomalaiset* (the "True Finns"), Finland's second largest party in parliament as of 2019, alongside overt Nazis.[10] Andersson is unashamedly Marxist and refers to her vision of "Tomorrow's Marxism."[11] She is also unmarried, but has an illegitimate child.

Finland's Millennial Ministers are young, they are reasonably attractive, and they are likely to be highly socially skilled, hence their progress in the world of Finnish politics. It is quite possible that Marin and Ohisalo have inherited some of the anti-social traits associated with alcoholism and poverty from their parents. Twin studies have found that alcoholism is approximately 0.5 heritable,[12] and it is predicted by such traits as low Conscientiousness, low Agreeableness[13] and high Neuroticism.[14] Poverty, in which they were raised, is predicted, in particular, by low Conscientiousness and high Neuroticism, as well as by low General Factor of Personality.[15] Thus, there may

---

10: Dan Kuivulaakso, Mikhael Brunila, and Li Andersson, *Äärioikeisto Suomessa* (Helsinki: Into, 2012).

11: Lena Skogberg, "Li Andersson—Marxisten Som Bara Måste," *HBL*, March 25, 2018): https://www.hbl.fi/artikel/li-andersson-marxisten-som-bara-maste/.

12: Brad Verhulst, Michael Neale, and K.S. Kendler, "The Heritability of Alcohol Use Disorders: A Meta-Analysis of Twin and Adoption Studies," *Psychological Medicine*, 45 (2015): 1061-1072.

13: Christian Hakulinen, Marko Elovaino, G. David Batty, *et al.*, "Personality and Alcohol Consumption: Pooled Analysis of 72,949 Adults from Eight Cohort Studies," *Drug and Alcohol Dependence*, 151 (2015): 110-114.

14: Susan Mosher-Ruiz, Marlene Oscar-Berman, Maaria Kemppainen, *et al.*, "Associations Between Personality and Drinking Motives Among Abstinent Adult Alcoholic Men and Women," *Alcohol and Alcoholism*, 52 (2017): 496-505.

15: Dimitri van der Linden, Jan te Nijenhuis, and Arnold Bakker, "The General Factor of Personality: A Meta-analysis of Big Five Inter-correlations and a Criterion Related Validity Study," *Journal of Research in Personality*, 44 (2010): 315–327.

be a degree to which Marin and Ohisalo are spiteful mutants. However, Finland's Millennial Ministers would appear to be very much the Head Girl type: socially skilled, conformist (though this may be less true of Li Andersson due to her relative extremism), and feminine, both in their looks and their worldviews. They can perhaps be said to have been inspired by people such as Andrea Dworkin, who are closer to the witch stereotype.

Interestingly, this is not the first time in Finnish history that young, attractive females have fought to push Finland in a fitness-damaging direction. It also happened in 1918. Finland became independent of Russia, by then the nascent Soviet Union, in December 1917. By January 1918, Finland was embroiled in a bloody civil war between the nationalist "Whites," who constituted its recognized government, and the socialist "Reds," who controlled much of the more industrialized south of the country. Their government was called "The Finnish People's Delegation." The Whites, narrowly, triumphed over the Reds, many of whom were ardent Communists and who were supported by Bolshevik troops.[16] It is widely accepted that many of the Reds, including their leadership, were Lenin-supporting Communists who wanted to make Finland part of the Soviet Union. When they were defeated, many fled over the Finnish border to Eastern Karelia (Western Karelia was part of Finland).[17] Had Finland become part of the Soviet Union, it is probable that there would have been mass starvation and purges, as occurred in Eastern Karelia, including to the Red Finns who ran Eastern Karelia until the "Great Purge" of 1937, so it clearly would have been a very bad turn of events.[18] Two of the cabinet ministers in the Red Government were Finland-Swede females in their early-40s: Hanna Karhinen (née Andelin, 1878-1938) was

16: Eyal Lewin, *National Resilience During War: Refining the Decision-making Model* (New York: Lexington Books, 2012), 159.

17: James Minahan, *The Former Soviet Union's Diverse Peoples: A Reference Source Book* (Oxford: ABC-Clio, 2004), 144.

18: See Jason Lavery, *The History of Finland* (Westport: Greenwood Publishing, 2006).

Deputy Interior Minister, while Hilja Pärssinen (née Lindgren, 1876-1935) was Social Affairs Minister. According to historians, "Never before had women gained such powerful positions in Finnish politics."[19] In addition, during the Finnish Civil War, the Reds employed a number of female-only battalions, with captured females stripping down to their underwear to avoid being identified as combatants and so summarily shot.[20] Their activities were considered so monstrous that newspapers called for them to be massacred, rather than treated as prisoners of war, and the Archbishop of Turku, Gustav Johansson (1844-1930), proclaimed that they should simply be "left in the hands of Satan" and not assisted in any way.[21]

Needless to say, the current Head Girls in charge of Finland are not likely to lead the country down a path towards state terror and death camps. It is remarkable, however, the degree to which a spiteful and foreign ideology (Bolshevism from Russia and "Woke-ism" from the U.S.) has captivated, inspired, and activated a generation of female leadership. The Head Girls seem to sense that now is their time to take charge.

The New Witches' Marks

We have already observed the importance of the "Witch's Mark," a deformity which implied suboptimal genetics and thus an

19: Judy Gottlieb, Judith Szapor, Tiina Lintunen, *et al.*, "Suffrage and Nationalism in Comparative Perspective: Britain, Hungary, Finland and the Transnational Experience of Rosika Schwimmer," in *Women Activists Between War and Peace: Europe, 1918-1923*, eds. Ingrid Sharp and Matthew Stibbe (London: Bloomsbury, 2017), 59.

20: Tiina Lintunen, "Women at War," in *The Finnish Civil War of 1918: History, Memory, Legacy*, eds. Tuomas Tepora and Aapo Roselius (Leiden: BRILL, 2014); Marjo Liukkonen, *Hennalan Naismurhat 1918* (Licentiate Thesis: University of Lapland, 2016).

21: Tiina Lintunen, "'She-wolves and Russian Brides': Women Enemies in War Propaganda," in *Proceedings of the 9th European Conference on Information Warfare and Security*, ed. J. Demergis (Thessaloniki: University of Macedonia, 2010).

elevated likelihood of espousing maladaptive, anti-patriarchal, and otherwise irreligious ideas. It might be argued that the tattoo, which has become gradually more prevalent since about the year 2000 in many Western countries, should be understood as a kind of "Witch's Mark." According to the Pew Research Center, in 2017, 40 percent of Americans born after 1980 had at least one tattoo.[22] An Australian study in 2012 found that women in their 20s were the most likely demographic to have a tattoo, with 29 percent of them having at least one.[23] Andrea Dworkin, as it happens, objected to the tattooing of females, mainly because she regarded tattooing, and other forms of body scarification, as a tribal means by which women were stamped as male property.[24] Though there are, of course, individual exceptions, we would not expect those who affirmed a traditional worldview to have tattoos in Western societies. This expectation is borne out in a variety of studies. When comparing those with tattoos to those without, those with tattoos tend to be weakly but significantly lower in Agreeableness and in Conscientiousness.[25] Those who are tattooed are also more likely to suffer from mental illness than are the non-tattooed, with the correlation being stronger among those with multiple, highly visible, or offensive tattoos.[26] It was found, using a sample of over 8,000 people, that those

---

22: Marsha Mercer, "Explosion in Tattooing, Piercing Tests State Regulators," *Pew Trusts*, June 14, 2017, https://www.pewtrusts.org/en/research-and-analysis/blogs/stateline/2017/06/14/explosion-in-tattooing-piercing-tests-state-regulators.

23: Wendy Heywood, Kent Patrick, Anthony Smith, *et al*, "Who Gets Tattoos? Demographic and Behavioral Correlates of Ever Being Tattooed in a Representative Sample of Men and Women," *Annals of Epidemiology*, 22 (2012): 51-56.

24: Wendy Steiner, *Venus in Exile: The Rejection of Beauty in Twentieth-Century Art* (Chicago: University of Chicago Press, 2002), 147.

25: James Tate and Britton Shelton, "Personality Correlates of Tattooing and Body Piercing in a College Sample: The Kids are Alright," *Personality and Individual Differences*, 45 (2008): 281-285.

26: Karoline Mortensen, Michael French, and Andrew Timming, "Are Tattoos Associated with Negative Health-related Outcomes and Risky Behaviors?" *International Journal of Dermatology*, 58 (2019): 816-824.

with tattoos are more likely to take serious risks.[27] This would be consistent with a fast Life History Strategy. Tattoos draw attention to the body, they stress individuality or membership of a tribe, they display the ability to endure pain, and they draw attention to oneself. These characteristics are all associated with a fast LHS. Men assume that tattooed women are more promiscuous than non-tattooed women.[28] And there is evidence from Poland that those with tattoos are slightly more sexually active than those without.[29] People with tattoos have been found to have a greater need for "uniqueness."[30]

Cosmetic surgery in females, to a lesser extent, might also be regarded as a modern day "Witch's Mark." Such surgery is usually visually obvious. Being dissatisfied with your body to the extent of presenting for cosmetic surgery has been found to be associated with a series of mental disorders. Indeed, 47 percent of those who present for cosmetic surgery have been found to have one and we can assume that many others are on the same scale but not high enough to be classified as mentally ill. One of the most common is Narcissistic Personality Disorder. Another is Histrionic Disorder.[31] This is characterized by excessive attention-seeking and an extreme need for approval.[32]

27: Heywood *et al.*, "Who Gets Tattoos?" *op cit.*

28: Nicolas Guéguen, "Effects of a Tattoo on Men's Behavior and Attitudes Toward Women: An Experimental Field Study," *Archives of Sexual Behavior*, 42 (2013): 1517-1524.

29: Krzysztof Nowosielski, Adam Sipiński, Ilona Kuczerawy, *et al.*, "Tattoos, Piercing, and Sexual Behaviors in Young Adults," *Journal of Sexual Medicine*, 9 (2012): 2307.

30: Viren Swami, Jajkob Pietschnig, Bianca Bertl, *et al.*, "Personality Differences Between Tattooed and Non-tattooed Individuals," *Psychological Reports*, 111 (2012): 97-106.

31: Viren Swami, Ulrich Tran, Louise Brooks *et al.*, "Body image and personality: associations between the Big Five Personality Factors, actual-ideal weight discrepancy, and body appreciation" *Scandinavian Journal of Psychology*, 54 (2013): 146-151.

32: Farah Malick, Josie Haward, and John Koo, "Understanding the psychology of the cosmetic patients," *Dermatologic Therapy*, 21 (2008): 47-53.

Consistent with this, there is evidence, from a female sample, that having a positive image of one's body—likely to be reflected in relatively low levels of beauty augmentation—is associated with low Neuroticism.

It should be noted that, based on a sample of 70,000, possessing a tattoo is negatively associated with IQ.[33] Thus, if someone has a tattoo in spite of likely having above average IQ, this is likely to be a reflection of an anti-social personality. If such a person has multiple or conspicuous tattoos, then there is every reason to see this as a Witch's Mark, and even the presence of a single tattoo is worth keeping in mind. It is also worth noting that Li Andersson, the most left-wing of the Millennial Ministers who began running Finland in December 2019, has a prominent tattoo on her left forearm. Mutants identify themselves to fellow-mutants, with whom they collaborate in destruction: unnatural hair colors, unattractive hair styles, and a general appearance that is intuitively bizarre and inducing of disgust.

Kali Yuga

Since the 17th century, the Western world can be said to have been turned on its head. In 1612, during the Pendle Witch Trials, the vast majority of people conformed to an evolutionarily adaptive form of religiousness. Those who did not conform were under threat of being persecuted for witchcraft. Today, the situation has reversed. Those who may well have been accused of witchcraft for their views and lifestyle were, as of December 2019, literally running a Nordic country. And those who question their views—the remnant normal population from pre-Industrial times—are persecuted in much the same way that religious people once were.

This situation, however, is not likely to be permanent, as alluded to in the fairytale that begins and ends this book.

33: Emil Kirkegaard, "Cognitive Ability and Tattoos and Piercings," *Clear Language, Clear Mind*, November 8, 2016, https://emilkirkegaard.dk/en/?p=5616.

The key predictors of passing on your genes are adhering to a patriarchal religion and being politically conservative, as well as low IQ. The heritability of religiousness is 0.4 and almost 0.7 on being "born again," while the heritability of political viewpoint is also around 0.4.[34] At the genetic level, we are becoming more religious and more ethnocentric, though also lower in intelligence.

There is even some evidence that the consequences of this selection for conservatism are manifesting themselves. Western society, although overtly moving ever-leftward, is increasingly polarizing based on a variety of measures and models. Some of the key factors are the following:

1. *Legitimacy Crisis*. Conservatives are, more and more, questioning the authority of the elite: politicians are roundly dismissed as out-of-touch or downright evil; respected newspapers are labeled "fake news" and journalists, ridiculed as "enemies of the people";

2. *Too many workers*. Immigration, offshoring, and automation have led to impoverishment, resentment, huge wage gaps, and angry masses;

3. *Intra-Elite Competition*. An over-educated, entitled society produces over-qualified people, who see many jobs as beneath them, and must battle over elite status.[35]

This polarization involves a movement to the political extremes, as people become more resentful and less trusting,[36]

34: John Alford, Carolyn Funk, and John Hibbing, "Are Political Orientations Genetically Transmitted?" *American Political Science Review*, 99 (2005): 153-167.

35: See Peter Turchin, *Ages of Discord: A Structural-Demographic Analysis of American History* (Beresta Books, 2016).

36: Peter Turchin, "A History of the Near Future: What history tells us about our Age of Discord," *Cliodynamica,* November 6, 2019, http://peterturchin.com/cliodynamica/a-history-of-the-near-future-what-history-tells-us-about-our-age-of-discord/.

including a growing nationalist subculture among young people[37] and the broader growth of populist nationalism in Europe.[38] Those who are referred to as part of generation *i-Gen*—born in the late 1990s and thus never having known a world without the Internet—appear to be more conservative than Millennials in a number of ways, despite environmental factors potentially pushing them in a leftward direction. They lose their virginity later, leave home later, they regard university as an extension of home, they start dating later, they are less sexually promiscuous, they have less sexual intercourse, and they are less inclined to drink alcohol.[39]

Our falling average intelligence would also push us towards being more instinctive—and thus more religious and more oriented towards our genetic interests—as well as more negatively ethnocentric. This is not reflected so starkly yet at the environmental level. This is because levels of stress are very low, making us less religious and less instinctive, and because spiteful mutants have undermined adaptive societal structures, such as religion and nationalism, and inculcated much of the population with fitness-damaging ideas, such as feminism and multiculturalism, to varying degrees.

The Collapse of the Human Zoo

There is every reason to think that our human zoo will collapse. Intelligence is declining. In terms of per capita innovations, Europe hit a low ebb in about 350 AD, remained stagnant,

37: See, J.P. Zúquete, *The Identitarians: The Movement Against Globalism and Islam* (Notre Dame: University of Notre Dame Press, 2018).

38: Roger Eatwell and Matthew Goodwin, *National Populism: The Revolt Against Liberal Democracy* (London: Penguin, 2018).

39: See, Jennifer Twenge, *iGen: Why Today's Super-Connected Kids Are Growing Up Less Rebellious, More Tolerant, Less Happy—and Completely Unprepared for Adulthood—and What That Means for the Rest of Us* (New York: Atria Books, 2017).

and then began to increasingly innovate from around 1100 onwards.[40] We reached a peak in about 1870 and have now returned to where we were in 1600. Based on current trends, a century from now, we will be back to where we were in 1100, at the end of the Dark Ages.[41] This decline is underpinned by our falling genetic intelligence, brought about by the collapse of selection for intelligence and then its reversal. Reaction times are lengthening. Indeed, between 1880 and the year 2000, their lengthening was consistent with a fall of 15 IQ points,[42] a trend that is also manifest across people born from 1959 to 1986 measured at the same time and with the same methods.[43] Currently, our living standards are still increasing because we are, in effect, living off capital accrued by our genius forbears. Only minor new innovations are required to maintain the capital. As intelligence falls further, we won't be able to do things that we once could, living standards will regress, and society will become more stressful, more disorganized, more instinctive, more religious and, of course, less feminist.

Also, as I showed in my book on Finland—*The Silent Rape Epidemic: How the Finns Were Groomed to Love Their Abusers*—multiculturalism inevitably leads to ethnic conflict and low-level war.[44] Multiculturalism is partly a product of spiteful mutants advocating for it, the collapse of religion (leading to

---

40: Edward Dutton and Michael A. Woodley of Menie, *At Our Wits' End: Why We're Becoming More Intelligent and What It Means for the Future* (Exeter, Imprint Academic, 2018).

41: Jonathan Huebner, "Response by Jonathan Huebner," *Journal of Technological Forecasting*, 10 (2005): 995-1000, 999.

42: Michael A. Woodley, Jan te Nijenhuis and Regan Murphy, "Were the Victorians cleverer than us? The decline in general intelligence estimated from a meta-analysis of the slowing of simple reaction time," *Intelligence*, 41 (2013): 843-850.

43: Guy Madison, Michael A. Woodley of Menie, and Justis Sänger, "Secular Slowing of Auditory Simple Reaction Time in Sweden (1959-1985)," *Frontiers in Human Neuroscience*, 10 (2016): 407.

44: Edward Dutton, *The Silent Rape Epidemic: How the Finns Were Groomed to Love Their Abusers* (Oulu, Finland: Thomas Edward Press, 2019).

the decline of ethnocentrism), and increased living standards, resulting in reduced stress, reduced religiousness, and reduced instinctiveness. However, the more ethnically diverse a society is, the more conflict-ridden it is—the correlation is 0.66[45]—and the less trusting it is, even among the natives. This is because trust is hard to earn and easy to lose, and the loss of it (partly due to the inability to predict the behaviors of people with other genotypes, cultures, and religions) spills over to their own ethnic group. Also, multiculturalism raises a fear that some among the natives may collaborate with the newcomers to gain power over their own people.[46] This means that, eventually, when a society is too diverse, it will gradually degenerate into conflict, increasing mortality salience, stress, and instinctive behavior. In addition, increasing genetic diversity would be expected to lead to an increasingly polarized and conflict-ridden society even between the native population, as genetic similarity predicts bonding and cooperation.[47] Accordingly, conflict and stress will increase, making people more religious and more instinctive. Thus, it is quite clear that the power of witches over European societies is merely a phase, just as is Kali Yuga, in which women dominate a society declining into chaos.

The Seasons of Civilization

All civilizations pass through the same phases of Spring, Summer, Autumn, and Winter. These parallel the intensity of individual and group selection. The people of that civilization, under intense Darwinian selection, become pro-social, highly

45: Tatu Vanhanen, *Ethnic Conflicts: Their Biological Roots in Ethnic Nepotism* (London: Ulster Institute for Social Research, 2012).

46: Robert Putnam, "*E Pluribus Unum*: Diversity and community in the twenty-first century. The 2006 Johan Skytte Prize Lecture," *Scandinavian Political Studies*, 30 (2007): 137–174.

47: J. Philippe Rushton, "Ethnic Nationalism, Evolutionary Psychology and Genetic Similarity Theory," *Nations and Nationalism*, 11 (2005): 489-507.

intelligent, religious, and ethnocentric. These traits permit them to survive the environment and dominate in conflict with other groups. Such civilizations also tend to become highly patriarchal, because this promotes positive ethnocentrism, as well as sexually puritanical. It has been suggested that the repression of sexuality is associated with the production of more creative work that might inspire the group, such as art.[48] Thus, the repression of sexuality would be beneficial at the level of group selection.

Accordingly, a high civilization is established. However, this tends to result in those at the top of society—who are also, on average, the most intelligent—experiencing luxurious conditions and becoming less religious, less instinctive, and less inclined to have children, as already discussed. Initially, this has many benefits and results in a period of considerable intellectual curiosity. Eventually, though, the intelligence of the society starts to fall. In these circumstances, with traditions being constantly questioned—due to the society's high intelligence and high comfort (and thus low religiousness)—the society as a whole becomes relatively more comfortable and also less religious, and less ethnocentric. People stop having children, partly because life no longer seems to have eternal importance, meaning they may as well just live hedonistic lives. Children increasingly become an accident, associated with low intelligence, and thus overall intelligence declines accordingly. This decline of religiosity also manifests in society becoming less sexually repressed, as well as less patriarchal. As we have discussed, both Judaism and Hinduism have highlighted high levels of female influence in a relatively advanced society as being a crucial sign of a civilization in decline. English anthropologist J. D. Unwin (1895-1936) looked at Athens in the fourth century BC, by which time girls were "choosing their own husbands," this having been unthinkable a century earlier. Unwin refers

48: Emily Kim, Veronika Zeppenfeld, and Dov Cohen, "Sublimation, Culture and Creativity," *Journal of Personal and Social Psychology,* 105 (2013): 639-666; J.D. Unwin, *Sex and Culture* (Oxford: Oxford University Press, 1934).

to a dialogue in which a "middle class" daughter explains to her mother that she simply cannot "control her desire for a certain man."[49] This was happening at a time when Greece was in decline and Rome was rising.

As Rome declined, female influence in Rome grew. English historian Patricia Southern summarizes that by the time of the late Republic and the Early Empire, there was a noticeable "rise in status of Roman women":

> *Some women had achieved considerable influence and wealth. They were on the verge of enjoying as much freedom of action as men, and worse still they had begun to voice their opinions.*

Fulvia (83 BC–40 BC) had led armies and interfered in politics. In 42 BC, Hortensia had successfully lobbied against the taxation of women. "It seemed that women as well as men preferred a life of freedom and choice, and they too were turning their backs on family life. . . ." This new generation of Roman aristocratic women were so "difficult to live with" that aristocratic men increasingly chose to marry their ex-slaves, who would be "docile," because they were forever in their husbands' debt. Senators asked Emperor Augustus (63 BC-14 AD) "how to curb the influence of women," to which he could give no satisfactory answer.[50] American theologian Frank Viola concurs that in around 44 BC, "a 'new' type of woman emerged in Rome." By the first century, they had spread throughout the Roman Empire. They were "liberated married women who pursued their social lives at the expense of their families and who defied previously accepted norms of marriage fidelity and chastity." Not only did they refuse to wear a veil in public (as had been the custom for married women) but they were also "sexually promiscuous and dressed in a seductive manner."[51] In

49: Unwin, *Sex and Culture, op cit.*, 391.

50: Patricia Southern, *Augustus* (London: Routledge, 2013).

51: Frank Viola, *The Untold Story of the New Testament Church* (Shippensburg: Destiny Image Publishing, 2005), 37, footnote 40.

terms of per-capita major innovations, the Ancient World was in overall decline from 350 BC to 350 AD,[52] coinciding with the increasing prominence and status of women.

The English historian Sir John Glubb (1897-1986) produced an analysis of how historical societies have risen and fallen, comparing Greece, Rome, Islam, and the British Empire. He found that they all follow the same process. As religiousness declines, people increasingly place material comfort over duty to the society, a move from "service to selfishness."[53] With the Empire wealthy but no longer religiously believing in its own superiority, it always permits "an influx of foreigners."[54] Pessimistic about the future, there is a focus on "frivolity" and sexual pleasure. Glubb finds that "the heroes of declining nations are always the same: the athlete, the singer, the actor," rather than a "statesman, a general, or a literary genius."[55] Glubb's description of the decline of the Arab Empire, centered on Baghdad, is particularly fascinating. Its decline began in about the year 861. Arab historians recorded a decline in sexual morality, and the rise in sexualized popular singing, especially by the 10th century. There was also an "increase in women in public life . . . with women demanding admission to professions hitherto monopolied by men," such as, according to historian Ibn Bassam (1058-1147), clerk, tax-collector, and imam. "Many women practiced law, while others obtained posts as university professors."[56]

This "decadent" situation, of low religiousness and low ethnocentrism and all that goes with it, allows the declining civilization to be invaded by the more religious, ethnocentric and adapted enemy society at its gate. Even in antiquity, scholars had already identified from history the way in which the same

52: Huebner, "Response of Jonathan Huebner," *op cit.*, 999.

53: John Glubb, *The Fate of Empires and the Search for Survival* (Edinburgh: William Blackwood & Sons, 1976), 9.

54: *Ibid*, 13.

55: *Ibid.*, 14.

56: *Ibid.*, 15.

process seemed to always occur again and again. One research group has gone so far as arguing that it is the reason why we have never seen aliens or time travelers. Even if there have been civilizations elsewhere in the universe, they have simply never managed to keep going for long enough to become sufficiently advanced to find civilizations on other planets.[57] A civilization can't get to the point of interstellar travel. It never does. World Religions—those that survived because they were adaptive—concur that if females are running a society, if society has shunned religion and patriarchy, then, in general, that society is well into its Winter or *Kali Yuga.* And, at the end of *Kali Yuga,* there is a great conflagration and a great flood; a purging of the world. When this happens, only the genetically healthy—the group-selected, the religious and the conservative—will survive.

Until then, we must understand that witches are real, and they must be avoided. As Roald Dahl put it: *"REAL WITCHES dress in ordinary clothes, and look very much like ordinary women."* They walk among us. The lead witches are likely to be prominent, articulate, and influential advocates of maladaptive, anti-traditional ideologies, especially combining this advocacy with an provocative and bizarre appearance and other markers of mutation. These are the necromancers of today. They aim to dissuade us from passing on our genes. They aim to dissuade us from investing energy in our extended genotype, our ethnic group. They aim to persuade us that life has no meaning. They aim to do us harm.

☾

57: Matthew Sarraf, Michael A. Woodley of Menie, and Colin Feltham, *Modernity and Cultural Decline: A Biobehavioral Perspective* (Basingstoke, Hants: Palgrave Macmillan, 2019).